Microsoft® Access®

2016
Level 1

Nita Rutkosky • Audrey Roggenkamp • Ian Rutkosky

PARADIGM
EDUCATION SOLUTIONS

St. Paul

Senior Vice President	Linda Hein
Editor in Chief	Christine Hurney
Director of Production	Timothy W. Larson
Production Editor	Jen Weaverling
Cover and Text Designer	Valerie King
Copy Editors	Communicáto, Ltd.; Page to Portal, LLC
Senior Design and Production Specialist	Jack Ross; PerfecType
Assistant Developmental Editors	Mamie Clark, Katie Werdick
Testers	Janet Blum, Fanshawe College; Traci Post
Instructional Support Writers	Janet Blum, Fanshawe College; Brienna McWade
Indexer	Terry Casey
Vice President Information Technology	Chuck Bratton
Digital Projects Manager	Tom Modl
Vice President Sales and Marketing	Scott Burns
Director of Marketing	Lara Weber McLellan

Trademarks: Microsoft is a trademark or registered trademark of Microsoft Corporation in the United States and/or other countries. Some of the product names and company names included in this book have been used for identification purposes only and may be trademarks or registered trade names of their respective manufacturers and sellers. The authors, editors, and publisher disclaim any affiliation, association, or connection with, or sponsorship or endorsement by, such owners.

We have made every effort to trace the ownership of all copyrighted material and to secure permission from copyright holders. In the event of any question arising as to the use of any material, we will be pleased to make the necessary corrections in future printings.

Cover Photo Credits: © Photomall/Dreamstime.com. **Getting Started Photo Credits**: Page 3: Leungchopan/Shutterstock.com.

Paradigm Publishing is independent from Microsoft Corporation, and not affiliated with Microsoft in any manner. While this publication may be used in assisting individuals to prepare for a Microsoft Office Specialist certification exam, Microsoft, its designated program administrator, and Paradigm Publishing do not warrant that use of this publication will ensure passing a Microsoft Office Specialist certification exam.

ISBN 978-0-76386-955-7 (print)
ISBN 978-0-76386-957-1 (digital)

© 2017 by Paradigm Publishing, Inc.
875 Montreal Way
St. Paul, MN 55102
Email: educate@emcp.com
Website: ParadigmCollege.com

Printed in the United States of America

23 22 21 20 19 18 17   2 3 4 5 6 7 8 9 10 11 12

Brief Contents

Contents

Preface

Benchmark Series: Microsoft® Access 2016 is designed for students who want to learn how to use this feature-rich data management tool to track, report, and share information. No prior knowledge of databases is required. After successfully completing a course using this textbook and digital courseware, students will be able to:

- Create database tables to organize business or personal records
- Modify and manage tables to ensure that data is accurate and up to date
- Perform queries to assist with decision making
- Plan, research, create, revise, and publish database information to meet specific communication needs
- Given a workplace scenario requiring the reporting and analysis of data, assess the information requirements and then prepare the materials that achieve the goal efficiently and effectively

Upon completing the text, students can expect to be proficient in using Access to organize, analyze, and present information.

Well-designed textbook pedagogy is important, but students learn technology skills through practice and problem solving. Technology provides opportunities for interactive learning as well as excellent ways to quickly and accurately assess student performance. To this end, this textbook is supported with SNAP 2016, Paradigm's web-based training and assessment learning management system. Details about SNAP as well as additional student courseware and instructor resources can be found on page xiv.

Achieving Proficiency in Access 2016

Since its inception several Office versions ago, the *Benchmark Series* has served as a standard of excellence in software instruction. Elements of the *Benchmark Series* function individually and collectively to create an inviting, comprehensive learning environment that produces successful computer users. The following visual tour highlights the structure and features that comprise the highly popular *Benchmark* model.

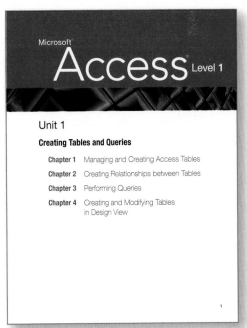

Unit Openers display the unit's four chapter titles. *Access Level 1* contains two units; each unit concludes with a comprehensive unit performance assessment.

Student Textbook and eBook

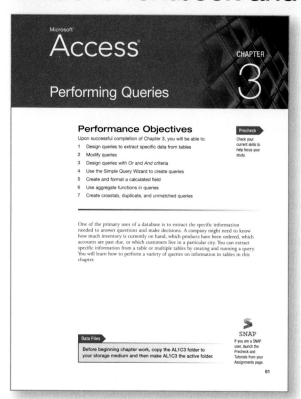

Chapter Openers present the performance objectives and an overview of the skills taught.

Precheck quizzes allow students to check their current skills before starting chapter work.

Data Files are provided for each chapter from the ebook. A prominent note reminds students to copy the appropriate chapter data folder and make it active.

Students with SNAP access are reminded to launch the Precheck quiz and chapter tutorials from their SNAP Assignments page.

Projects Build Skill Mastery within Realistic Context

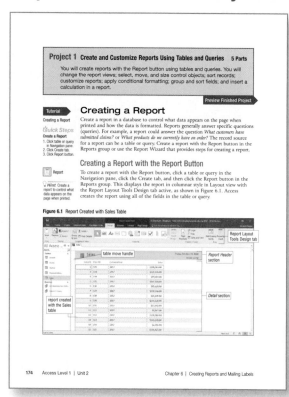

Multipart Projects provide a framework for instruction and practice on software features. A project overview identifies tasks to accomplish and key features to use in completing the work.

Preview Finished Project shows how the file will look after students complete the project.

Tutorials provide interactive, guided training and measured practice.

Quick Steps provide feature summaries for reference and review.

Hint margin notes offer useful tips on how to use features efficiently and effectively.

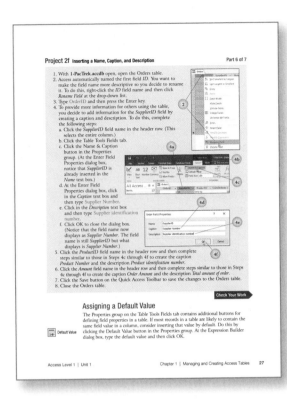

Step-by-Step Instructions guide students to the desired outcome for each project part. Screen captures illustrate what the screen should look like at key points.

Magenta Text identifies material to type.

Check Your Work allows students to confirm they have completed the project activity correctly.

Typically, a file remains open throughout all parts of the project. Students save their work incrementally. At the end of the project, students save, print, and then close the file.

Between project parts, the text presents instruction on the features and skills necessary to accomplish the next section of the project.

Chapter Review Tools Reinforce Learning

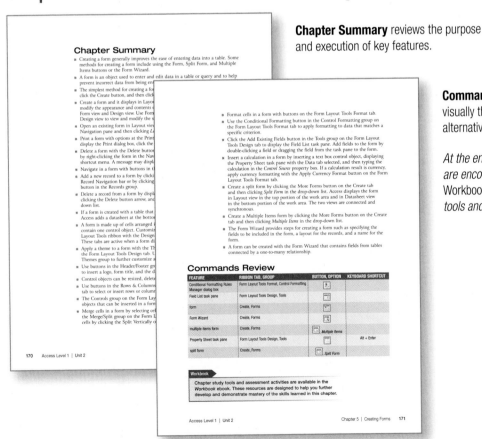

Chapter Summary reviews the purpose and execution of key features.

Commands Review summarizes visually the major features and alternative methods of access.

At the end of each chapter, students are encouraged to go to the Workbook ebook to access study tools and assessment activities.

Workbook eBook Activities Provide a Hierarchy of Learning Assessments

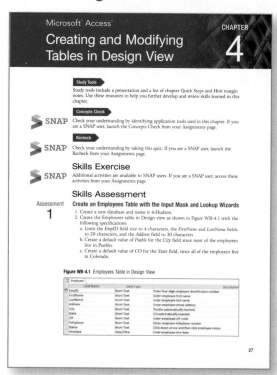

Study Tools are presentations with audio support and a list of chapter Quick Steps and Hint margin notes designed to help students further develop and review skills learned in the chapter.

Concepts Check is an objective completion exercise that allows students to assess their comprehension and recall of application features, terminology, and functions.

Recheck concept quizzes for each chapter enable students to check how their skills have improved after completing chapter work.

Skills Exercises are available to SNAP 2016 users. SNAP will automatically score student work, which is preformed live in the application, and provide detailed feedback.

Skills Assessment exercises ask students to develop both standard and customized types of databases without how-to directions.

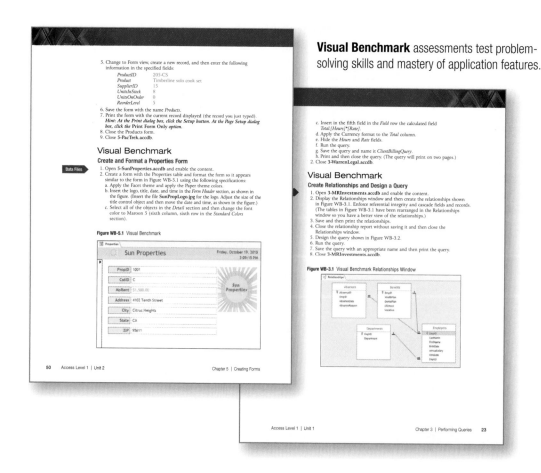

Visual Benchmark assessments test problem-solving skills and mastery of application features.

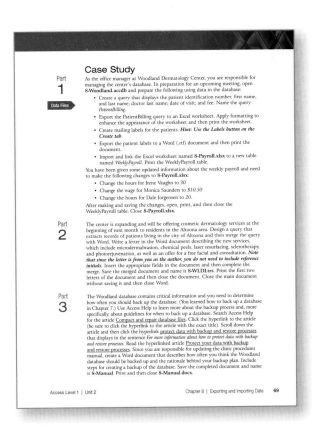

Case Study requires analyzing a workplace scenario and then planning and executing a multipart project.

Students search the web and/or use the program's Help feature to locate additional information required to complete the Case Study.

Unit Performance Assessments Deliver Cross-Disciplinary, Comprehensive Evaluation

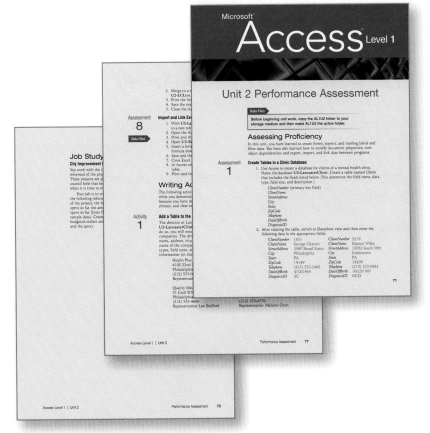

Assessing Proficiency exercises check mastery of features.

Writing Activities involve applying application skills in a communication context.

Internet Research projects reinforce research and information processing skills.

Job Study at the end of Unit 2 presents a capstone assessment requiring critical thinking and problem solving.

SNAP Training and Assessment

SNAP is a web-based training and assessment program and learning management system (LMS) for learning Microsoft Office 2016. SNAP is comprised of rich content, a sophisticated grade book, and robust scheduling and analytics tools. SNAP courseware supports the *Benchmark Series* content and delivers live-in-the-application assessments for students to demonstrate their skills mastery. Interactive tutorials increase skills-focused moments with guided training and measured practice. SNAP provides automatic scoring and detailed feedback on the many activities, exercises, and quizzes to help identify areas where additional support is needed, evaluating student performance both at an individual and course level. The *Benchmark Series* SNAP course content is also available to export into any LMS system that supports LTI tools.

Paradigm Education Solutions provides technical support for SNAP through 24-7 chat at ParadigmCollege.com. In addition, an online User Guide and other SNAP training tools for using SNAP are available.

Student eBook and *Workbook* eBook

The student ebook and *Workbook* ebook available through SNAP or online at Paradigm.bookshelf.emcp.com provide access to the *Benchmark Series* content from any device (desktop, tablet, and smartphone) anywhere, through a live Internet connection. The versatile ebook platform features dynamic navigation tools including a linked table of contents and the ability to jump to specific pages, search for terms, bookmark, highlight, and take notes. The ebooks offer live links to the interactive content and resources that support the print textbook, including the student data files, Precheck and Recheck quizzes, and interactive tutorials. The *Workbook* ebook also provides access to presentations with audio support and to end-of-section Concept Check, Skills Assessment, Visual Benchmark, Case Study, and end-of-unit Performance Assessment activities.

Instructor eResources eBook

All instructor resources are available digitally through a web-based ebook at Paradigm.bookshelf.emcp.com. The instructor materials include these items:

- Planning resources, such as lesson plans, teaching hints, and sample course syllabi
- Presentation resources, such as PowerPoint slide shows with lecture notes
- Assessment resources, including live and annotated PDF model answers for chapter work and workbook activities, rubrics for evaluating student work, and chapter-based exam banks

Office

Getting Started in Office 2016

Several computer applications are combined to make the Microsoft Office 2016 application suite. The applications are known as *software*, and they contain instructions that tell the computer what to do. Some of the applications in the suite include Word, a word processing applicaton; Excel, a spreadsheet applicaton; Access, a database applicaton; and PowerPoint, a presentation applicaton.

Identifying Computer Hardware

The Microsoft Office suite can run on several types of computer equipment, referred to as *hardware*. You will need access to a laptop or a desktop computer system that includes a PC/tower, monitor, keyboard, printer, drives, and mouse. If you are not sure what equipment you will be operating, check with your instructor. The computer systems shown in Figure G.1 consists of six components. Each component is discussed separately in the material that follows.

Figure G.1 Computer System

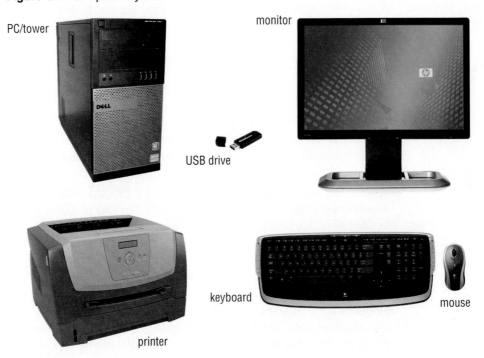

PC/tower

monitor

USB drive

printer

keyboard

mouse

Figure G.2 PC/Tower

PC/Tower

The PC, also known as the *tower*, is the brain of the computer and is where all processing occurs. A PC/tower consists of components such as the Central Processing Unit (CPU), hard drives, and video cards plugged into a motherboard. The motherboard is mounted inside the case, which includes input and output ports for attaching external peripherals (as shown in Figure G.2). When a user provides input through the use of peripherals, the PC/tower computes that input and outputs the results. Similar hardware is included in a laptop, but the design is more compact to allow for mobility.

Monitor

Hint Monitor size is measured diagonally. For example, the distance from the bottom left corner to the top right corner of the monitor.

A computer monitor looks like a television screen. It displays the visual information that the computer is outputting. The quality of display for monitors varies depending on the type of monitor and the level of resolution. Monitors can also vary in size—generally from 13 inches to 26 inches or larger.

Keyboard

The keyboard is used to input information into the computer. The number and location of the keys on a keyboard can vary. In addition to letters, numbers, and symbols, most computer keyboards contain function keys, arrow keys, and a numeric keypad. Figure G.3 shows an enhanced keyboard.

The 12 keys at the top of the keyboard, labeled with the letter F followed by a number, are called *function keys*. Use these keys to perform functions within each of the Office applications. To the right of the regular keys is a group of special or dedicated keys. These keys are labeled with specific functions that will be performed when you press the key. Below the special keys are arrow keys. Use these keys to move the insertion point in the document screen.

Some keyboards include mode indicator lights. When you select certain modes, a light appears on the keyboard. For example, if you press the Caps Lock key, which disables the lowercase alphabet, a light appears next to Caps Lock. Similarly, pressing the Num Lock key will disable the special functions on the numeric keypad, which is located at the right side of the keyboard.

Figure G.3 Keyboard

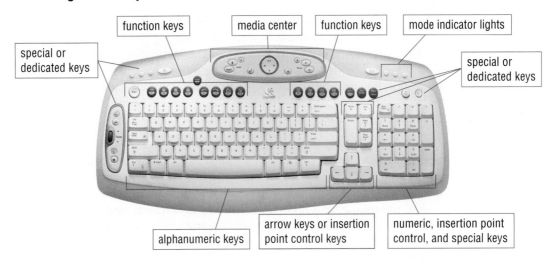

function keys

media center

function keys

mode indicator lights

special or dedicated keys

special or dedicated keys

alphanumeric keys

arrow keys or insertion point control keys

numeric, insertion point control, and special keys

Drives and Ports

A PC includes drives and ports that allow you to input and output data. For example, a hard drive is a disk drive inside of the PC that stores data that may have been inputted or outputted. Other drives may include CD, DVD and BluRay disc drives, although newer computers may not include these drives, because USB flash drives are becoming the preferred technology. Ports are the "plugs" on the PC, and are used to connect devices to the computer, such as the keyboard and mouse, the monitor, speakers, a USB flash drive and so on. Most PCs will have a few USB ports, at least one display port, an audio cable port, and possibly an ethernet port (used to physically connect to the Internet or a network).

Printer

An electronic version of a file is known as a *soft copy*. If you want to create a hard copy of a file, you need to print it. To print documents you will need to access a printer (as shown in Figure G.4), which will probably be either a laser printer or an ink-jet printer. A laser printer uses a laser beam combined with heat and pressure to print documents, while an ink-jet printer prints a document by spraying a fine mist of ink on the page.

Figure G.4 Printer

Mouse

Most functions and commands in the Microsoft Office suite are designed to be performed using a mouse or a similar pointing device. A mouse is an input device that sits on a flat surface next to the computer. You can operate a mouse with your left or right hand. Moving the mouse on the flat surface causes a corresponding pointer to move on the screen, and clicking the left or right mouse buttons allows you to select various objects and commands. Figure G.5 shows an example of a mouse.

Using the Mouse The applications in the Microsoft Office suite can be operated with the keyboard and a mouse. The mouse generally has two buttons on top, which you press to execute specific functions and commands. A mouse may also contain a wheel, which can be used to scroll in a window or as a third button. To use the mouse, rest it on a flat surface or a mouse pad. Put your hand over it with your palm resting on top of the mouse and your index finger resting on the left mouse button. As you move your hand, and thus the mouse, a corresponding pointer moves on the screen.

When using the mouse, you should understand four terms — point, click, double-click, and drag. When operating the mouse, you may need to point to a specific command, button, or icon. To *point* means to position the mouse pointer on the desired item. With the mouse pointer positioned on the item, you may need to click a button on the mouse to select the item. To *click* means to quickly tap a button on the mouse once. To complete two steps at one time, such as choosing and then executing a function, double-click the mouse button. To *double-click* means to tap the left mouse button twice in quick succession. The term *drag* means to click and hold down the left mouse button, move the mouse pointer to a specific location, and then release the button.

 Hint This textbook will use the verb *click* to refer to the mouse and the verb press to refer to a key on the keyboard.

Using the Mouse Pointer The mouse pointer will look different depending on where you have positioned it and what function you are performing. The following are some of the ways the mouse pointer can appear when you are working in the Office suite:

- The mouse pointer appears as an I-beam (called the *I-beam pointer*) when you are inserting text in a file. The I-beam pointer can be used to move the insertion point or to select text.
- The mouse pointer appears as an arrow pointing up and to the left (called the *arrow pointer*) when it is moved to the Title bar, Quick Access Toolbar, ribbon, or an option in a dialog box, among other locations.
- The mouse pointer becomes a double-headed arrow (either pointing left and right, pointing up and down, or pointing diagonally) when you perform certain functions such as changing the size of an object.

Figure G.5 Mouse

- In certain situations, such as when you move an object or image, the mouse pointer displays with a four-headed arrow attached. The four-headed arrow means that you can move the object left, right, up, or down.

- When a request is being processed or when an application is being loaded, the mouse pointer may appear as a moving circle. The moving circle means "please wait." When the process is completed, the circle is replaced with a normal mouse pointer.

- When the mouse pointer displays as a hand with a pointing index finger, it indicates that more information is available about an item. The mouse pointer also displays as a hand with a pointing index finger when you hover the mouse over a hyperlink.

Touchpad

If you are working on a laptop computer, you may use a touchpad instead of a mouse. A *touchpad* allows you to move the mouse pointer by moving your finger across a surface at the base of the keyboard. You click and right-click by using your thumb to press the buttons located at the bottom of the touchpad. Some touchpads have special features such as scrolling or clicking something by tapping the surface of the touchpad instead of pressing a button with a thumb.

TouchScreen

Smartphones, tablets, and touch monitors all use TouchScreen technology (as shown in Figure G.6), which allows users to directly interact with the objects on the screen by touching them with fingers, thumbs, or a stylus. Multiple fingers or both thumbs can be used on most modern touchscreens, giving users the ability to zoom, rotate, and manipulate items on the screen. While a lot of activities in this textbook can be completed using a device with a touchscreen, a mouse or touchpad might be required to complete a few activities.

Figure G.6 Touchscreen

Choosing Commands

Once an application is open, you can use several methods in the application to choose commands. A command is an instruction that tells the application to do something. You can choose a command using the mouse or the keyboard. When an application such as Word or PowerPoint is open, the ribbon contains buttons and options for completing tasks, as well as tabs you can click to display additional buttons and options. To choose a button on the Quick Access Toolbar or on the ribbon, position the tip of the mouse arrow pointer on the button and then click the left mouse button.

The Office suite provides accelerator keys you can press to use a command in an application. Press the Alt key on the keyboard to display KeyTips that identify the accelerator key you can press to execute a command. For example, if you press the Alt key in a Word document with the Home tab active, KeyTips display as shown in Figure G.7. Continue pressing accelerator keys until you execute the desired command. For example, to begin checking the spelling in a document, press the Alt key, press the R key on the keyboard to display the Review tab, and then press the letter S on the keyboard.

Choosing Commands from Drop-Down Lists

To choose a command from a drop-down list with the mouse, position the mouse pointer on the option and then click the left mouse button. To make a selection from a drop-down list with the keyboard, type the underlined letter in the option.

Some options at a drop-down list may appear in gray (dimmed), indicating that the option is currently unavailable. If an option at a drop-down list displays preceded by a check mark, it means the option is currently active. If an option at a drop-down list displays followed by an ellipsis (...), clicking that option will display a dialog box.

Choosing Options from a Dialog Box

A dialog box contains options for applying formatting or otherwise modifying a file or data within a file. Some dialog boxes display with tabs along the top that provide additional options. For example, the Font dialog box shown in Figure G.8 contains two tabs—the Font tab and the Advanced tab. The tab that displays in the front is the active tab. To make a tab active using the mouse, position the arrow pointer on the tab and then click the left mouse button. If you are using the keyboard, press Ctrl + Tab or press Alt + the underlined letter on the tab.

To choose an option from a dialog box with the mouse, position the arrow pointer on the option and then click the left mouse button. If you are using the keyboard, press the Tab key to move the insertion point forward from option to option. Press Shift + Tab to move the insertion point backward from option to option. You can also press and hold down the Alt key and then press the

Figure G.7 Word Home Tab KeyTips

Figure G.8 Word Font Dialog Box

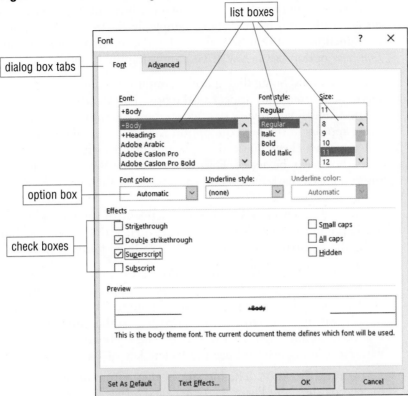

underlined letter of the option. When an option is selected, it displays with a blue background or surrounded by a dashed box called a *marquee*. A dialog box contains one or more of the following elements: list boxes, option boxes, check boxes, text boxes, option buttons, measurement boxes, and command buttons.

List Boxes and Option Boxes The fonts available in the Font dialog box, shown in Figure G.8, are contained in a list box. To make a selection from a list box with the mouse, move the arrow pointer to the option and then click the left mouse button.

Some list boxes may contain a scroll bar. This scroll bar will display at the right side of the list box (a vertical scroll bar) or at the bottom of the list box (a horizontal scroll bar). Use a vertical scroll bar or a horizontal scroll bar to move through the list if the list is longer (or wider) than the box. To move down a list using a vertical scroll bar, position the arrow pointer on the down arrow, and then click and hold down the left mouse button. To scroll up through the list, position the arrow pointer on the up arrow, and then click and hold down the left mouse button. You can also move the arrow pointer above the scroll box and click the left mouse button to scroll up the list or move the arrow pointer below the scroll box and click the left mouse button to move down the list. To navigate in a list with a horizontal scroll bar, click the left arrow to scroll to the left of the list or click the right arrow to scroll to the right of the list.

To use the keyboard to make a selection from a list box, move the insertion point into the box by holding down the Alt key and pressing the underlined letter of the desired option. Press the Up and/or Down Arrow keys on the keyboard to move through the list, and press the Enter key when the desired option is selected.

In some dialog boxes where there is not enough room for a list box, lists of options are contained in a drop-down list box called an *option box*. Option boxes display with a down arrow. For example, in Figure G.8, the font color options are contained in an option box. To display the different color options, click the *Font color* option box arrow. If you are using the keyboard, press Alt + C.

Check Boxes Some dialog boxes contain options preceded by a box. A check mark may or may not appear in the box. The Word Font dialog box shown in Figure G.8 displays a variety of check boxes within the *Effects* section. If a check mark appears in the box, the option is active (turned on). If the check box does not contain a check mark, the option is inactive (turned off). Any number of check boxes can be active. For example, in the Word Font dialog box, you can insert a check mark in several of the boxes in the *Effects* section to activate the options.

To make a check box active or inactive with the mouse, position the tip of the arrow pointer in the check box and then click the left mouse button. If you are using the keyboard, press Alt + the underlined letter of the option.

Text Boxes Some options in a dialog box require you to enter text. For example, the boxes below the *Find what* and *Replace with* options at the Excel Find and Replace dialog box shown in Figure G.9 are text boxes. In a text box, type text or edit existing text. Edit text in a text box in the same manner as normal text. Use the Left and Right Arrow keys on the keyboard to move the insertion point without deleting text and use the Delete key or Backspace key to delete text.

Command Buttons The buttons at the bottom of the Excel Find and Replace dialog box shown in Figure G.9 are called *command buttons*. Use a command button to execute or cancel a command. Some command buttons display with an ellipsis (...), which means another dialog box will open if you click that button. To choose a command button with the mouse, position the arrow pointer on the button and then click the left mouse button. To choose a command button with the keyboard, press the Tab key until the command button is surrounded by a marquee and then press the Enter key.

Option Buttons The Word Insert Table dialog box shown in Figure G.10 contains options in the *AutoFit behavior* section preceded by option buttons. Only one option button can be selected at any time. When an option button is selected, a blue or black circle displays in the button. To select an option button with the mouse, position the tip of the arrow pointer inside the option button or on the option and then click the left mouse button. To make a selection with the keyboard, press and hold down the Alt key, press the underlined letter of the option, and then release the Alt key.

Figure G.9 Excel Find and Replace Dialog Box

Figure G.10 Word Insert Table Dialog Box

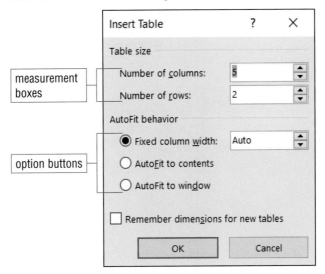

Measurement Boxes Some options in a dialog box contain measurements or amounts you can increase or decrease. These options are generally located in a measurement box. For example, the Word Insert Table dialog box shown in Figure G.10 contains the *Number of columns* and *Number of rows* measurement boxes. To increase a number in a measurement box, position the tip of the arrow pointer on the up arrow at the right of the measurement box and then click the left mouse button. To decrease the number, click the down arrow. If you are using the keyboard, press and hold down the Alt key and then press the underlined letter for the option, press the Up Arrow key to increase the number or the Down Arrow key to decrease the number, and then release the Alt key.

💡 **Hint** In addition to using the up and down arrows, you can change the current measurement by selecting it and then typing the new measurement using the keyboard.

Choosing Commands with Keyboard Shortcuts

Applications in the Office suite offer a variety of keyboard shortcuts you can use to execute specific commands. Keyboard shortcuts generally require two or more keys. For example, the keyboard shortcut to display the Open dialog box in an application is Ctrl + F12. To use this keyboard shortcut, press and hold down the Ctrl key, press the F12 function on the keyboard, and then release the Ctrl key. For a list of keyboard shortcuts, refer to the Help files.

Choosing Commands with Shortcut Menus

The software applications in the Office suite include shortcut menus that contain commands related to different items. To display a shortcut menu, position the mouse pointer over the item for which you want to view more options, and then click the right mouse button or press Shift + F10. The shortcut menu will appear wherever the insertion point is positioned. For example, if the insertion point is positioned in a paragraph of text in a Word document, clicking the right mouse button or pressing Shift + F10 will cause the shortcut menu shown in Figure G.11 to display in the document screen (along with the Mini toolbar).

To select an option from a shortcut menu with the mouse, click the option. If you are using the keyboard, press the Up or Down Arrow key until the option is selected and then press the Enter key. To close a shortcut menu without choosing an option, click outside the shortcut menu or press the Esc key.

Figure G.11 Word Shortcut Menu

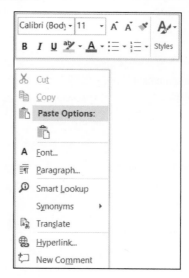

Working with Multiple Programs

As you learn the various applications in the Microsoft Office suite, you will notice many similarities between them. For example, the steps to save, close, and print are virtually the same whether you are working in Word, Excel, or PowerPoint. This consistency between applications greatly enhances your ability to transfer knowledge learned in one application to another within the suite. Another benefit to using Microsoft Office is the ability to have more than one application open at the same time and to integrate content from one program with another. For example, you can open Word and create a document, open Excel and create a spreadsheet, and then copy the Excel spreadsheet into Word.

When you open an application, a button containing an icon representing the application displays on the taskbar. If you open another application, a button containing an icon representing that application displays to the right of the first application button on the taskbar. Figure G.12 shows the taskbar with Word, Excel, Access, and PowerPoint open. To move from one program to another, click the taskbar button representing the desired application.

Customizing Settings

Before beginning computer projects in this textbook, you may need to customize your monitor's settings, change the DPI display setting, and turn on the display of file extensions. Projects in the chapters in this textbook assume that the monitor display is set at 1600×900 pixels, the DPI set at 125%, and that the display of file extensions is turned on. If you are unable to make changes to the monitor's resolution or the DPI settings, the projects can still be completed successfully. Some references in the text might not perfectly match what you see on your

Figure G.12 Taskbar with Word, Excel, Access, and PowerPoint Open

screen, so some mental adjustments may need to be made for certain steps. For example, an item in a drop-down gallery might appear in a different column or row than what is indicated in the step instructions.

Before you begin learning the applications in the Microsoft Office 2016 suite, take a moment to check the display settings on the computer you are using. Your monitor's display settings are important because the ribbon in the Microsoft Office suite adjusts to the screen resolution setting of your computer monitor. A computer monitor set at a high resolution will have the ability to show more buttons in the ribbon than will a monitor set to a low resolution. The illustrations in this textbook were created with a screen resolution display set at 1600 × 900 pixels. In Figure G.13, the Word ribbon is shown three ways: at a lower screen resolution (1366 × 768 pixels), at the screen resolution featured throughout this textbook, and at a higher screen resolution (1920 × 1080 pixels). Note the variances in the ribbon in all three examples. If possible, set your display to 1600 × 900 pixels to match the illustrations you will see in this textbook.

Figure G.13 The Home Tab Displayed on a Monitor Set at Different Screen Resolutions

1366 × 768 screen resolution

1600 × 900 screen resolution

1920 × 1080 screen resolution

Project 1 Setting Monitor Display to 1600 × 900

Note: The resolution settings may be locked on lab computers. Also, some laptop screens and small monitors may not be able to display in a 1600 × 900 resolution.

1. At the Windows 10 desktop, right-click in a blank area of the screen.
2. At the shortcut menu, click the *Display settings* option.

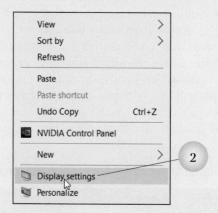

3. At the Settings window with the SYSTEM screen active, scroll down and then click *Advanced display settings*.

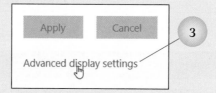

4. Scroll down the Settings window until the *Resolution* option box is visible and take note of the current resolution setting. If the current resolution is already set to 1600 × 900, skip ahead to Step 8.
5. Click in the Resolution option box and then click the 1600 × 900 option at the drop-down list.

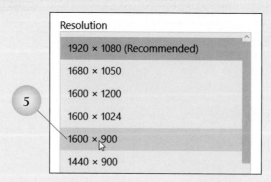

6. Click the Apply button.
7. Click the Keep Changes button.
8. Click the Close button.

Project 2 Changing the DPI Setting

Note: The DPI settings may be locked on lab computers. Also, some laptop screens and small monitors may not allow the DPI settings to be changed.

1. At the Windows 10 desktop, right-click in a blank area of the screen.
2. At the shortcut menu, click the *Display settings* option.
3. At the Settings window, take note of the current DPI percentage next to the text *Change the size of text, apps, and other items*. If the percentage is already set to 125%, skip to Step 5.
4. Click the slider bar below the text *Change the size of text, apps, and other items* and hold down the left mouse button, drag to the right until the DPI percentage is 125%, and then release the mouse button.

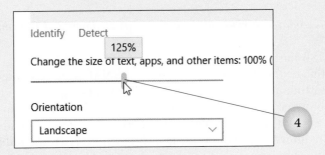

5. Close the computer window.

Project 3 Displaying File Extensions

1. At the Windows 10 desktop, click the File Explorer button on the taskbar.

2. At the File Explorer window, click the View tab.
3. Click the *File name extensions* check box in the Show/hide group to insert a check mark.

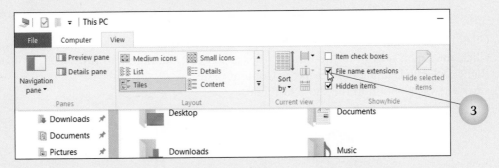

4. Close the computer window.

Completing Computer Projects

Some projects in this textbook require that you open an existing file. Project files are saved on OneDrive in a zip file. Before beginning projects and assessments in this book and the accompanying ebook, copy the necessary folder from the zip file to your storage medium (such as a USB flash drive) using File Explorer. Begin downloading the files for this book by going to the ebook and clicking the Ancillary Links button that displays when the ebook displays this page or any chapter opener page with the Data Files tab on it.

Project 4 Downloading Files to a USB Flash Drive

Note: OneDrive is updated periodically, so the steps to download files may vary from the steps below.

1. Insert your USB flash drive into an available USB port.
2. Navigate to this textbook's ebook. If you are a SNAP user, navigate to the ebook by clicking the textbook ebook link on your Assignments page. If you are not a SNAP user, launch your browser and go to http://paradigm.bookshelf.emcp.com, log in, and then click the textbook ebook thumbnail. *Note: The steps in this activity assume you are using the Microsoft Edge browser. If you are using a different browser, the following steps may vary.*
3. Navigate to the ebook page that corresponds to this textbook page.
4. Click the Ancillary Links button in the menu. The menu that appears may be at the top of the window or along the side of the window, depending on the size of the window.

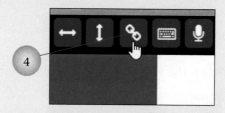

5. At the Ancillary Links dialog box, click the Data Files: All Files hyperlink.

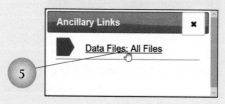

6. Click the Download hyperlink at the top of the window.
7. Click the Open button in the message box when the DataFiles.zip finishes downloading.
8. Right-click the DataFiles folder in the Content pane.
9. Click the *Copy* option in the shortcut menu.

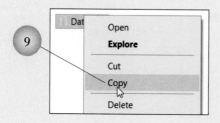

10. Click the USB flash drive that displays in the Navigation pane at the left side of the File Explorer window.
11. Click the Home tab in the File Explorer window.
12. Click the Paste button in the Clipboard group.

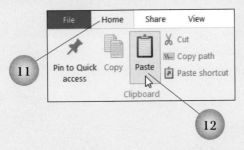

13. Close the File Explorer window by clicking the Close button in the upper right corner of the window.

Project 5 Deleting a File

Note: Check with your instructor before deleting a file.

1. At the Windows 10 desktop, open File Explorer by clicking the File Explorer button on the taskbar.
2. Click the *Downloads* folder in the navigation pane.
3. Right-click *DataFiles.zip*.
4. Click the *Delete* option at the shortcut menu.

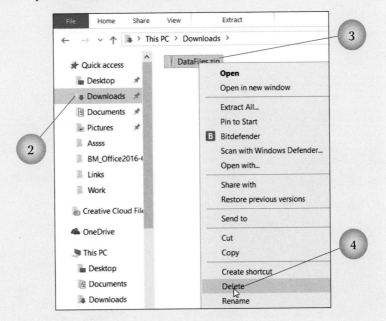

Microsoft® Access® Level 1

Unit 1

Creating Tables and Queries

Microsoft®

Access®

Managing and Creating Access Tables

Performance Objectives

Upon successful completion of Chapter 1, you will be able to:

1 Open and close objects in a database
2 Insert, delete, and move fields in a table
3 Hide, unhide, freeze, and unfreeze fields
4 Adjust table column width
5 Preview and print a table
6 Design and create a table
7 Rename fields
8 Insert a field name, caption, and description
9 Insert Quick Start fields
10 Assign a default value and field size

Precheck

Check your current skills to help focus your study.

Managing information is an integral part of operating a business. Information can come in a variety of forms, such as data about customers, including names, addresses, and telephone numbers; product data; and purchasing and buying data. Most companies today manage data using system software. Microsoft Office Professional Plus includes a database management system software program named *Access*. With Access, you can organize, store, maintain, retrieve, sort, and print all types of business data.

This chapter contains just a few ideas on how to manage data with Access. A properly designed and maintained database management system can help a company operate smoothly.

SNAP

If you are a SNAP user, launch the Precheck and Tutorials from your Assignments page.

Data Files

Before beginning chapter work, copy the AL1C1 folder to your storage medium and then make AL1C1 the active folder.

Project 1 **Explore an Access Database**   **1 Part**

You will open a database and open and close objects in the database, including tables, queries, forms, and reports.

Exploring a Database

A database is comprised of a series of objects (such as tables, queries, forms, and reports) used to enter, manage, view, and print data. Data in a database is organized into tables, which contain information for related items (such as customers, employees, orders, and products).

To create a new database or open a previously created database, click the Windows 10 Start button and then click the Access 2016 tile. (These steps may vary depending on your system configuration.) This displays the Access 2016 opening screen, as shown in Figure 1.1. At this screen, open a recently opened database, a blank database, a database from the Open backstage area, or a database based on a template.

To create a new blank database, click the *Blank desktop database* template. At the Blank desktop database window, type a name for the database in the *File Name* text box, and then click the Create button. To save the database in a particular location, click the Browse button at the right side of the *File Name* text box. At the File New Database dialog box, navigate to the desired location or folder, type the database name in the *File name* text box, and then click OK.

Create

Opening a Database

A previously saved database can be opened at the Open dialog box. To display this dialog box, display the Open backstage area and then click the *Browse* option.

Figure 1.1 Access 2016 Opening Screen

Click this template to create a blank database.

Click the Open Other Files hyperlink to display the Open backstage area, navigate to the folder and then double-click the name of the database file.

Quick Steps
Open a Database
1. Open Access.
2. Click Open Other Files hyperlink.
3. Click *Browse* option.
4. Navigate to location.
5. Double-click database.

Display the Open backstage area by clicking the <u>Open Other Files</u> hyperlink at the Access 2016 opening screen. Or, click the File tab at the blank Access screen and then click the *Open* option. Other methods for displaying the Open backstage area include using the keyboard shortcut, Ctrl + O, or inserting an Open button on the Quick Access Toolbar.

At the Open backstage area, click the *Browse* option and the Open dialog box displays. At the Open dialog box, navigate to the desired location, such as the drive containing your storage medium, open the folder containing the database, and then double-click the database name in the Content pane. When a database is open, the Access screen looks similar to what is shown in Figure 1.2. Refer to Table 1.1 for descriptions of the Access screen elements.

Only one Access database can be open at a time. If a new database is opened in the current Access window, the existing database closes. However, multiple instances of Access can be opened and a database can be opened in each instance. In other applications in the Microsoft Office suite, a revised file must be saved after changes are made to the file. In an Access database, any changes made to data are saved automatically when moving to a new record, closing a table, or closing the database.

Hint The active database is saved automatically on a periodic basis and when you make another record active, close the table, or close the database.

Enabling Content

A security warning message bar may appear below the ribbon if Access determines the file being opened did not originate from a trusted location on the computer and may contain viruses or other security hazards. This often occurs when an Access database is copied from another medium (such as a CD or the web). Active content in the file is disabled until the Enable Content button is clicked. The message bar closes when the database is identified as a trusted source. Before making any changes to the database, the Enable Content button must be clicked.

Figure 1.2 Access Screen

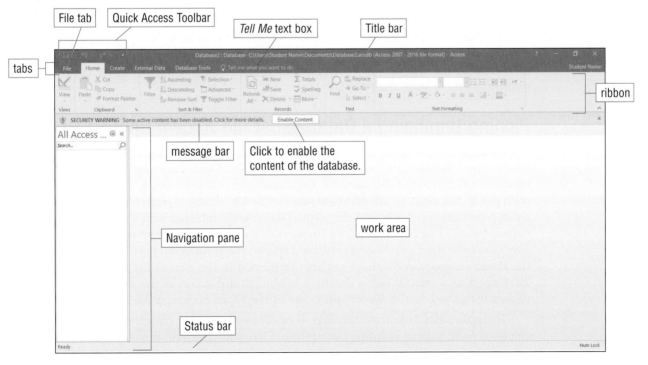

Table 1.1 Access Screen Elements

Feature	Description
File tab	when clicked, displays the backstage area that contains options for working with and managing databases
message bar	displays security alerts if the database being opened contains potentially unsafe content
Navigation pane	displays the names of objects within the database grouped by categories
Quick Access Toolbar	contains buttons for commonly used commands
ribbon	contains tabs with commands and buttons divided into groups
Status bar	displays messages, the current view, and view buttons
tabs	contain commands and features organized into groups
Tell Me text box	provides information as well as guidance on how to perform a function
Title bar	displays the database name followed by the program name
work area	displays opened objects

Tutorial

Managing the
Recent Option List

Opening a Database from the *Recent* Option List

At the Open backstage area with the *Recent* option selected, a list of the most recently opened databases displays. Access displays 25 of the most recently opened databases and groups them into categories such as *Today*, *Yesterday*, and perhaps another category such as *Last Week*. Click the database name in the *Recent* option list to open the database.

(Note: If opening a database from a OneDrive account, Access requires that a copy of the database be saved to a location such as the computer's hard drive or a USB flash drive. Any changes made to the database will be saved to the local copy of the database but not the database in the OneDrive account. To save a database back to the OneDrive account, the database will need to be uploaded by opening a web browser, going to onedrive.com, logging in to the OneDrive account, and then clicking the Upload link. Microsoft constantly updates the OneDrive.com website, so these steps may vary.)

Pinning/Unpinning a Database at the *Recent* Option List

If a database is opened on a regular basis, consider pinning it to the *Recent* option list. To pin a database to the *Recent* option list at the Open backstage area, hover the mouse pointer over the database name and then click the small left-pointing push pin to the right of the database name. The left-pointing push pin changes to a down-pointing push pin and the pinned database is inserted into a new category named *Pinned*. The *Pinned* category displays at the top of the *Recent* option list. The next time the Open backstage area displays, the pinned database displays in the *Pinned* category. A database can also be pinned to the Recent list at the Access 2016 opening screen. When a database is pinned, it displays at the top of the Recent list as well as the *Recent* option list at the Open backstage area.

To unpin a database from the Recent or *Recent* option list, click the pin to change it from a down-pointing push pin to a left-pointing push pin. More than one database can be pinned to a list. Another method for pinning and unpinning databases is to use the shortcut menu. Right-click a database name and then click the *Pin to list* or *Unpin from list* option.

Opening and Closing Objects

Tutorial

Opening and Closing an Object

The Navigation pane at the left side of the Access screen displays the objects contained in the database. Some common objects found in a database include tables, queries, forms, and reports. Refer to Table 1.2 for descriptions of these four types of objects.

Control what displays in the pane by clicking the menu bar at the top of the Navigation pane and then clicking an option at the drop-down list or by clicking the button on the menu bar containing the down arrow. (The name of this button changes depending on what is selected.) For example, to display a list of all saved objects in the database, click the *Object Type* option at the drop-down list. This view displays the objects grouped by type: *Tables, Queries, Forms,* and *Reports.* To open an object, double-click the object in the Navigation pane. The object opens in the work area and a tab displays with the object name at the left side of the object. An object can also be opened with the shortcut menu by right-clicking the object in the Navigation pane and then clicking the *Open* option at the shortcut menu.

Shutter Bar Open/Close Button

To view more of an object, consider closing the Navigation pane by clicking the Shutter Bar Open/Close Button in the upper right corner of the Navigation pane or by pressing the F11 function key. Click the button or press F11 again to reopen the Navigation pane. More than one object can be opened in the work area. Each object opens with a visible tab. Navigate to objects by clicking the object tab.

Hint Hide the Navigation pane by clicking the Shutter Bar Open/Close Button or by pressing F11.

To close an object, click the Close button in the upper right corner of the work area or use the keyboard shortcut Ctrl + F4. The shortcut menu can also be used to close an object by right-clicking the object and then clicking *Close* at the shortcut menu. Close multiple objects by right-clicking an object tab and then clicking *Close All* at the shortcut menu.

Closing a Database

Tutorial

Closing a Database and Closing Access

To close a database, click the File tab and then click the *Close* option. Close Access by clicking the Close button in the upper right corner of the screen or with the keyboard shortcut Alt + F4.

 Close

Table 1.2 Database Objects

Object Type	Description
table	Organizes data in fields (columns) and records (rows). A database must contain at least one table. The table is the base upon which other objects are created.
query	Displays data from a table or related tables that meets a conditional statement and/or performs calculations. For example, all records from a specific month can be displayed or only those records containing a specific city.
form	Allows fields and records to be presented in a layout different from the datasheet. Used to facilitate data entry and maintenance.
report	Prints data from tables or queries.

1. Open Access by clicking the Windows Start button and then clicking the Access 2016 tile in the Start menu.
2. At the Access 2016 opening screen, click the Open Other Files hyperlink.
3. At the Open backstage area, click the *Browse* option.
4. At the Open dialog box, navigate to the AL1C1 folder on your storage medium and then double-click *1-SampleDatabase.accdb*. (This database contains data on orders, products, and suppliers for a specialty hiking and backpacking outfitters store named Pacific Trek.)
5. Click the Enable Content button in the message bar if a security warning message appears. (The message bar will display immediately below the ribbon.)
6. With the database open, click the Navigation pane menu bar and then click *Object Type* at the drop-down list. (This option displays the objects grouped by type: *Tables*, *Queries*, *Forms*, and *Reports*.)
7. Double-click *Suppliers* in the Tables group in the Navigation pane. This opens the Suppliers table in the work area, as shown in Figure 1.3.
8. Close the Suppliers table by clicking the Close button in the upper right corner of the work area.

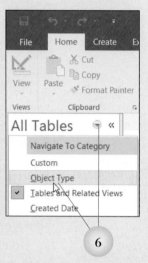

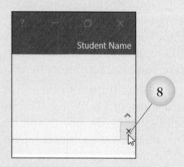

9. Double-click *OrdersOver$500* in the Queries group in the Navigation pane. A query displays data that meets a conditional statement. This query displays orders that meet the criterion of being more than $500.
10. Close the query by clicking the Close button in the upper right corner of the work area.
11. Right-click *SuppliersNotVancouver* in the Queries group in the Navigation pane and then click *Open* at the shortcut menu. This query displays information about suppliers but excludes those in Vancouver.
12. Right-click the SuppliersNotVancouver tab in the work area and then click *Close* at the shortcut menu.
13. Double-click *Orders* in the Forms group in the Navigation pane. This displays an order form. A form is used to view and edit data in a table one record at a time.
14. Double-click *Orders* in the Reports group in the Navigation pane. The Orders form is still open and the report opens in the work area over the Orders form. The Orders report displays information about orders and order amounts.

15. Close the Navigation pane by clicking the Shutter Bar Open/Close Button in the upper right corner of the pane.
16. After viewing the report, click the Shutter Bar Open/Close Button again to open the Navigation pane.
17. Right-click the Orders tab and then click *Close All* at the shortcut menu. (This closes both open objects.)
18. Close the database by clicking the File tab and then clicking the *Close* option.
19. Close Access by clicking the Close button in the upper right corner of the screen.

Figure 1.3 Suppliers Table

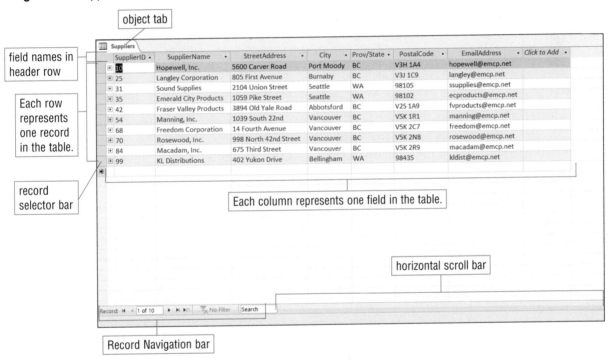

Project 2 Manage Tables in a Database   7 Parts

Pacific Trek is an outfitting store specializing in hiking and backpacking gear. Information about the store, including suppliers and products, is contained in a database. You will open the database and then insert and delete records; insert, move, and delete fields; preview and print tables; rename and delete a table; and create two new tables for the database.

Preview Finished Project

Managing Tables

In a new database, tables are the first objects created, since all other database objects rely on a table as the source for their data. Managing the tables in the database is important for keeping the database up to date and may include inserting or deleting records, inserting or deleting fields, renaming fields, creating a hard copy of the table by printing the table, and renaming and deleting tables.

Adding and Deleting Records

Tutorial

Adding and Deleting Records in a Table

When a table is opened, it displays in Datasheet view in the work area. The Datasheet view displays the contents of a table in a column and row format similar to an Excel worksheet. Columns contain field data, with the field names in the header row at the top of the table, and rows contain records. A Record Navigation bar displays at the bottom of the screen just above the Status bar and contains buttons to navigate in the table. Figure 1.4 identifies the buttons and other elements on the Record Navigation bar.

 New

To add a new record to the open table, make sure the Home tab is active and then click the New button in the Records group. This moves the insertion point to the first field in the blank row at the bottom of the table and the *Current Record* box on the Record Navigation bar indicates what record is being created (or edited). A new record can also be added by clicking the New (blank) record button on the Record Navigation bar.

Quick Steps

Add a New Record
1. Open table.
2. Click New button on Home tab.
3. Type data.
OR
1. Open table.
2. Click New (blank) record button on Record Navigation bar.
3. Type data.

When working in a table, press the Tab key to make the next field in the current record active or press Shift + Tab to make the previous field in the current record active. Make a field active with the mouse by clicking in the field. When typing data for the first field in the record, another row of cells is automatically inserted below the current row and a pencil icon displays in the record selector bar at the beginning of the current record. The pencil icon indicates that the record is being edited and that the changes to the data have not been saved. When data is entered in the last field and the insertion point is moved out of the field, the pencil icon is removed, indicating that the data has been saved.

 Delete

To delete a record, click in one of the fields in the record, make sure the Home tab is active, click the Delete button arrow, and then click *Delete Record* at the drop-down list. At the message asking to confirm the deletion, click Yes. Click in a field in a record and the Delete button displays in a dimmed manner unless specific data is selected.

Quick Steps

Delete a Record
1. Click a field in the record.
2. Click Delete button arrow.
3. Click *Delete Record*.
4. Click Yes.

Data entered in a table is automatically saved, however, changes to the layout of a table are not automatically saved. For example, if a column is deleted in a table, a deletion confirmation message will display when the table is closed.

Figure 1.4 Record Navigation Bar

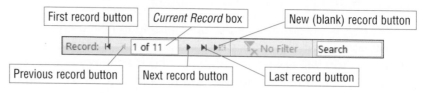

1. Open Access.
2. At the Access 2016 opening screen, click the <u>Open Other Files</u> hyperlink.
3. At the Open backstage area, click the *Browse* option.
4. At the Open dialog box, navigate to the AL1C1 folder on your storage medium and then double-click *1-PacTrek.accdb*.
5. Click the Enable Content button in the message bar if a security warning message appears. (The message bar will display immediately below the ribbon.)
6. With the database open, make sure the Navigation pane displays object types. (If it does not, click the Navigation pane menu bar and then click *Object Type* at the drop-down list.)
7. Double-click *Suppliers* in the Tables group in the Navigation pane. (This opens the table in Datasheet view.)
8. With the Suppliers table open and the Home tab active, add a new record by completing the following steps:

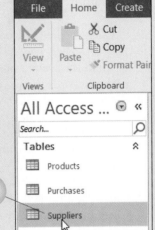

    a. Click the New button in the Records group on the Home tab. (This moves the insertion point to the first field in the blank record at the bottom of the table and the *Current Record* box in the Record Navigation bar indicates what record you are creating or editing.)

    b. Type 38. (This inserts *38* in the field immediately below *99*.)
    c. Press the Tab key (to make the next field in the current record active) and then type Hadley Company.
    d. Press the Tab key and then type 5845 Jefferson Street.
    e. Press the Tab key and then type Seattle.
    f. Press the Tab key and then type WA.
    g. Press the Tab key and then type 98107.
    h. Press the Tab key and then type hcompany@emcp.net.
    i. Press the Tab key and then type Jurene Miller.

SupplierID	SupplierNam	StreetAddres	City	Prov/State	PostalCode	EmailAddress	Contact	Click to Add
10	Hopewell, Inc.	5600 Carver Ro	Port Moody	BC	V3H 1A4	hopewell@emc	Jacob Hopewell	
25	Langley Corpor	805 First Avenu	Burnaby	BC	V3J 1C9	langley@emcp.	Mandy Shin	
31	Sound Supplies	2104 Union Stre	Seattle	WA	98105	ssupplies@emc	Regan Levine	
35	Emerald City Pr	1059 Pike Street	Seattle	WA	98102	ecproducts@en	Howard Greer	
42	Fraser Valley Pr	3894 Old Yale R	Abbotsford	BC	V2S 1A9	fvproducts@em	Layla Adams	
54	Manning, Inc.	1039 South 22n	Vancouver	BC	V5K 1R1	manning@emcp	Jack Silverstein	
68	Freedom Corpo	14 Fourth Avent	Vancouver	BC	V5K 2C7	freedom@emcp	Opal Northwoo	
70	Rosewood, Inc.	998 North 42nd	Vancouver	BC	V5K 2N8	rosewood@em	Clint Rivas	
84	Macadam, Inc.	675 Third Street	Vancouver	BC	V5K 2R9	macadam@emc	Hans Reiner	
99	KL Distributions	402 Yukon Drive	Bellingham	WA	98435	kldist@emcp.ne	Noland Danniso	
38	Hadley Compan	5845 Jefferson	Seattle	WA	98107	hcompany@em	Jurene Miller	

9. Close the Suppliers table by clicking the Close button in the work area.
10. Open the Products table by double-clicking *Products* in the Tables group in the Navigation pane. (This opens the table in Datasheet view.)
11. Insert two new records by completing the following steps:
    a. Click the New button in the Records group and then enter the data for a new record as shown in Figure 1.5. (See the record that begins with *901-S*.)

b. After typing the last field entry in the record for product number 901-S, press the Tab key. This moves the insertion point to the blank field below *901-S*.

c. Type the new record as shown in Figure 1.5. (See the record that begins with *917-S*.)

12. With the Products table open, delete a record by completing the following steps:

a. Click in the field containing the data *780-2*.

b. Click the Delete button arrow in the Records group (notice that the button displays in a dimmed manner) and then click *Delete Record* at the drop-down list.

c. At the message asking if you want to delete the record, click Yes.

13. Close the Products table by clicking the Close button in the work area.

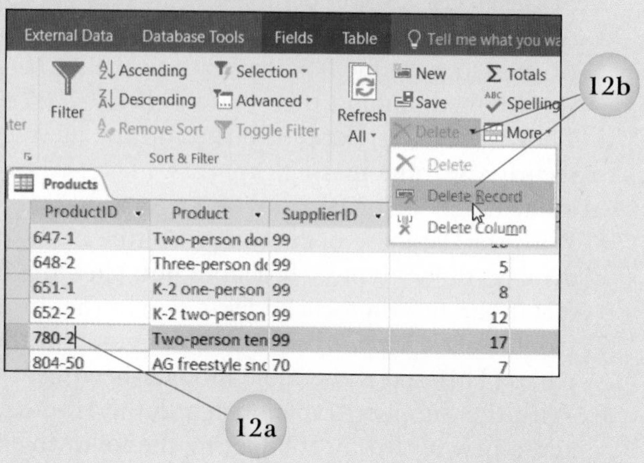

Check Your Work

Figure 1.5 Project 2a, Step 11

Step 11

Tutorial

Managing Fields in Datasheet View

Quick Steps

Insert a New Field
1. Open table.
2. Click in first cell below *Click to Add*.
3. Type data.

Inserting, Moving, and Deleting Fields

When managing a database, an additional field may need to be added to a table. For example, a field column may need to be added for contact information, one for cell phone numbers, or for the number of items in stock. To insert a new field column in a table, open the table in Datasheet view and then click in the first cell below *Click to Add* in the header row. Type the data in the cell, press the Down Arrow key, and then type the data for the second row. Continue in this manner until all data has been entered for the new field. In addition to pressing the Down Arrow key to move the insertion point down to the next cell, click in the desired cell using the mouse or press the Tab key until the desired cell is active.

A new field column is added to the right of existing field columns. Move a field column by positioning the mouse pointer on the field name in the header row until the pointer displays as a down-pointing black arrow and then click the left mouse button. This selects the entire field column. With the field column selected, position the mouse pointer on the field name; click and hold down the left mouse button; drag to the left or right until a thick, black vertical line displays in the desired location; and then release the mouse button. The thick, black vertical line indicates where the field column will be positioned when the mouse button is released. In addition, the pointer displays with the outline of a gray box attached to it, indicating that a move operation is being performed.

Delete a field column in a manner similar to deleting a row. Click in one of the fields in the column, make sure the Home tab is active, click the Delete button arrow, and then click *Delete Column* at the drop-down list. At the message asking to confirm the deletion, click Yes.

Project 2b   Inserting, Moving, and Deleting Fields

1. With **1-PacTrek.accdb** open, add a new field to the Suppliers table by completing the following steps:
   a. Double-click *Suppliers* in the Tables group in the Navigation pane.
   b. Click in the field immediately below *Click to Add* in the header row.
   c. Type (604) 555-3843 and then press the Down Arrow key on the keyboard.
   d. Type the remaining telephone numbers as shown below and at the right.

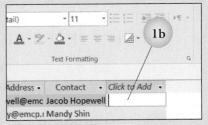

2. Move the *Field1* field column so it is positioned immediately left of the *EmailAddress* field column by completing the following steps:
   a. Position the mouse pointer on the *Field1* field name in the header row until the pointer displays as a down-pointing black arrow and then click the left mouse button. (This selects the field column.)
   b. Position the mouse pointer on the *Field1* field name. (The pointer displays as the normal, white arrow pointer.) Click and hold down the left mouse button; drag to the left until the thick, black vertical line displays immediately left of the *EmailAddress* field column; and then release the mouse button.

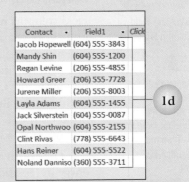

3. Delete the *Contact* field by completing the following steps:
   a. Position the mouse pointer on the *Contact* field name in the header row until the pointer displays as a down-pointing black arrow and then click the left mouse button. (This selects the field column.)
   b. Click the Delete button arrow in the Records group and then click *Delete Column* at the drop-down list.

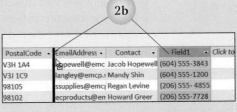

c. At the message asking if you want to permanently delete the selected field(s) click Yes.

4. Close the Suppliers table. At the message asking if you want to save the changes to the layout of the table, click Yes.

Check Your Work

Hiding, Unhiding, Freezing, and Unfreezing Field Columns

A field column in a table can be hidden if the column is not needed for data entry or editing purposes or to make viewing easier for two nonadjacent field columns containing data to be compared. To hide a field column, click in any field in the column, click the More button in the Records group on the Home tab, and then click *Hide Fields* at the drop-down list. Hide adjacent field columns by selecting the columns, clicking the More button in the Records group, and then clicking *Hide Fields* at the drop-down list. To unhide field columns, click the More button and then click *Unhide Fields*. At the Unhide Columns dialog box insert a check mark in the check boxes for those field columns that should remain visible.

More

Another method for comparing field columns side by side is to freeze a column. Freezing a field column is also helpful when not all of the columns of data are visible at one time. To freeze a field column, click in any field in the column, click the More button, and then click *Freeze Fields* at the drop-down list. To freeze adjacent field columns, select the columns first, click the More button, and then click *Freeze Fields* at the drop-down list. To unfreeze all field columns in a table, click the More button and then click *Unfreeze All Fields* at the drop-down list.

Tutorial

Adjusting Field Column Width

Adjusting Field
Column Width

Field columns have a default width of 13.111 characters, which is the approximate number of characters that will display in a field in the column. Depending on the data entered in a field in a field column, not all of the data will be visible. Or, data entered in a field may take up only a portion of the field. Change a field's column width with options at the Column Width dialog box. Display the dialog box by clicking the More button in the Records group on the Home tab and then clicking the *Field Width* option. Enter a measurement in the *Column Width* measurement box or click the Best Fit button to adjust the column width to accommodate the longest entry.

Quick Steps

Adjust Field Column Width
1. Click More button.
2. Click *Field Width*.
3. Type measurement
4. Click OK.
OR
1. Click More button.
2. Click *Field Width*.
3. Click Best Fit button.
OR
Double-click column boundary line.
OR
Select field columns and then double-click column boundary line.
OR
Drag column boundary line to new position.

The width of a field column also can be adjusted to accommodate the longest entry by positioning the arrow pointer on the column boundary line at the right side of the column in the header row until the pointer turns into a left-and-right-pointing arrow with a vertical line in the middle and then double-clicking the left mouse button. Adjust the widths of adjacent field columns by selecting the columns first and then double-clicking one of the selected column boundary lines in the header row. To select adjacent field columns, position the arrow pointer on the first field name to be selected in the header row until the pointer turns into a down-pointing black arrow, click and hold down the left mouse button, drag to the last field name to be selected, and then release the mouse button. With the field columns selected, double-click one of the field column boundary lines.

Another method for adjusting the width of a field column is to drag a boundary line to the desired position. To do this, position the arrow pointer on the column boundary line (until the pointer turns into a left-and-right-pointing arrow with a vertical line in the middle), click and hold down the left mouse button, drag until the field column is the desired width, and then release the mouse button.

1. With **1-PacTrek.accdb** open, open the Suppliers table.
2. Hide the *PostalCode* field column by clicking the *PostalCode* field name in the header row, clicking the More button in the Records group on the Home tab, and then clicking *Hide Fields* at the drop-down list.

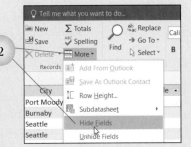

3. Unhide the field column by clicking the More button and then clicking *Unhide Fields* at the drop-down list. At the Unhide Columns dialog box, click the *PostalCode* check box to insert a check mark, and then click the Close button.

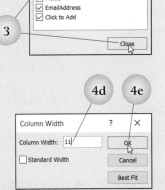

4. Adjust the width of the *SupplierID* field column by completing the following steps:
   a. Click the *SupplierID* field name in the header row.
   b. Click the More button in the Records group on the Home tab.
   c. Click the *Field Width* option.
   d. Type 11 in the *Column Width* measurement box.
   e. Click OK.
5. Adjust the *SupplierName* field column by completing the following steps:
   a. Click the *SupplierName* field name in the header row.
   b. Click the More button in the Records group.
   c. Click the *Field Width* option.
   d. Click the Best Fit button.
6. Adjust the width of the remaining columns by completing the following steps:
   a. Position the arrow pointer on the *StreetAddress* field name in the header row until the pointer turns into a down-pointing black arrow, click and hold down the left mouse button, drag to the *EmailAddress* field name, and then release the mouse button.
   b. With the columns selected, double-click one of the column boundary lines in the header row.
   c. Click in any field in the table to deselect the field columns.
7. Increase the width of the *EmailAddress* field column by positioning the arrow pointer on the column boundary line in the header row at the right side of the *EmailAddress* field column until it turns into a left-and-right-pointing arrow with a vertical line in the middle, clicking and holding down the left mouse button, dragging all of the way to the right side of the screen, and then releasing the mouse button. (Check the horizontal scroll bar at the bottom of the table and notice that the scroll bar contains a scroll box.)
8. Position the mouse pointer on the scroll box on the horizontal scroll bar and then drag to the left until the *SupplierID* field is visible.
9. Freeze the *SupplierID* field column by clicking in any field in the *SupplierID* field column, clicking the More button in the Records group, and then clicking *Freeze Fields* at the drop-down list.

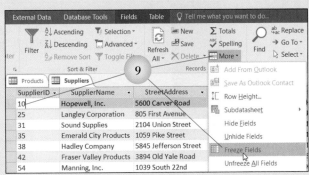

10. Using the mouse, drag the scroll box along the horizontal scroll to the right and left to view that the *SupplierID* field column remains visible on the screen.
11. Unfreeze the field column by clicking the More button in the Records group and then clicking *Unfreeze All Fields* at the drop-down list.
12. Double-click the column boundary line in the header row at the right side of the *EmailAddress* field column.
13. Close the Suppliers table and click Yes at the message that asks if you want to save the changes to the layout.
14. Open the Products table and then complete steps similar to those in Step 6 to select and then adjust the field column widths.
15. Close the Products table and click Yes at the message that asks if you want to save the changes to the layout.

Check Your Work

Tutorial

Renaming and
Deleting Objects

Quick Steps

Rename a Table
1. Right-click table name in Navigation pane.
2. Click *Rename*.
3. Type new name.
4. Press Enter.

Delete a Table
1. Right-click table name in Navigation pane.
2. Click *Delete*.
3. Click Yes, if necessary.

Renaming and Deleting a Table

Managing tables might include actions such as renaming and deleting a table. Rename a table by right-clicking the table name in the Navigation pane, clicking *Rename* at the shortcut menu, typing the new name, and then pressing the Enter key. Delete a table from a database by clicking the table name in the Navigation pane, clicking the Delete button in the Records group on the Home tab, and then clicking Yes at the message asking to confirm the deletion. Another method is to right-click the table in the Navigation pane, click *Delete* at the shortcut menu, and then click Yes at the message. If a table is deleted from the computer's hard drive, the message asking to confirm the deletion does not display. This is because Access automatically sends the deleted table to the Recycle Bin, where it can be retrieved if necessary.

Tutorial

Previewing and
Printing a Table

Quick Steps

Print a Table
1. Click File tab.
2. Click *Print*.
3. Click *Quick Print*.
OR
1. Click File tab.
2. Click *Print*.
3. Click *Print*.
4. Click OK.

Printing Tables

Click the File tab and then click the *Print* option to display the Print backstage area as shown in Figure 1.6. Click the *Quick Print* option to send the table directly to the printer without making any changes to the printer setup or the table formatting. Click the *Print* option to display the Print dialog box, with options for specifying the printer, page range, and specific records to print. Click OK to close the dialog box and send the table to the printer. By default, Access prints a table on letter-size paper in portrait orientation.

Figure 1.6 Print Backstage Area

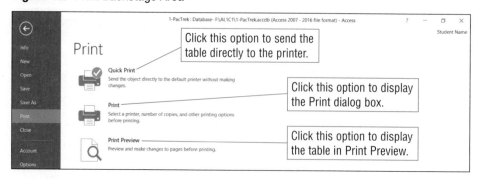

Previewing a Table

Quick Steps

Preview a Table
1. Click File tab.
2. Click *Print* option.
3. Click *Print Preview* option.

Print Preview

Print

Close Print Preview

Before printing a table, consider displaying the table in Print Preview to see how the table will print on the page. To display a table in Print Preview, as shown in Figure 1.7, click the *Print Preview* option at the Print backstage area.

Use options in the Zoom group on the Print Preview tab to increase or decrease the size of the page display. The size of the page display can also be changed using the Zoom slider bar at the right side of the Status bar. If a table spans more than one page, use buttons on the Navigation bar to display the next or previous page.

Print a table from Print Preview by clicking the Print button at the left side of the Print Preview tab. Click the Close Print Preview button to close Print Preview and continue working in the table without printing it.

Changing Page Size and Margins

Size

Margins

By default, Access prints a table in standard letter size (8.5 inches wide and 11 inches tall). Click the Size button in the Page Size group on the Print Preview tab and a drop-down list displays with options for changing the page size to legal, executive, envelope, and so on. Access uses default top, bottom, left, and right margins of 1 inch. Change these default margins by clicking the Margins button in the Page Size group and then clicking one of the predesigned margin options.

Figure 1.7 Print Preview

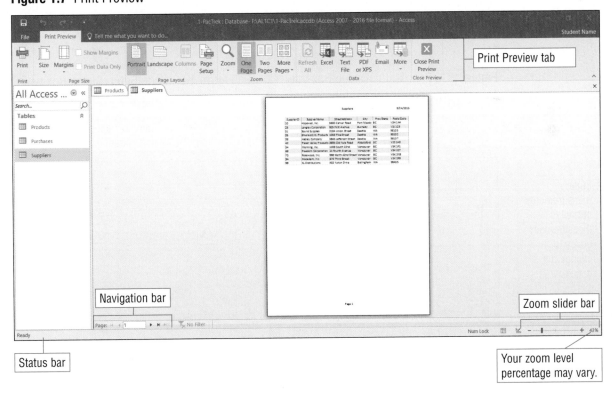

Changing Page Layout

The Print Preview tab contains the Page Layout group with buttons for controlling how data is printed on the page. By default, Access prints a table in portrait orientation, which prints the text on the page so that it is taller than it is wide (like a page in this textbook). If a table contains a number of columns, changing to landscape orientation allows more columns to fit on a page. Landscape orientation rotates the printout to be wider than it is tall. To change from the default portrait orientation to landscape orientation, click the Landscape button in the Page Layout group on the Print Preview tab.

Click the Page Setup button in the Page Layout group and the Page Setup dialog box displays as shown in Figure 1.8. At the Page Setup dialog box with the Print Options tab selected, notice that the default margins are 1 inch. Change these defaults by typing different numbers in the margin measurement boxes. By default, the table name prints at the top center of the page and the current date prints in the upper right corner of the page. In addition, the word *Page* followed by the page number prints at the bottom of the page. To specify that the name of the table, date, and page number should not print, remove the check mark from the *Print Headings* option at the Page Setup dialog box with the Print Options tab selected.

Click the Page tab at the Page Setup dialog box and the dialog box displays as shown in Figure 1.9. Change the orientation with options in the *Orientation* section and change the paper size with options in the *Paper* section. Click the *Size* option box arrow and a drop-down list displays with paper sizes similar to the options available at the *Size* button drop-down list in the Page Size group on the Print Preview tab. Specify the printer with options in the *Printer for (table name)* section of the dialog box.

Landscape

Page Setup

Figure 1.8 Page Setup Dialog Box with Print Options Tab Selected

Figure 1.9 Page Setup Dialog Box with Page Tab Selected

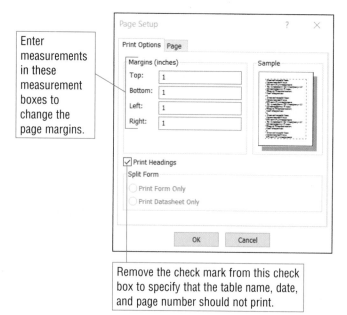

Enter measurements in these measurement boxes to change the page margins.

Remove the check mark from this check box to specify that the table name, date, and page number should not print.

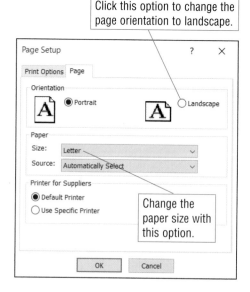

Click this option to change the page orientation to landscape.

Change the paper size with this option.

1. With **1-PacTrek.accdb** open, open the Suppliers table.
2. Preview and then print the Suppliers table in landscape orientation by completing the following steps:

   a. Click the File tab and then click the *Print* option.

   b. At the Print backstage area, click the *Print Preview* option.

   c. Click the Two Pages button in the Zoom group on the Print Preview tab. (This displays two pages of the table.)

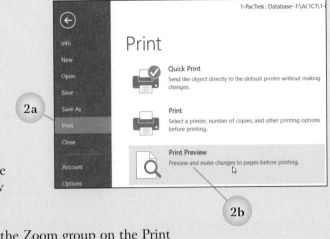

   d. Click the Zoom button arrow in the Zoom group on the Print Preview tab and then click *75%* at the drop-down list.

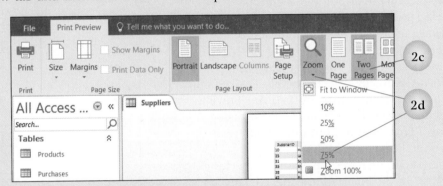

   e. Position the arrow pointer on the Zoom slider bar button at the right side of the Status bar, click and hold down the left mouse button, drag to the right until *100%* displays at the right of the Zoom slider bar, and then release the mouse button.

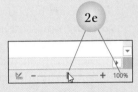

   f. Return the display to a full page by clicking the One Page button in the Zoom group on the Print Preview tab.

   g. Click the Margins button in the Page Size group on the Print Preview tab and then click the *Narrow* option at the drop-down list. (Notice how the data will print on the page with the narrow margins.)

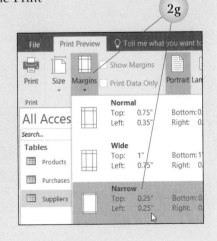

   h. Change the margins back to the default by clicking the Margins button in the Page Size group and then clicking the *Normal* option at the drop-down list.

   i. Change to landscape orientation by clicking the Landscape button in the Page Layout group. (Check the Next Page button on the Record Navigation bar and notice that it is dimmed. This indicates that the table will print on only one page.)

   j. Print the table by clicking the Print button at the left side of the Print Preview tab and then clicking OK at the Print dialog box.

3. Close the Suppliers table.
4. Open the Products table and then print the table by completing the following steps:
   a. Click the File tab and then click the *Print* option.
   b. At the Print backstage area, click the *Print Preview* option.
   c. Click the Page Setup button in the Page Layout group on the Print Preview tab. (This displays the Page Setup dialog box with the Print Options tab selected.)
   d. At the Page Setup dialog box, click the Page tab.
   e. Click the *Landscape* option.

   f. Click the Print Options tab.
   g. Select the current measurement in the *Top* measurement box and then type 0.5.
   h. Select the current measurement in the *Bottom* measurement box and then type 0.5.
   i. Select the current measurement in the *Left* measurement box and then type 1.5.
   j. Click OK to close the dialog box.
   k. Click the Print button on the Print Preview tab and then click OK at the Print dialog box. (This table will print on two pages.)

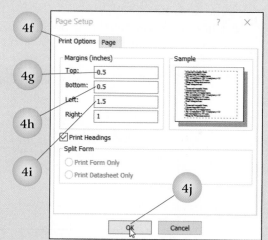

5. Close the Products table.
6. Rename the Purchases table by right-clicking *Purchases* in the Navigation pane, clicking *Rename* at the shortcut menu, typing Orders, and then pressing the Enter key.
7. Delete the Orders table by right-clicking *Orders* in the Tables group in the Navigation pane and then clicking *Delete* at the shortcut menu. If a message displays asking if you want to permanently delete the table, click Yes.

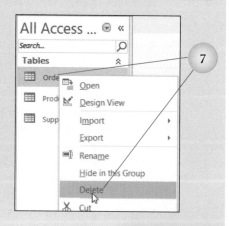

Check Your Work

Designing a Table

Tables are the first objects created in a new database and all other objects in a database rely on tables for data. Designing a database involves planning the number of tables needed and the fields that will be included in each table. Each table in a database should contain information about only one subject. For example, the Suppliers table in the 1-PacTrek.accdb database contains data only about suppliers and the Products table contains data only about products.

Database designers often create a visual representation of the database's structure in a diagram similar to the one shown in Figure 1.10. Each table is represented by a box with the table name at the top. Within each box, the fields that will be stored in the table are listed with the field names that will be used when the table is created.

Notice that one field in each table has an asterisk next to its name. The field with the asterisk is called the *primary key field*. A primary key field holds data that uniquely identifies each record in a table and is usually an identification number. The lines drawn between each table in Figure 1.10 are called *join lines,* and they represent links established between tables (called *relationships*) so that data can be extracted from one or more tables. The join lines point to a common field name included in each table that is to be linked. (Joining tables is covered in Chapter 2.) A database with related tables is called a *relational database.*

The join line in the database diagram connects the *SupplierID* field in the Suppliers table with the *SupplierID* field in the Products table and another join line connects the *SupplierID* field in the Suppliers table with the *SupplierID* field in the Orders table. A join line connects the *ProductID* field in the Products table with the *ProductID* field in the Orders table.

Consider certain design principles when designing a database. The first principle is to reduce redundant (duplicate) data. Redundant data increases the amount of data entry required, increases the chances for errors and inconsistencies, and takes up additional storage space. The Products table contains a *SupplierID* field and that field reduces the duplicate data needed in the table by keeping the data in one table instead of two and then joining the tables by a common field.

💡 **Hint** Join tables to minimize or eliminate data duplication.

Figure 1.10 Database Diagram

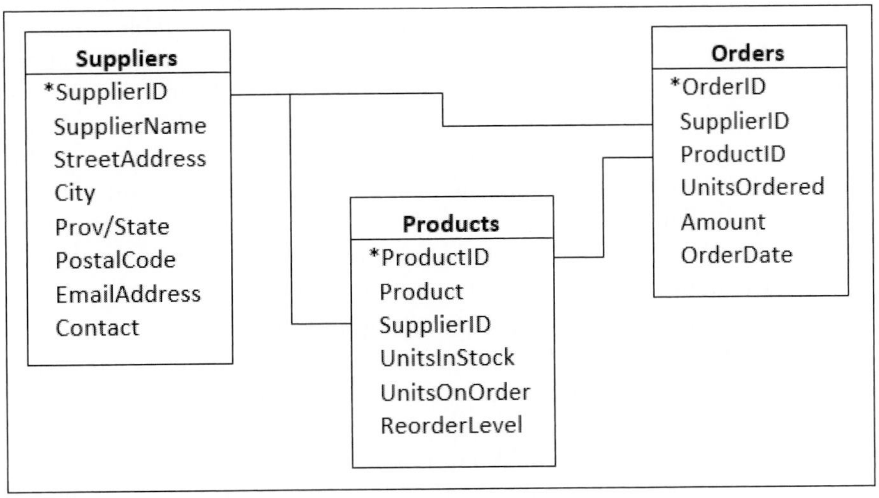

For example, rather than typing the supplier information in the Suppliers table *and* the Products table, type the information once in the Suppliers table and then join the tables with the connecting field *SupplierID*. If information is needed on suppliers as well as specific information about products, the information can be drawn into one object, such as a query or report using data from both tables. When creating the Orders table, the *SupplierID* field and the *ProductID* field will be used rather than typing all of the information for the suppliers and the product description. Typing a two-letter unique identifier number for a supplier greatly reduces the amount of typing required to create the Orders table. Inserting the *ProductID* field in the Orders table eliminates the need to type the product description for each order; instead, a unique five-, six-, or seven-digit identifier number is typed.

Creating a Table

Tutorial

Creating a Table in Datasheet View

Creating a new table generally involves determining fields, assigning a data type to each field, modifying properties, designating the primary key field, and naming the table. This process is referred to as defining the table structure.

The first step in creating a table is to determine the fields. A field, commonly called a column, is one piece of information about a person, place, or item. Each field contains data about one aspect of the table subject, such as a company name or product number. All fields for one unit, such as a customer or product, are considered a record. For example, in the Suppliers table in the 1-PacTrek.accdb database, a record is all of the information pertaining to one supplier. A collection of records becomes a table.

💡 **Hint** A database table contains fields that can describe a person, customer, client, object, place, idea, or event.

When designing a table, determine the fields to be included based on how the information will be used. When organizing fields be sure to consider not only the current needs for the data but also any future needs. For example, a company may need to keep track of customer names, addresses, and telephone numbers for current mailing lists. In the future, the company may want to promote a new product to customers who purchase a specific type of product. For this information to be available at a later date, a field that identifies product type must be included in the database. When organizing fields, consider all potential needs for the data but also try to keep the fields logical and manageable.

 Table

A table can be created in Datasheet view or Design view. To create a table in Datasheet view, open the desired database (or create a new database), click the Create tab, and then click the Table button in the Tables group. This inserts a blank table in the work area with the tab labeled *Table1*, as shown in Figure 1.11. Notice the column with the field name *ID* has been created automatically. Access creates *ID* as an AutoNumber data type field in which the field value is assigned automatically by Access as each record is entered in the table. In many tables, this AutoNumber data type field is used to create the unique identifier for the table. For example, in Project 2e, you will create an Orders table and use the *ID* AutoNumber data type field to assign automatically a number to each order, since each order must contain a unique number.

💡 **Hint** Assign a data type to each field that determines the type of information that can be entered into the field.

When creating a new field (column), determine the type of data to be inserted in the field. For example, one field might contain text such as a name or product description, another field might contain an amount of money, and another might contain a date. The data type defines the type of information Access will allow to be entered into the field. For example, Access will not allow alphabetic characters to be entered into a field with a data type set to Date & Time.

Figure 1.11 Blank Table in Datasheet View

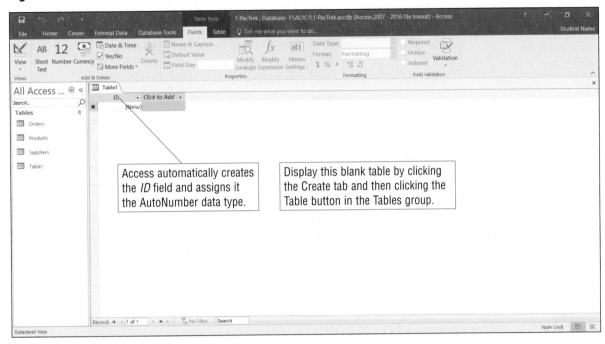

Access automatically creates the *ID* field and assigns it the AutoNumber data type.

Display this blank table by clicking the Create tab and then clicking the Table button in the Tables group.

More Fields

The Add & Delete group on the Table Tools Fields tab contains five buttons for assigning data types plus a More Fields button. Descriptions of the five data types assigned by the buttons are provided in Table 1.3.

Table 1.3 Data Types

Button	Description
Short Text	Alphanumeric data up to 255 characters in length—for example, a name, an address, or a value such as a telephone number or social security number that is used as an identifier and not for calculating.
Number	Positive or negative values that can be used in calculations; not to be used for values that will calculate monetary amounts (see Currency).
Currency	Values that involve money; Access will not round off during calculations.
Date & Time	Used to ensure dates and times are entered and sorted properly.
Yes/No	Data in the field will be either *Yes* or *No*; *True* or *False*, *On* or *Off*.

In Project 2e, you will create the Orders table, as shown in Figure 1.12. Looking at the diagram in Figure 1.10, you will assign the following data types to the columns:

OrderID:	AutoNumber (Access automatically assigns this data type to the first column)
SupplierID:	Short Text (the supplier numbers are identifiers, not numbers for calculating)
ProductID:	Short Text (the product numbers are identifiers, not numbers for calculating)
UnitsOrdered:	Number (the unit numbers are values for calculating)
Amount:	Currency
OrderDate:	Date & Time

Click a data type button and Access inserts a field to the right of the *ID* field and selects the field heading *Field1*. Type a name for the field; press the Enter key; and Access selects the next field heading, named *Click to Add*, and displays a drop-down list of data types. This drop-down list contains the same five data types as the buttons in the Add & Delete group as well as additional data types. Click the data type at the drop-down list, type the field name, and then press the Enter key. Continue in this manner until all field names have been entered for the table. When naming a field, consider the following guidelines:

- Each field must have a unique name.
- The name should describe the contents of the field.
- A field name can contain up to 64 characters.
- A field name can contain letters and numbers. Some symbols are permitted but others are excluded, so avoid using symbols other than the underscore (to separate words) and the number symbol (to indicate an identifier number).

- Do not use spaces in field names. Although a space is an accepted character, most database designers avoid using spaces in field names and object names. Use field compound words for field names or the underscore character as a word separator. For example, a field name for a person's last name could be named *LastName*, *Last_Name*, or *LName*.
- Abbreviate field names so that they are as short as possible but still easily understood. For example, a field such as *CompanyName* could be shortened to *CoName* and a field such as *EmailAddress* could be shortened to *Email*.

Project 2e Creating a Table and Entering Data

Part 5 of 7

1. With **1-PacTrek.accdb** open, create a new table and specify data types and field names by completing the following steps:
   a. Click the Create tab.
   b. Click the Table button in the Tables group.
   c. Click the Short Text button in the Add & Delete group.

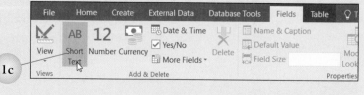

1c

d. With the *Field1* field name selected, type SupplierID and then press the Enter key. (This displays a drop-down list of data types below the *Click to Add* heading.)

e. Click the *Short Text* option at the drop-down list.

f. Type ProductID in the next field name and then press the Enter key.

g. Click *Number* at the drop-down list, type UnitsOrdered in the next field name, and then press the Enter key.

h. Click *Currency* at the drop-down list, type Amount for the next field, and then press the Enter key.

i. Click *Date & Time* at the drop-down list and then type OrderDate. (Do not press the Enter key since this is the last field in the table.)

2. Enter the first record in the table, as shown in Figure 1.12, by completing the following steps:

a. Click two times in the first field below the *SupplierID* field name. (The first time you click the mouse button, the row is selected. Clicking the second time makes only the field below *SupplierID* active.)

b. Type the data in the fields as shown in Figure 1.12. Press the Tab key to move to the next field or press Shift + Tab to move to the previous field. Access will automatically insert the next number in the sequence in the first field column (the *ID* field column). When typing the money amounts in the *Amount* field column, you do not need to type the dollar symbol or the comma. Access will automatically insert them when you make the next field active. Make sure to proofread the data after you type it to ensure it is accurate.

3. When the 14 records have been entered, click the Save button on the Quick Access Toolbar.

4. At the Save As dialog box, type Orders and then press the Enter key. (This saves the table with the name *Orders*.)

5. Close the Orders table by clicking the Close button in the upper right corner of the work area.

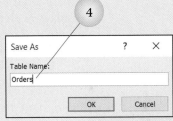

Check Your Work

Figure 1.12 Project 2e

ID	SupplierID	ProductID	UnitsOrdered	Amount	OrderDate	Click to Add
1	54	101-S3	10	$1,137.50	1/5/2018	
2	68	209-L	25	$173.75	1/5/2018	
3	68	209-XL	25	$180.00	1/5/2018	
4	68	209-XXL	20	$145.80	1/5/2018	
5	68	210-M	15	$97.35	1/5/2018	
6	68	210-L	25	$162.25	1/5/2018	
7	31	299-M2	10	$887.90	1/19/2018	
8	31	299-M3	10	$887.90	1/19/2018	
9	31	299-M5	10	$887.90	1/19/2018	
10	31	299-W1	8	$602.32	1/19/2018	
11	31	299-W3	10	$752.90	1/19/2018	
12	31	299-W4	10	$752.90	1/19/2018	
13	31	299-W5	10	$752.90	1/19/2018	
14	35	602-XR	5	$2,145.00	1/19/2018	
*	(New)		0	$0.00		

Renaming a Field

Click a data type button or click a data type at the data type drop-down list and the default field name (such as *Field1*) is automatically selected. With the default field name selected, type a name for the field. To change a field name, right-click the name, click *Rename Field* at the shortcut menu (which selects the current field name), and then type the new name.

Modifying Field
Properties in
Datasheet View

Name &
Caption

Inserting a Name, Caption, and Description

When creating a table that others will use, consider providing additional information so users understand the fields in the table and what should be entered in each one. Along with the field name, provide a caption and description for each field with options at the Enter Field Properties dialog box, shown in Figure 1.13. Display this dialog box by clicking the Name & Caption button in the Properties group on the Table Tools Fields tab.

At the Enter Field Properties dialog box, type the desired name for the field in the *Name* text box. To provide a more descriptive name for the field, type the descriptive name in the *Caption* text box. The text typed will display as the field caption but the actual field name will still be part of the table structure. Creating a caption is useful if the field name is abbreviated or to show spaces between words in a field name. The field name is what Access uses for the table and the caption is what displays to users.

The *Description* text box is another source for providing information about the field to others using the database. Type information in the text box that specifies what should be entered in the field. The text typed in the *Description* text box displays at the left side of the Status bar when a field in a column is active. For example, type *Enter the total amount of the order* in the *Description* text box for the *Amount* field and that text will display at the left side of the Status bar when a field in the column is active.

Figure 1.13 Enter Field Properties Dialog Box

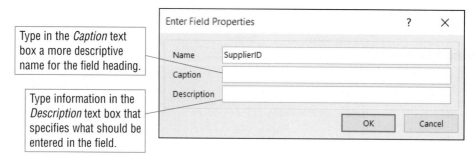

Type in the *Caption* text box a more descriptive name for the field heading.

Type information in the *Description* text box that specifies what should be entered in the field.

1. With **1-PacTrek.accdb** open, open the Orders table.
2. Access automatically named the first field *ID*. You want to make the field name more descriptive so you decide to rename it. To do this, right-click the *ID* field name and then click *Rename Field* at the drop-down list.
3. Type OrderID and then press the Enter key.
4. To provide more information for others using the table, you decide to add information for the *SupplierID* field by creating a caption and description. To do this, complete the following steps:
   a. Click the *SupplierID* field name in the header row. (This selects the entire column.)
   b. Click the Table Tools Fields tab.
   c. Click the Name & Caption button in the Properties group. (At the Enter Field Properties dialog box, notice that *SupplierID* is already inserted in the *Name* text box.)
   d. At the Enter Field Properties dialog box, click in the *Caption* text box and then type Supplier Number.
   e. Click in the *Description* text box and then type Supplier identification number.
   f. Click OK to close the dialog box. (Notice that the field name now displays as *Supplier Number*. The field name is still *SupplierID* but what displays is *Supplier Number*.)

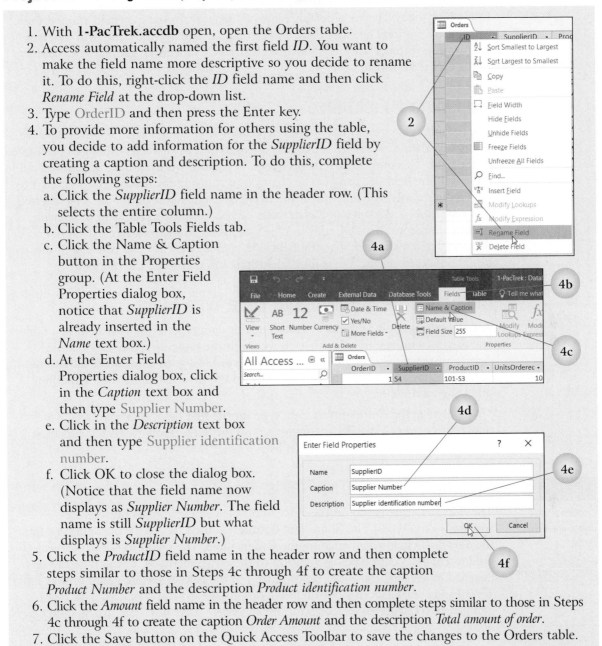

5. Click the *ProductID* field name in the header row and then complete steps similar to those in Steps 4c through 4f to create the caption *Product Number* and the description *Product identification number*.
6. Click the *Amount* field name in the header row and then complete steps similar to those in Steps 4c through 4f to create the caption *Order Amount* and the description *Total amount of order*.
7. Click the Save button on the Quick Access Toolbar to save the changes to the Orders table.
8. Close the Orders table.

Check Your Work

Assigning a Default Value

The Properties group on the Table Tools Fields tab contains additional buttons for defining field properties in a table. If most records in a table are likely to contain the same field value in a column, consider inserting that value by default. Do this by clicking the Default Value button in the Properties group. At the Expression Builder dialog box, type the default value and then click OK.

 Default Value

For example, in Project 2g, you will create a new table in the 1-PacTrek database containing information on customers, most of whom live in Vancouver, British Columbia. You will create a default value of *Vancouver* for the *City* field and a default value of *BC* for the *Prov/State* field. You can replace the default value with different text, so if a customer lives in Abbotsford instead of Vancouver, simply type *Abbotsford* in the *City* field instead.

Assigning a Field Size

The default field size property varies depending on the data type. For example, the Short Text data type assigns a maximum length of 255 characters that can be entered in the field. This number can be decreased depending on what data will be entered in the field. The field size can also be changed to control how much data is entered to help reduce errors. For example, if the two-letter state abbreviation is to be inserted in a state field, a field size of 2 characters can be assigned to the field. If someone entering data into the table tries to type more than two letters, Access will not accept the additional text. To change the field size, click in the *Field Size* text box in the Properties group on the Table Tools Fields tab and then type the number.

Changing the AutoNumber Data Type Field

Access automatically applies the AutoNumber data type to the first field in a table and assigns a unique number to each record in the table. In many cases, letting Access automatically assign a number to a record is a good idea. Some situations may arise, however, when the unique value in the first field should be something other than a number.

To change the AutoNumber data type for the first field, click the *Data Type* option box arrow in the Formatting group on the Table Tools Fields tab and then click the data type at the drop-down list.

Inserting Quick Start Fields

The Add & Delete group on the Table Tools Fields tab contains buttons for specifying data types. The Short Text button was used to specify the data type for the *SupplierID* field when creating the Orders table. The field drop-down list was also used to choose a data type. In addition to these two methods, a data type can be assigned by clicking the More Fields button in the Add & Delete group on the Table Tools Fields tab. Click this button and a drop-down list displays with data types grouped into categories such as *Basic Types*, *Number*, *Date and Time*, *Yes/No*, and *Quick Start*.

The options in the *Quick Start* category not only define a data type but also assign a field name. Additionally, with options in the *Quick Start* category, a group of related fields can be added in one step. For example, click the *Name* option in the *Quick Start* category and Access inserts the *LastName* field in one column and the *FirstName* field in the next column. Both fields are automatically assigned a Short Text data type. Click the *Address* option in the *Quick Start* category and Access inserts five fields, including *Address*, *City*, *StateProvince*, *ZIPPostal*, and *CountryRegion*—all with the Short Text data type assigned.

1. The owners of Pacific Trek have decided to publish a semiannual product catalog and have asked customers who want to receive the catalog to fill out a form and include on the form whether or not they want to receive notices of upcoming sales in addition to the catalog. Create a table to store the data for customers by completing the following steps:

   a. With **1-PacTrek.accdb** open, click the Create tab.

   b. Click the Table button in the Tables group.

   c. With the *Click to Add* field active, click the More Fields button in the Add & Delete group on the Table Tools Fields tab.

   d. Scroll down the drop-down list and then click *Name* in the *Quick Start* category. (This inserts the captions *Last Name* and *First Name* in the table. The actual field names are *LastName* and *FirstName*.)

   e. Click *Click to Add* immediately right of the *First Name* field name in the header row. (Although the data type drop-down list displays, you are going to use the More Fields button rather than the drop-down list to create the next fields.)

   f. Click the More Fields button, scroll down the drop-down list, and then click *Address* in the *Quick Start* category. (This inserts five more fields in the table.)

   g. Scroll to the right in the table to display *Click to Add* that follows the *Country Region* field name in the header row. (You can scroll in the table using the horizontal scroll bar to the right of the Record Navigation bar.)

   h. Click *Click to Add* and then click *Yes/No* at the drop-down list.

   i. With the name *Field1* selected, type Mailers. (When entering records in the table, you will insert a check mark in the field check box if a customer wants to receive sales promotion mailers. If a customer does not want to receive the mailers, you will leave the check box blank.)

2. Rename and create a caption and description for the *ID* field by completing the following steps:

   a. Scroll to the beginning of the table and then click the *ID* field name in the header row. (You can scroll in the table using the horizontal scroll bar to the right of the Record Navigation bar.)

   b. Click the Name & Caption button in the Properties group on the Table Tools Fields tab.

   c. At the Enter Field Properties dialog box, select the text *ID* in the *Name* text box and then type CustomerID.

d. Press the Tab key and then type Customer Number in the *Caption* text box.

e. Press the Tab key and then type Access will automatically assign the record the next number in the sequence.

f. Click OK to close the Enter Field Properties dialog box. (Notice the description at the left side of the Status bar.)

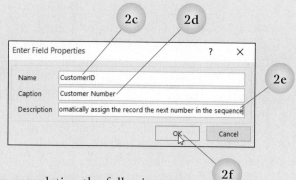

3. Add a description to the *Last Name* field by completing the following steps:

a. Click the *Last Name* field name in the header row.

b. Click the Name & Caption button in the Properties group.

c. At the Enter Field Properties dialog box notice that Access named the field *LastName* but provided the caption *Last Name*. You do not want to change the name and caption so press the Tab key two times to make the *Description* text box active and then type Customer last name.

d. Click OK to close the dialog box.

4. You know that a customer's last name will not likely exceed 30 characters, so you decide to limit the field size. To do this, click in the *Field Size* text box in the Properties group (this selects *255*), type 30, and then press the Enter key.

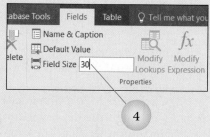

5. Click the *First Name* field name in the header row and then complete steps similar to those in Steps 3 and 4 to create the description *Customer first name* and change the field size to 30 characters.

6. Since most of Pacific Trek's customers live in the city of Vancouver, you decide to make it the default field value. To do this, complete the following steps:

a. Click the *City* field name in the header row.

b. Click the Default Value button in the Properties group.

c. At the Expression Builder dialog box, type Vancouver.

d. Click the OK button to close the dialog box.

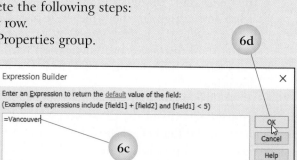

7. Change the *State Province* field name and insert a default value by completing the following steps:

a. Right-click the *State Province* field name in the header row and then click *Rename Field* at the shortcut menu.

b. Type Province.

c. Click the Default Value button in the Properties group.

d. Type BC in the Expression Builder dialog box and then click the OK button.

8. Click the *ZIP Postal* field name in the header row and then limit the field size to 7 characters by clicking in the *Field Size* text box (which selects *255*), typing 7, and then pressing the Enter key.

9. Since most customers want to be sent the sales promotional mailers, you decide to insert a check mark as the default value in the check boxes in the *Yes/No* column. To do this, complete the following steps:
   a. Click the *Mailers* field name in the header row.
   b. Click the Default Value button in the Properties group.
   c. At the Expression Builder dialog box, press the Backspace key two times to delete *No* and then type Yes.
   d. Click OK to close the dialog box.
10. Delete the *Country Region* field by clicking the *Country Region* field name in the header row and then clicking the Delete button in the Add & Delete group.
11. Save the table by completing the following steps:
    a. Click the Save button on the Quick Access Toolbar.
    b. At the Save As dialog box, type Customers and then press the Enter key.
12. Enter the six records in the table shown in Figure 1.14. To remove a check mark in the *Mailers* column, press the spacebar.
13. Adjust the field column widths to accommodate the longest entry in each column by completing the following steps:
    a. Position the arrow pointer on the *Customer Number* field name in the header row until the pointer turns into a down-pointing black arrow, click and hold down the left mouse button, drag to the *Mailers* field name, and then release the mouse button.
    b. With the columns selected, double-click one of the column boundary lines in the header row.
14. Click the Save button on the Quick Access Toolbar to save the Customers table.
15. Print the Customers table by completing the following steps:
    a. Click the File tab and then click the *Print* option.
    b. At the Print backstage area, click the *Print Preview* option.
    c. Click the Landscape button in the Page Layout group on the Print Preview tab.
    d. Click the Print button at the left side of the Print Preview tab.
    e. At the Print dialog box, click OK.
16. Close the Customers table.
17. Open the Orders table.
18. Automatically adjust the field column widths to accommodate the longest entry in each column.
19. Click the Save button to save the Orders table.
20. Print the table in landscape orientation (refer to Step 15) and then close the table.
21. Close **1-PacTrek.accdb**.

Check Your Work

Figure 1.14 Project 2g

Customer Number ▾	Last Name ▾	First Name ▾	Address ▾	City ▾	Province ▾	ZIP Postal ▾	Mailers ▾
1	Blakely	Mathias	7433 224th Ave. E	Vancouver	BC	V5K 2M7	✓
2	Donato	Antonio	18225 Victoria Dr.	Vancouver	BC	V5K 1H4	☐
3	Girard	Stephanie	430 Deer Lake Pl.	Burnaby	BC	V3J 1E4	✓
4	Hernandez	Angelica	1233 E. 59th Ave.	Vancouver	BC	V5K 3H3	✓
5	Ives-Keller	Shane	9055 Gilbert Rd.	Richmond	BC	V6Y 1B2	☐
6	Kim	Keung	730 West Broadway	Vancouver	BC	V5K 5B2	✓
* (New)				Vancouver	BC		✓

Chapter Summary

- Microsoft Access is a database management system software program that can organize, store, maintain, retrieve, sort, and print all types of business data.

- In Access, open an existing database by clicking the <u>Open Other Files</u> hyperlink at the Access 2016 opening screen. At the Open backstage area, click the *Browse* option. At the Open dialog box, navigate to the location of the database and then double-click the database.

- Some common objects found in a database include tables, queries, forms, and reports.

- The Navigation pane displays at the left side of the Access screen and displays the objects that are contained in the database.

- Open a database object by double-clicking the object in the Navigation pane or by right-clicking the object and then clicking *Open* at the shortcut menu.

- Close an object by clicking the Close button in the upper right corner of the work area or right-clicking the object tab and then clicking *Close* at the shortcut menu.

- When a table is open, the Record Navigation bar displays at the bottom of the screen and contains buttons for displaying records in the table.

- Insert a new record in a table by clicking the New button in the Records group on the Home tab or by clicking the New (blank) record button in the Record Navigation bar.

- Delete a record by clicking in a field in the record to be deleted, clicking the Delete button arrow on the Home tab, and then clicking *Delete Record* at the drop-down list.

- Add a field column to a table by clicking in the first field below *Click to Add* and then typing the data.

- Move a field column by selecting the column and then using the mouse to drag a thick, black, vertical line (representing the column) to the desired location.

- Delete a field column by clicking in any field in the column, clicking the Delete button arrow, and then clicking *Delete Column* at the drop-down list.

- Data entered in a table is automatically saved while changes to the layout of a table are not automatically saved.

- Hide, unhide, freeze, and unfreeze field columns with options at the More button drop-down list. Display this list by clicking the More button in the Records group on the Home tab.

- Adjust the width of a field column with options at the Column Width dialog box. Display the dialog box by clicking the More button and then clicking *Field Width* at the drop-down list. Enter a column measurement in the *Column Width* measurement box or click the Best Fit button.

- Adjust the width of a field column by dragging the column boundary line in the header row. Or, adjust the width of a column (or selected columns) to accommodate the longest entry by double-clicking the column boundary line.

- Rename a table by right-clicking the table name in the Navigation pane, clicking *Rename*, and then typing the new name. Delete a table by right-clicking the table name in the Navigation pane and then clicking *Delete*.

- Print a table by clicking the File tab, clicking the *Print* option, and then clicking the *Quick Print* option. Preview a table before printing by clicking the *Print Preview* option at the Print backstage area.

- Use buttons and options on the Print Preview tab to change the page size, orientation, and margins.
- The first principle in database design is to reduce redundant data, because redundant data increases the amount of data entry required and the potential for errors, as well as takes up additional storage space.
- A data type defines the type of data Access will allow in the field. Assign a data type to a field with buttons in the Add & Delete group on the Table Tools Fields tab, by clicking an option from the field drop-down list, or with options at the More Fields button drop-down list.
- Rename a field by right-clicking the field name, clicking *Rename Field* at the shortcut menu, and then typing the new name.
- Type a name, caption, and description for a field with options at the Enter Field Properties dialog box.
- Use options in the *Quick Start* category in the More Fields button drop-down list to define a data type and assign a field name to a group of related fields.
- Insert a default value in a field with the Default Value button and assign a field size with the *Field Size* text box in the Properties group on the Table Tools Fields tab.
- Use the *Data Type* option box in the Formatting group on the Table Tools Fields tab to change the AutoNumber data type for the first column in a table.

Commands Review

FEATURE	RIBBON TAB, GROUP/OPTION	BUTTON, OPTION	KEYBOARD SHORTCUT
close Access		✕	Alt + F4
close database	File, *Close*		
create table	Create, Tables	⊞	
Currency data type	Table Tools Fields, Add & Delete		
Date & Time data type	Table Tools Fields, Add & Delete		
delete column	Home, Records	✕, *Delete Column*	
delete record	Home, Records	✕, *Delete Record*	
Enter Field Properties dialog box	Table Tools Fields, Properties		
Expression Builder dialog box	Table Tools Fields, Properties		
freeze column	Home, Records	, *Freeze Fields*	
hide column	Home, Records	, *Hide Fields*	

Chapter 1 | Managing and Creating Access Tables

FEATURE	RIBBON TAB, GROUP/OPTION	BUTTON, OPTION	KEYBOARD SHORTCUT
landscape orientation	File, *Print*	*Print Preview*, ▭	
new record	Home, Records	▭	Ctrl + +
next field			Tab
Number data type	Table Tools Fields, Add & Delete	12	
Page Setup dialog box	File, *Print*	*Print Preview*, ▭	
page size	File, *Print*	*Print Preview*, ▭	
page margins	File, *Print*	*Print Preview*, ▭	
portrait orientation	File, *Print*	*Print Preview*, ▭	
previous field			Shift + Tab
Print backstage area	File, *Print*		
Print dialog box	File, *Print*	*Print*	Ctrl + P
Print Preview	File, *Print*	*Print Preview*	
Short Text data type	Table Tools Fields, Add & Delete	AB	
unfreeze column	Home, Records	▭, *Unfreeze Fields*	
unhide column	Home, Records	▭, *Unhide Fields*	
Yes/No data type	Table Tools Fields, Add & Delete	☑	

Microsoft®

Access®
Creating Relationships between Tables

CHAPTER

2

Performance Objectives

Upon successful completion of Chapter 2, you will be able to:

1 Define a primary key field in a table

2 Create a one-to-many relationship

3 Specify referential integrity

4 Print, edit, and delete relationships

5 Create a one-to-one relationship

6 View and edit a subdatasheet

Precheck

Check your current skills to help focus your study.

Access is a relational database program you can use to create tables that are related or connected within the same database. When a relationship is established between tables, you can view and edit records in related tables with a subdatasheet. In this chapter, you will learn how to identify a primary key field in a table that is unique to that table, how to join tables by creating a relationship between them, and how to view and edit subdatasheets.

SNAP

If you are a SNAP user, launch the Precheck and Tutorials from your Assignments page.

Data Files

Before beginning chapter work, copy the AL1C2 folder to your storage medium and then make AL1C2 the active folder.

You will specify the primary keys field in tables, establish one-to-many relationships between tables, specify referential integrity, and print the relationships. You will also edit and delete a relationship.

Preview Finished Project

Relating Tables

Hint Defining a relationship between tables is one of the most powerful features of a relational database management system.

Generally, a database management system fits into one of two categories: a file management system (also sometimes referred to as a *flat file database*) or a relational database management system. A flat file management system stores all data in a single directory and cannot contain multiple tables. This type of management system is a simple way to store data but becomes inefficient as more data is added. In a relational database management system, like Access, relationships are defined between sets of data, allowing greater flexibility in manipulating data and eliminating data redundancy (entering the same data in more than one place).

In Project 1, you will define relationships between tables in the Pacific Trek database. Because the tables in the database will be related, information on the same product does not need to be repeated in multiple tables. If you used a flat file management system to maintain product information, you would need to repeat that product description each time.

Determining Relationships

Taking time to plan a database is extremely important. Creating a database with related tables takes even more consideration. Determine how to break down the required data and what tables to create to eliminate redundancies. One idea to help determine what tables are necessary in a database is to think of the word *about*. For example, the Pacific Trek store needs a table *about* products, another *about* suppliers, and another *about* orders. A table should be about only one subject, such as products, suppliers, or orders.

Along with determining the necessary tables for a database, determine the relationship between those tables. The ability to relate, or "join," tables is what makes Access a relational database management system. As explained in Chapter 1, database designers often create a visual representation of the database's structure in a diagram. Figure 2.1 displays the database diagram for the Pacific Trek database. (Some of the fields in tables have been modified slightly from the database used in Chapter 1.)

Tutorial

Setting the Primary Key Field

Setting the Primary Key Field

A database table can contain two different types of key fields: a primary key field and a foreign key field. In the database diagram in Figure 2.1, notice that one field in each table contains an asterisk. The asterisk indicates a primary key field, which is a field that holds data that uniquely identifies each record in a table. For example, the *SupplierID* field in the Suppliers table contains a unique supplier number for each record in the table and the *ProductID* field in the Products table contains a unique product number for each product. A table can have only one primary key field and it is the field by which the table is sorted whenever the table is opened.

Figure 2.1 Pacific Trek Database Diagram

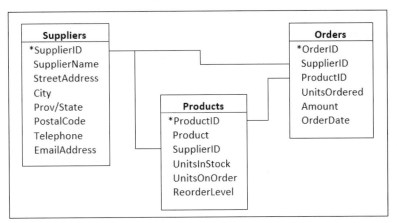

Quick Steps

Define a Primary Key Field
1. Open table.
2. Click View button.
3. Click field.
4. Click Primary Key button.
5. Click Save button

Primary Key

Hint Access uses a primary key field to associate data from multiple tables.

When a new record is added to a table, Access checks to ensure that there is no existing record with the same data in the primary key field. If there is, Access displays an error message indicating there are duplicate values and does not allow the record to be saved. When adding a new record to a table, the primary key field cannot be left blank. Access expects a value in each record in the table and this is referred to as *entity integrity*. If a value is not entered in a field, Access actually enters a null value. A null value cannot be given to a primary key field. Access will not allow a database to be closed that contains a primary key field with a null value.

By default, Access includes the *ID* field as the first field in a table, assigns the AutoNumber data type, and identifies the field as the primary key field. The AutoNumber data type assigns the first record a field value of *1* and each new record is assigned the next sequential number. Use this default field as the primary key field or define a different primary key field. To determine what field is the primary key field or to define a primary key field, display the table in Design view. To do this, open the table and then click the View button at the left side of the Home tab. A table also can be opened in Design view by clicking the View button arrow and then clicking *Design View* at the drop-down list. To add or remove a primary key designation from a field, click the desired field in the *Field Name* column and then click the Primary Key button in the Tools group on the Table Tools Design tab. A key icon is inserted in the field selector bar (the blank column to the left of the field names) for the desired field. Figure 2.2 displays the Products table in Design view with the *ProductID* field identified as the primary key field.

Typically, a primary key field in one table becomes the foreign key field in a related table. For example, the primary key field *SupplierID* in the Suppliers table is considered the foreign key field in the Orders table. In the Suppliers table, each entry in the *SupplierID* field must be unique since it is the primary key field but the same supplier number may appear more than once in the *SupplierID* field in the Orders table (for instance, in a situation when more than one product is ordered from the same supplier).

Hint You must enter a value in the primary key field in every record.

Data in the foreign key field must match data in the primary key field of the related table. For example, any supplier number entered in the *SupplierID* field in the Orders table must also be contained in the Suppliers table. In other words, an order would not be placed by a supplier that does not exist in the Suppliers table. Figure 2.3 identifies the primary and foreign key fields in the tables in the Pacific Trek database. Primary key fields are identified with *(PK)* and foreign key fields are identified with *(FK)* in the figure.

Figure 2.2 Products Table in Design View

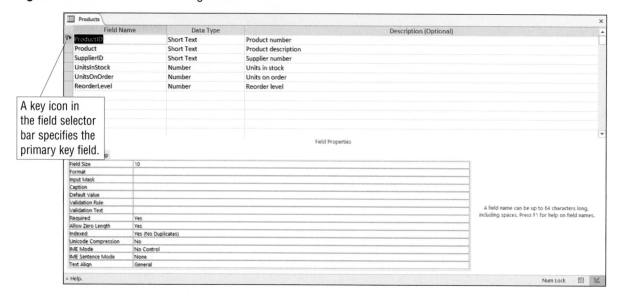

A key icon in the field selector bar specifies the primary key field.

Figure 2.3 Pacific Trek Database Diagram with Primary and Foreign Key Fields Identified

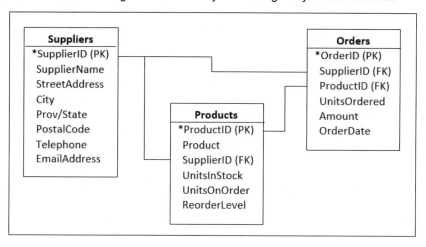

Project 1a Defining a Primary Key Field

Part 1 of 4

1. Open Access.
2. At the Access 2016 opening screen, click the <u>Open Other Files</u> hyperlink at the left side of the screen.
3. At the Open backstage area, click the *Browse* option.
4. At the Open dialog box, navigate to the AL1C2 folder on your storage medium and then double-click the database *2-PacTrek.accdb*.
5. Click the Enable Content button in the message bar if the security warning message appears. (The message bar will display immediately below the ribbon.)
6. Open the Products table.

7. View the primary key field by completing the following steps:
   a. Click the View button at the left side of the Home tab. (This displays the table in Design view.)

   b. In Design view, notice the *Field Name*, *Data Type*, and *Description* columns and the information that displays for each field. The first field, *ProductID*, is the primary key field and is identified by the key icon in the field selector bar.
   c. Click the View button to return to the Datasheet view.
   d. Close the Products table.
8. Open the Suppliers table, click the View button to display the table in Design view, and then notice the *SupplierID* field is defined as the primary key field.
9. Click the View button to return to Datasheet view and then close the table.
10. Open the Orders table. (The first field in the Orders table has been changed from the AutoNumber data type field automatically assigned by Access, to a Short Text data type field.)
11. Define the *OrderID* field as the primary key field by completing the following steps:
    a. Click the View button at the left side of the Home tab.
    b. With the table in Design view and the *OrderID* field selected in the *Field Name* column, click the Primary Key button in the Tools group on the Table Tools Design tab.

    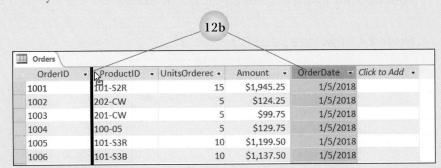

    c. Click the Save button on the Quick Access Toolbar.
    d. Click the View button to return the table to Datasheet view.
12. Move the *OrderDate* field by completing the following steps:
    a. Click the *OrderDate* field name in the header row. (This selects the column.)
    b. Position the mouse pointer on the field name in the header row; click and hold down the left mouse button; drag to the left until the thick, black vertical line displays immediately left of the *ProductID* field; and then release the mouse button.

12b

OrderID	ProductID	UnitsOrdered	Amount	OrderDate	Click to Add
1001	101-S2R	15	$1,945.25	1/5/2018	
1002	202-CW	5	$124.25	1/5/2018	
1003	201-CW	5	$99.75	1/5/2018	
1004	100-05	5	$129.75	1/5/2018	
1005	101-S3R	10	$1,199.50	1/5/2018	
1006	101-S3B	10	$1,137.50	1/5/2018	

13. Automatically adjust the column widths.
14. Save and then close the Orders table.

Check Your Work

Relating Tables in a One-to-Many Relationship

In Access, one table can be related to another, which is generally referred to as performing a join. When tables with a common field are joined, data can be extracted from both tables as if they were one large table. Relating tables helps to ensure the integrity of the data by avoiding entering the same data in multiple tables. For example, in Project 1b, a relationship will be established between the Suppliers table and the Products table. The relationship will ensure that a supplier number cannot be entered in the Products table without first being entered in the Suppliers table. This type of relationship is called a *one-to-many relationship*, which means that one record in the Suppliers table will match zero, one, or many records in the Products table.

In a one-to-many relationship, the table containing the "one" is referred to as the *primary table* and the table containing the "many" is referred to as the *related table*. Access follows a set of rules that provide referential integrity, which enforces consistency between related tables. These rules are enforced when data is updated in related tables. The referential integrity rules ensure that a record added to a related table has a matching record in the primary table.

 Relationships

To create a one-to-many relationship, open the database containing the tables to be related. Click the Database Tools tab and then click the Relationships button in the Relationships group. This displays the Show Table dialog box, as shown in Figure 2.4. (If the Show Table dialog box is not visible, click the Show Table button in the Relationships group.) At the Show Table dialog box, each table that will be related must be added to the Relationships window. To do this, click the first table name to be included and then click the Add button (or double-click the table name). This inserts the fields of the table in a table field list box. Continue in this manner until all necessary tables (in table field list boxes) have been added to the Relationships window and then click the Close button.

At the Relationships window, such as the one shown in Figure 2.5, use the mouse to drag the common field from the primary table's table field list box (the "one") to the related table's table field list box (the "many"). This causes the Edit Relationships dialog box to display, as shown in Figure 2.6. At the Edit Relationships dialog box, check to make sure the correct field name displays in the *Table/Query* and *Related Table/Query* list boxes and the relationship type at the bottom of the dialog box displays as *One-To-Many*.

Quick Steps

Create a One-to-Many Relationship
1. Click Database Tools tab.
2. Click Relationships button.
3. Add tables.
4. Drag "one" field from primary table to "many" field in related table.
5. At Edit Relationships dialog box, click Create button.
6. Click Save button.

Figure 2.4 Show Table Dialog Box

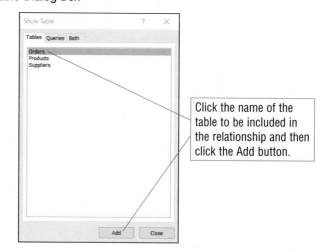

Click the name of the table to be included in the relationship and then click the Add button.

Figure 2.5 Relationships Window

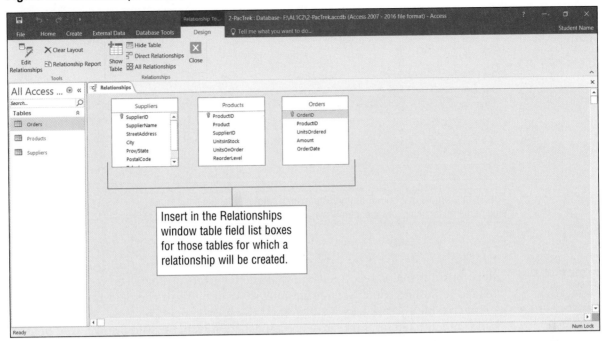

Insert in the Relationships window table field list boxes for those tables for which a relationship will be created.

Figure 2.6 Edit Relationships Dialog Box

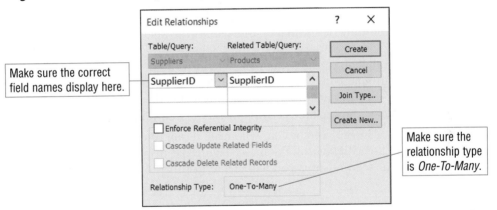

Make sure the correct field names display here.

Make sure the relationship type is *One-To-Many*.

Specify the relationship options by choosing *Enforce Referential Integrity*, as well as *Cascade Update Related Fields* and/or *Cascade Delete Related Records*, and then click the Create button. This causes the Edit Relationships dialog box to close and the Relationships window to display showing the relationship between the tables.

In Figure 2.7, the Suppliers table field list box displays with a black line attached along with the number *1* (signifying the "one" side of the relationship). The black line is connected to the Products table field list box along with the infinity symbol, ∞ (signifying the "many" side of the relationship). The black line, called the *join line*, is thick at both ends if the *Enforce Referential Integrity* option is chosen. If this option is not chosen, the line is thin at both ends. Click the Save button on the Quick Access Toolbar to save the relationship. Close the Relationships window by clicking the Close button in the upper right corner of the window.

Figure 2.7 One-to-Many Relationship

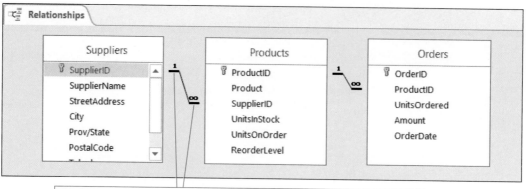

This is an example of a one-to-many relationship, where 1 identifies the "one" side of the relationship and the infinity symbol (∞) identifies the "many" side.

Hint Referential integrity ensures that a record exists in the "one" table before the record can be entered in the "many" table.

Specifying Referential Integrity Choose *Enforce Referential Integrity* at the Edit Relationships dialog box to ensure that the relationships between records in related tables are valid. Referential integrity can be set if the field from the primary table is a primary key field and the related fields have the same data type. When referential integrity is established, a value for the primary key field must first be entered in the primary table before it can be entered in the related table.

If only *Enforce Referential Integrity* is selected and the related table contains a record, a primary key field value in the primary table cannot be changed. A record in the primary table cannot be deleted if its key value equals a foreign key field in the related table. Select *Cascade Update Related Fields* and, if changes are made to the primary key field value in the primary table, Access will automatically update the matching value in the related table. Choose *Cascade Delete Related Records* and, if a record is deleted in the primary table, Access will delete any related records in the related table.

In Project 1b, you will create a one-to-many relationship between tables in the C2-PacTrek.accdb database. Figure 2.8 displays the Relationships window showing the relationships you will create in this project.

Figure 2.8 Relationships in the 2-PacTrek Database

A one-to-many relationship with referential integrity and cascade updated and deleted records selected.

A one-to-many relationship with referential integrity selected. (Notice the join line is thick in the middle, indicating that cascade updated and cascade deleted records are not selected.)

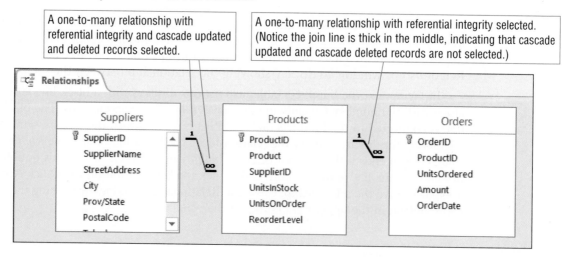

Ǫuick Steps

Create a Relationship Report
1. Click Database Tools tab.
2. Click Relationships button.
3. Click Relationship Report button.

Creating and Printing a Relationship Report Once all relationships have been created in a database, printing a hard copy of the relationships is a good idea. The documentation is a quick reference of all of the table names, fields within each table, and relationships between tables. To print a relationship report, display the Relationships window and then click the Relationship Report button in the Tools group. This displays a relationship report in Print Preview. Click the Print button in the Print group on the Print Preview tab and then click OK at the Print dialog box. After printing the relationship report, click the Close button to close the relationship report.

Project 1b Relating Tables

1. With **2-PacTrek.accdb** open, click the Database Tools tab and then click the Relationships button in the Relationships group. (The Show Table dialog box should display in the Relationships window. If it does not display, click the Show Table button in the Relationships group on the Relationship Tools Design tab.)

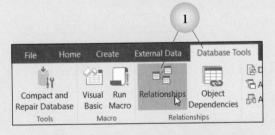

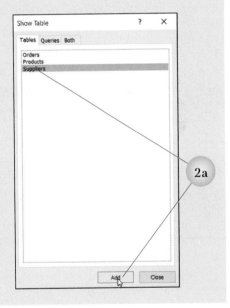

2. At the Show Table dialog box with the Tables tab selected, add the Suppliers, Products, and Orders tables to the Relationships window by completing the following steps:
   a. Click *Suppliers* in the list box and then click the Add button.
   b. Click *Products* in the list box and then click the Add button.
   c. Double-click *Orders* in the list box.
3. Click the Close button to close the Show Table dialog box.

4. At the Relationships window, drag the *SupplierID* field from the Suppliers table field list box to the Products table field list box by completing the following steps:

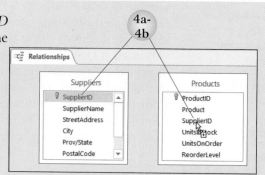

a. Position the arrow pointer on the *SupplierID* field in the Suppliers table field list box.

b. Click and hold down the left mouse button, drag the arrow pointer (with a field icon attached) to the *SupplierID* field in the Products table field list box, and then release the mouse button. (This causes the Edit Relationships dialog box to display.)

5. At the Edit Relationships dialog box, make sure *SupplierID* displays in the *Table/Query* and *Related Table/Query* list boxes and the relationship type at the bottom of the dialog box displays as *One-To-Many*.

6. Enforce the referential integrity of the relationship by completing the following steps:

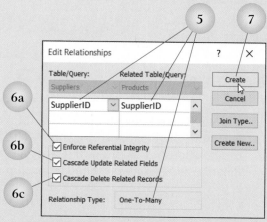

a. Click the *Enforce Referential Integrity* check box to insert a check mark. (This makes the other two options available.)

b. Click the *Cascade Update Related Fields* check box to insert a check mark.

c. Click the *Cascade Delete Related Records* check box to insert a check mark.

7. Click the Create button. (This causes the Edit Relationships dialog box to close and the Relationships window to display, showing a black join line [thick on the ends and thin in the middle] connecting the *SupplierID* field in the Suppliers table field list box to the *SupplierID* field in the Products table field list box. A *1* appears on the join line on the Suppliers table side and an infinity symbol [∞] appears on the join line on the Products table side.)

8. Click the Save button on the Quick Access Toolbar to save the relationship.

9. Create a one-to-many relationship between the Products table and the Orders table with the *ProductID* field by completing the following steps:

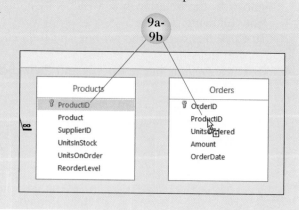

a. Position the arrow pointer on the *ProductID* field in the Products table field list box.

b. Click and hold down the left mouse button, drag the arrow pointer (with a field icon attached) to the *ProductID* field in the Orders table field list box, and then release the mouse button.

c. At the Edit Relationships dialog box, make sure *ProductID* displays in the *Table/Query* and *Related Table/Query* list boxes and the relationship type displays as *One-To-Many*.

d. Click the *Enforce Referential Integrity* check box to insert a check mark. (Do not insert check marks in the other two check boxes.)

e. Click the Create button.

10. Click the Save button on the Quick Access Toolbar to save the relationships.

11. Print the relationships by completing the following steps:

a. At the Relationships window, click the Relationship Report button in the Tools group. This displays the relationship report in Print Preview. (If a security notice displays, click the Open button.)

b. Click the Print button in the Print group at the left side of the Print Preview tab.

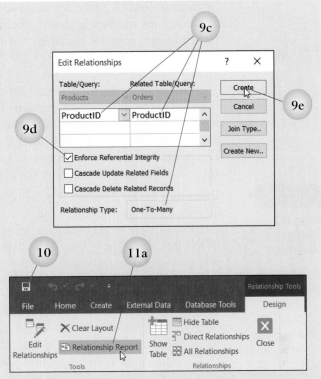

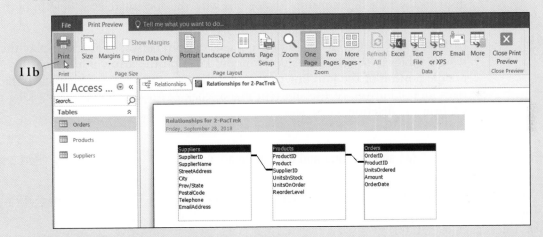

c. Click OK at the Print dialog box.

d. Close the report by clicking the Close button in the upper right corner of the work area.

e. At the message asking if you want to save changes to the design of the report, click No.

12. Close the Relationships window by clicking the Close button in the upper right corner of the work area.

Check Your Work

Show Table

Showing Tables Once a relationship is established between tables and the Relationships window is closed, clicking the Relationships button causes the Relationships window to display without the Show Table dialog box. To display the Show Table dialog box, click the Show Table button in the Relationships group.

Pacific Trek offers a discount on one product each week. Keep track of this information by creating a Discounts table that includes the discount item for each week of the first three months of the year. A new record will be added to this field each week when the discount item is chosen. (In Project 1c, you will create the Discounts table shown in Figure 2.9 on page 49 and then relate the Products table with the Discounts table using the *ProductID* field.)

Tutorial

Editing and
Deleting a
Relationship

Edit Relationships

Quick Steps

Edit a Relationship
1. Click Database Tools tab.
2. Click Relationships button.
3. Click Edit Relationships button.
4. Make changes at Edit Relationships dialog box.
5. Click OK.

Editing a Relationship A relationship between tables can be edited or deleted. To edit a relationship, open the database containing the tables with the relationship, click the Database Tools tab, and then click the Relationships button in the Relationships group. This displays the Relationships window with the related tables. Click the Edit Relationships button in the Tools group to display the Edit Relationships dialog box. The dialog box will be similar to the one shown in Figure 2.6 on page 41. Identify the relationship to be edited by clicking the *Table/Query* option box arrow and then clicking the table name containing the "one" field. Click the *Related Table/Query* option box arrow and then click the table name containing the "many" field.

To edit a specific relationship, position the arrow pointer on the middle portion of the join line that connects the related tables and then click the right mouse button. At the shortcut menu, click the *Edit Relationship* option. This displays the Edit Relationships dialog box with the specific related field in both list boxes.

Deleting a Relationship To delete a relationship between tables, display the related tables in the Relationships window. Position the arrow pointer on the middle portion of the join line connecting the related tables and then click the right mouse button. At the shortcut menu, click *Delete*. At the message asking to confirm the deletion, click Yes.

Project 1c Creating a Table and Creating and Editing Relationships

Part 3 of 4

1. With **2-PacTrek.accdb** open, create the Discounts table shown in Figure 2.9 on page 49 by completing the following steps:
   a. Click the Create tab.
   b. Click the Table button in the Tables group.
   c. Click the Short Text button in the Add & Delete group. (This creates and then selects *Field1* at the right of the *ID* column.)

d. Type ProductID and then press the Enter key.

e. Click the *Short Text* option at the drop-down list and then type Discount.

f. Click the *ID* field name (in the first column), click the *Data Type* option box arrow in the Formatting group, and then click *Date/Time* at the drop-down list.

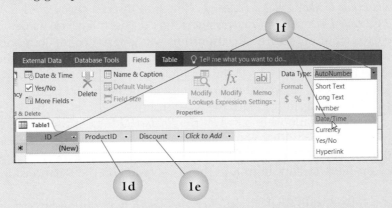

g. Right-click the *ID* field name, click *Rename Field* at the shortcut menu, type Week, and then press the Enter key.

h. Type the 13 records in the Discounts table shown in Figure 2.9 on page 49.

2. After typing the records, save the table by completing the following steps:

a. Click the Save button on the Quick Access Toolbar.

b. At the Save As dialog box, type Discounts and then press the Enter key.

3. Close the Discounts table.

4. Display the Relationships window and add the Discounts table to the window by completing the following steps:

a. Click the Database Tools tab and then click the Relationships button in the Relationships group.

b. Display the Show Table dialog box by clicking the Show Table button in the Relationships group.

c. At the Show Table dialog box, double-click the *Discounts* table.

d. Click the Close button to close the Show Table dialog box.

5. At the Relationships window, create a one-to-many relationship between the Products table and the Discounts table with the *ProductID* field by completing the following steps:

a. Drag the *ProductID* field from the Products table field list box to the *ProductID* field in the Discounts table field list box.

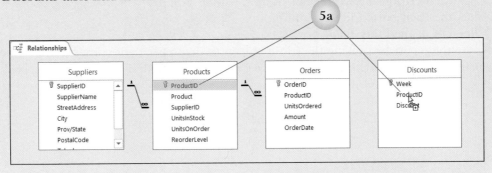

b. At the Edit Relationships dialog box, make sure *ProductID* displays in the *Table/Query* and *Related Table/Query* list boxes and the relationship type at the bottom of the dialog box displays as *One-To-Many*.

c. Click the *Enforce Referential Integrity* check box to insert a check mark.

d. Click the *Cascade Update Related Fields* check box to insert a check mark.

e. Click the *Cascade Delete Related Records* check box to insert a check mark.

f. Click the Create button. (At the Relationships window, notice the join line between the Products table and the Discounts table. If a message occurs stating that the relationship cannot be created, click the Cancel button. Open the Discounts table, check to make sure the product numbers are entered correctly in the *ProductID* field, and then close the Discounts table. Try again to create the relationship.)

6. Edit the one-to-many relationship between the *ProductID* field in the Products table and the Orders table and specify that you want to cascade updated and related fields and cascade and delete related records by completing the following steps:

a. Click the Edit Relationships button in the Tools group on the Relationship Tools Design tab.

b. At the Edit Relationships dialog box, click the *Table/Query* option box arrow and then click *Products* at the drop-down list.

c. Click the *Related Table/Query* option box arrow and then click *Orders* at the drop-down list.

d. Click the *Cascade Update Related Fields* check box to insert a check mark.

e. Click the *Cascade Delete Related Records* check box to insert a check mark.

f. Click the OK button.

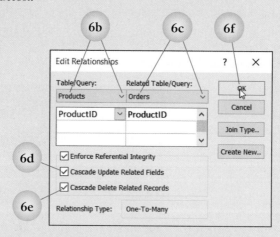

7. Click the Save button on the Quick Access Toolbar to save the relationship.

8. Print the relationships by completing the following steps:

a. Click the Relationship Report button in the Tools group.

b. Click the Print button in the Print group.

c. Click OK at the Print dialog box.

d. Close the report by clicking the Close button in the upper right corner of the work area.

e. At the message asking if you want to save changes to the design of the report, click No.

9. Delete the relationship between the Products table and the Discounts table by completing the following steps:

   a. Position the arrow pointer on the thin portion of the join line connecting the *ProductID* field in the Products table field list box with the *ProductID* field in the Discounts table field list box and then click the right mouse button.

   b. Click the *Delete* option at the shortcut menu.

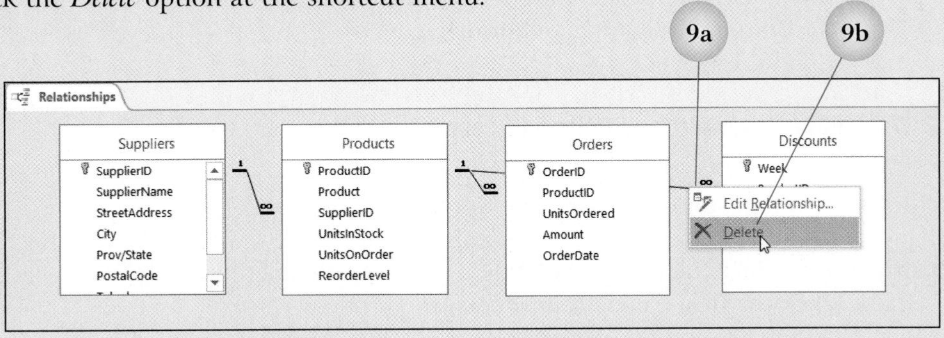

   c. At the message asking if you are sure you want to permanently delete the selected relationship from your database, click Yes.

10. Click the Save button on the Quick Access Toolbar to save the relationship.

11. Print the relationships by completing the following steps:

   a. Click the Relationship Tools Design tab and then click the Relationship Report button in the Tools group.

   b. Click the Print button in the Print group.

   c. Click OK at the Print dialog box.

   d. Close the report by clicking the Close button in the upper right corner of the work area.

   e. At the message asking if you want to save changes to the design of the report, click No.

12. Close the Relationships window by clicking the Close button in the upper right corner of the work area.

Check Your Work

Figure 2.9 Discounts Table in Datasheet View

Week	ProductID	Discount	Click to Add
1/7/2018	155-45	20%	
1/14/2018	652-2	15%	
1/21/2018	443-1A	20%	
1/28/2018	202-CW	15%	
2/4/2018	804-60	10%	
2/11/2018	652-2	15%	
2/18/2018	101-S1B	5%	
2/25/2018	560-TL	20%	
3/4/2018	652-2	20%	
3/11/2018	602-XX	15%	
3/18/2018	100-05	10%	
3/25/2018	652-2	15%	
4/1/2018	202-CW	15%	

Inserting and Deleting Records in Related Tables In the relationship established in Project 1b, a record must first be added to the Suppliers table before a related record can be added to the Products table. This is because the *Enforce Referential Integrity* option was selected at the Edit Relationships dialog box. Because the two options, *Cascade Update Related Fields* and *Cascade Delete Related Records*, were also selected, records in the Suppliers table (the primary table) can be updated or deleted and related records in the Products table (the related table) are automatically updated or deleted.

Project 1d Editing, Inserting, and Deleting Records

Part 4 of 4

1. With **2-PacTrek.accdb** open, open the Suppliers table.
2. Change two supplier numbers in the Suppliers table (Access will automatically change them in the Products table and the Orders table) by completing the following steps:
   a. Double-click the field value *15* in the *SupplierID* field.
   b. Type *33*.
   c. Double-click the field value *42* in the *SupplierID* field.
   d. Type *51*.
   e. Click the Save button on the Quick Access Toolbar.
   f. Close the Suppliers table.
   g. Open the Products table and notice that supplier number *15* changed to *33* and supplier number *42* changed to *51*.
   h. Close the Products table.
3. Open the Suppliers table and then add the following records:

SupplierID	16	SupplierID	28
SupplierName	Olympic Suppliers	SupplierName	Gorman Company
StreetAddress	1773 50th Avenue	StreetAddress	543 26th Street
City	Seattle	City	Vancouver
Prov/State	WA	Prov/State	BC
PostalCode	98101	PostalCode	V5K 3C5
Telephone	(206) 555-9488	Telephone	(778) 555-4550
EmailAddress	olysuppliers@emcp.net	EmailAddress	gormanco@emcp.net

4. Delete the record for supplier number 38 (Hadley Company). At the message stating that relationships that specify cascading deletes are about to cause records in this table and related tables to be deleted, click Yes.

5. Display the table in Print Preview, change to landscape orientation, and then print the table.

6. Close the Suppliers table.

7. Open the Products table and then add the following records to the table:

ProductID	701-BK	*ProductID*	703-SP
Product	Basic first aid kit	*Product*	Medical survival pack
SupplierID	33	*SupplierID*	33
UnitsInStock	8	*UnitsInStock*	8
UnitsOnOrder	0	*UnitsOnOrder*	0
ReorderLevel	5	*ReorderLevel*	5
ProductID	185-10	*ProductID*	185-50
Product	Trail water filter	*Product*	Trail filter replacement cartridge
SupplierID	51	*SupplierID*	51
UnitsInStock	4	*UnitsInStock*	14
UnitsOnOrder	10	*UnitsOnOrder*	0
ReorderLevel	10	*ReorderLevel*	10

8. Display the Products table in Print Preview, change to landscape orientation, change the top and bottom margins to 0.5 inch and then print the table. (The table will print on two pages.)

9. Close the Products table.

10. Open the Orders table and then add the following record:

OrderID	1033
OrderDate	2/15/2018
ProductID	185-10
UnitsOrdered	10
Amount	$310.90

11. Print and then close the Orders table.

12. Close **2-PacTrek.accdb**.

Check Your Work

Project 2 Create Relationships and Display Subdatasheets in a Database

2 Parts

You will open a company database and then create one-to-many relationships between tables, as well as a one-to-one relationship. You will also display and edit subdatasheets.

Preview Finished Project

Tutorial

Creating a One-to-One Relationship

Creating a One-to-One Relationship

A one-to-one relationship can be created between tables in which each record in the first table matches only one record in the second table and one record in the second table matches only one record in the first table. (One-to-one relationships exist between primary key fields.) A one-to-one relationship is not as common as a one-to-many relationship, since the type of information used to create the relationship can be stored in one table. A one-to-one relationship is generally used to break a large table with many fields into two smaller tables.

Hint The
Relationships
window displays any
relationship you have
defined between tables.

In Project 2a, you will create a one-to-one relationship between the Employees table and the Benefits table in the Griffin database. Each record in the Employees table and each record in the Benefits table pertains to one employee. These two tables could be merged into one but the data in each table is easier to manage when separated. Figure 2.10 shows the relationships you will define between the tables in the Griffin database. The Benefits table and the Departments table have been moved down so you can more easily see the relationships.

Figure 2.10 Griffin Database Table Relationships

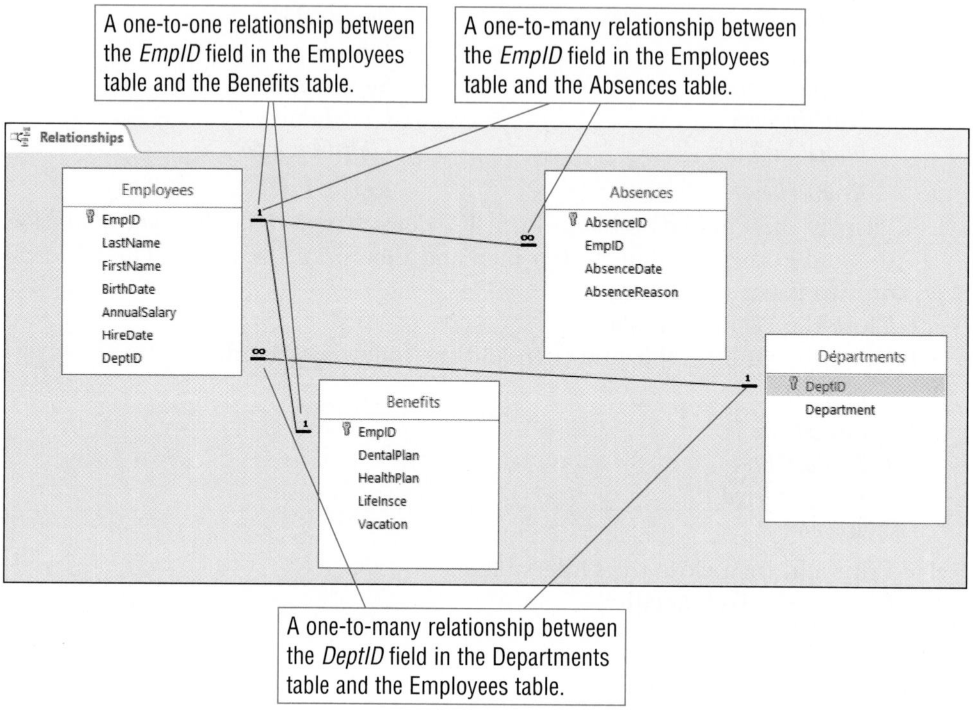

A one-to-one relationship between the *EmpID* field in the Employees table and the Benefits table.

A one-to-many relationship between the *EmpID* field in the Employees table and the Absences table.

A one-to-many relationship between the *DeptID* field in the Departments table and the Employees table.

Project 2a Creating One-to-Many and One-to-One Relationships

Part 1 of 2

1. Open **2-Griffin.accdb** and enable the content.
2. Click the Database Tools tab.
3. Click the Relationships button in the Relationships group.
4. At the Show Table dialog box with the Tables tab selected, add all of the tables to the Relationships window by completing the following steps:
   a. Double-click *Employees* in the list box. (This inserts the table in the Relationships window.)
   b. Double-click *Benefits* in the list box.
   c. Double-click *Absences* in the list box.
   d. Double-click *Departments* in the list box.
   e. Click the Close button to close the Show Table dialog box.
5. At the Relationships window, create a one-to-many relationship with the *EmpID* field in the Employees table as the "one" and the *EmpID* field in the Absences table the "many" by completing the following steps:
   a. Position the arrow pointer on the *EmpID* field in the Employees table field list box.

b. Click and hold down the left mouse button, drag the arrow pointer (with a field icon attached) to the *EmpID* field in the Absences table field list box, and then release the mouse button. (This causes the Edit Relationships dialog box to display.)

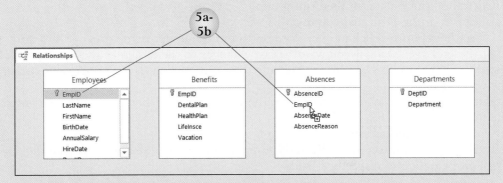

c. At the Edit Relationships dialog box, make sure *EmpID* displays in the *Table/Query* and *Related Table/Query* list boxes and the relationship type at the bottom of the dialog box displays as *One-To-Many*.

d. Click the *Enforce Referential Integrity* check box to insert a check mark.

e. Click the *Cascade Update Related Fields* check box to insert a check mark.

f. Click the *Cascade Delete Related Records* check box to insert a check mark.

g. Click the Create button. (A *1* appears at the Employees table field list box side and an infinity symbol (∞) appears at the Absences table field list box side of the black line.)

6. Complete steps similar to those in Step 5 to create a one-to-many relationship with the *DeptID* field in the Departments table the "one" and the *DeptID* field in the Employees table the "many." (You may need to scroll down the Employees table field list box to display the *DeptID* field.)

7. Create a one-to-one relationship with the *EmpID* field in the Employees table and the *EmpID* field in the Benefits table by completing the following steps:

a. Position the arrow pointer on the *EmpID* field in the Employees table field list box.

b. Click and hold down the left mouse button, drag the arrow pointer to the *EmpID* field in the Benefits table field list box, and then release the mouse button. (This displays the Edit Relationships dialog box; notice at the bottom of the dialog box that the relationship type displays as *One-To-One*.)

c. Click the *Enforce Referential Integrity* check box to insert a check mark.

d. Click the *Cascade Update Related Fields* check box to insert a check mark.

e. Click the *Cascade Delete Related Records* check box to insert a check mark.

f. Click the Create button. (Notice that a *1* appears at both the side of the Employees table field list box and at the side of the *Benefits* field list box, indicating a one-to-one relationship.)

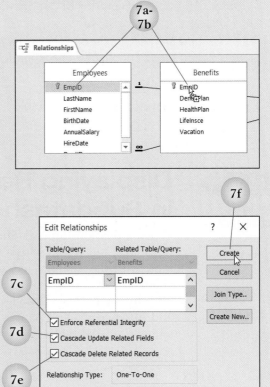

8. Click the Save button on the Quick Access Toolbar to save the relationships.
9. Print the relationships by completing the following steps:
   a. Click the Relationship Report button in the Tools group.
   b. Click the Print button in the Print group.
   c. Click OK at the Print dialog box.
   d. Close the report by clicking the Close button in the upper right corner of the work area.
   e. At the message asking if you want to save changes to the design of the report, click No.
10. Close the Relationships window by clicking the Close button in the upper right corner of the work area.
11. Add a record to and delete a record from the Employees and Benefits tables by completing the following steps:
    a. Open the Employees table.
    b. Click the New button in the Records group on the Home tab and then type the following data in the specified field:

EmpID	1096
LastName	Schwartz
FirstName	Bryan
BirthDate	5/21/1983
DeptID	IT
AnnualSalary	$45,000.00
HireDate	1/15/2010

    c. Delete the record for Trevor Sargent (employee number 1005). At the message stating that relationships that specify cascading deletes are about to cause records in this table and related tables to be deleted, click Yes.
    d. Print and then close the Employees table.
12. Open the Benefits table and notice that the record for Trevor Sargent is deleted but the new employee record you entered in the Employees table is not reflected in the Benefits table. Add a new record for Bryan Schwartz with the following information:

EmpID	1096
Dental Plan	(Press spacebar to remove check mark.)
Health Plan	(Leave check mark.)
Life Insurance	$100,000.00
Vacation	2 weeks

13. Print and then close the Benefits table.

Check Your Work

Tutorial

Viewing a Subdatasheet

Displaying Related Records in Subdatasheets

When a relationship is established between tables, records in related tables can be viewed and edited with a subdatasheet. Figure 2.11 displays the Employees table with the subdatasheet displayed for employee Kate Navarro. The subdatasheet displays the fields in the Benefits table related to Kate Navarro. Use this subdatasheet to view and edit information in both the Employees table and Absences table. Changes made to fields in a subdatasheet affect the table and any related tables.

Quick Steps

Display a Subdatasheet
1. Open table.
2. Click expand indicator at left side of record.
3. Click table at Insert Subdatasheet dialog box.
4. Click OK.

Access automatically inserts a plus symbol (referred to as an *expand indicator*) before each record in a table that is joined to another table by a one-to-many relationship. Click the expand indicator and, if the table is related to only one other table, a subdatasheet containing fields from the related table displays below the record, as shown in Figure 2.11. To close the subdatasheet, click the minus symbol (referred to as a *collapse indicator*) preceding the record. (The plus symbol turns into the minus symbol when a subdatasheet displays.)

If a table has more than one relationship defined, clicking the expand indicator will display the Insert Subdatasheet dialog box, as shown in Figure 2.12. At this dialog box, click the desired table in the Tables list box and then click OK. The Insert Subdatasheet dialog box can also be displayed by clicking the More button in the Records group on the Home tab, pointing to *Subdatasheet*, and then clicking *Subdatasheet*. Display subdatasheets for all records by clicking the More button, pointing to *Subdatasheet*, and then clicking *Expand All*. Close all subdatasheets by clicking the More button, pointing to *Subdatasheet*, and then clicking *Collapse All*.

If a table is related to two or more tables, specify the subdatasheet at the Insert Subdatasheet dialog box. To display a different subdatasheet, remove the subdatasheet first, before selecting the next subdatasheet. Do this by clicking the More button, pointing to *Subdatasheet*, and then clicking *Remove*.

Figure 2.11 Table with Subdatasheet Displayed in Datasheet View

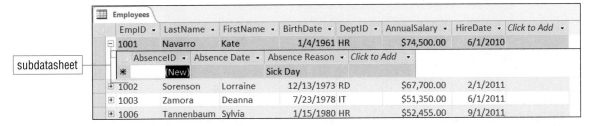

Figure 2.12 Insert Subdatasheet Dialog Box

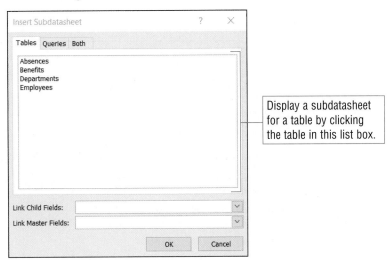

Display a subdatasheet for a table by clicking the table in this list box.

1. With **2-Griffin.accdb** open, open the Employees table.
2. Display a subdatasheet by clicking the expand indicator (plus symbol) at the left side of the first row (the row for Kate Navarro).
3. Close the subdatasheet by clicking the collapse indicator (minus symbol) at the left side of the record for Kate Navarro.
4. Display subdatasheets for all of the records by clicking the More button in the Records group, pointing to *Subdatasheet*, and then clicking *Expand All*.

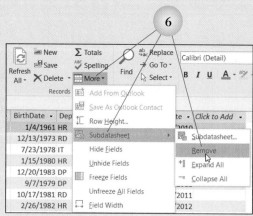

5. Remove the display of all subdatasheets by clicking the More button, pointing to *Subdatasheet*, and then clicking *Collapse All*.
6. Remove the connection between the Employees table and Absences table by clicking the More button, pointing to *Subdatasheet*, and then clicking *Remove*. (Notice that the expand indicators [plus symbols] no longer display before each record.)

7. Suppose that the employee, Diane Michaud, has moved to a different department and has had an increase in salary. You would like to update her record in the tables. Display the Benefits subdatasheet and make changes to fields in the Employees table and Benefits table by completing the following steps:

a. Click the More button in the Records group, point to *Subdatasheet*, and then click *Subdatasheet* at the side menu.

b. At the Insert Subdatasheet dialog box, click *Benefits* in the list box and then click OK.

c. Change the department ID for the record for *Diane Michaud* from *DP* to *A*.

d. Change the salary from *$56,250.00* to *$57,500.00*.

e. Click the expand indicator (plus symbol) at the left side of the record for Diane Michaud.

f. Insert a check mark in the *Dental Plan* check box and change the vacation from 3 weeks to 4 weeks.

g. Click the collapse indicator (minus symbol) at the left side of the record for Diane Michaud.

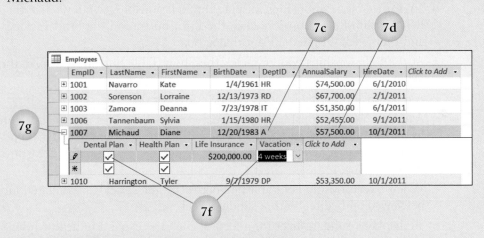

8. Click the Save button on the Quick Access Toolbar.
9. Print and then close the Employees table.
10. Open, print, and then close the Benefits table.
11. Close **2-Griffin.accdb**.

Check Your Work

Chapter Summary

- Access is a relational database software program in which tables can be created that are related or connected.

- When planning a table, take time to determine how to break down the required data and what relationships need to be defined to eliminate data redundancies.

- Generally, one field in a table must be unique so that one record can be distinguished from another. A field with a unique value is considered a primary key field.

- A table can have only one primary key field and it is the field by which the table is sorted whenever it is opened.

- In a field defined as a primary key field, duplicate values are not allowed. Access also expects a value in each record in the primary key field.

- Typically, a primary key field in one table becomes the foreign key field in a related table. Data in a foreign key field must match data in the primary key field of the related tables.

- Tables are related by performing a join. When tables that have a common field are joined, data can be extracted from both tables as if they were one large table.

- A one-to-many relationship can be created between tables. In this relationship, a record must be added to the "one" table before it can be added to the "many" table.

- To print table relationships, display the Relationships window, click the Relationship Report button, click the Print button on the Print Preview tab, and then click OK at the Print dialog box.

- At the Relationships window, click the Show Table button to display the Show Table dialog box.

- A relationship between tables can be edited or deleted.

- A one-to-one relationship can be created between tables in which each record in the first table matches only one record in the related table. This type of relationship is generally used to break a large table with many fields into two smaller tables.

- When a relationship is established between tables, fields in a related table can be viewed and edited with a subdatasheet.

- To display a subdatasheet for a record, click the expand indicator (plus symbol) at the left of the record in Datasheet view. To display subdatasheets for all records, click the More button in the Records group on the Home tab, point to *Subdatasheet*, and then click *Expand All*.

- Display the Insert Subdatasheet dialog box by clicking the More button in the Reports group on the Home tab, pointing to *Subdatasheet*, and then clicking *Subdatasheet*.

- Turn off the display of a subdatasheet by clicking the collapse indicator (minus symbol) at the left of the record. To turn off the display of subdatasheets for all records, click the More button, point to *Subdatasheet*, and then click *Collapse All*.

Commands Review

FEATURE	RIBBON, GROUP	BUTTON, OPTION
Edit Relationships dialog box	Relationship Tools Design, Tools	
Insert Subdatasheet dialog box	Home, Records	*Subdatasheet, Subdatasheet*
primary key field	Table Tools Design, Tools	
print relationships report	Relationship Tools Design, Tools	
Relationships window	Database Tools, Relationships	
Show Table dialog box	Relationship Tools Design, Relationships	

> **Workbook**
>
> Chapter study tools and assessment activities are available in the *Workbook* ebook. These resources are designed to help you further develop and demonstrate mastery of the skills learned in this chapter.

Microsoft®
Access®

Performing Queries

Performance Objectives

Upon successful completion of Chapter 3, you will be able to:

1   Design queries to extract specific data from tables

2   Modify queries

3   Design queries with *Or* and *And* criteria

4   Use the Simple Query Wizard to create queries

5   Create and format a calculated field

6   Use aggregate functions in queries

7   Create crosstab, duplicate, and unmatched queries

Precheck

Check your current skills to help focus your study.

One of the primary uses of a database is to extract the specific information needed to answer questions and make decisions. A company might need to know how much inventory is currently on hand, which products have been ordered, which accounts are past due, or which customers live in a particular city. You can extract specific information from a table or multiple tables by creating and running a query. You will learn how to perform a variety of queries on information in tables in this chapter.

Data Files

Before beginning chapter work, copy the AL1C3 folder to your storage medium and then make AL1C3 the active folder.

SNAP

If you are a SNAP user, launch the Precheck and Tutorials from your Assignments page.

Project 1 Design Queries

8 Parts

You will design and run a number of queries including queries with fields from one table and queries with fields from more than one table. You will also use the Simple Query Wizard to design queries and create and format a calculated field.

Preview Finished Project

Designing Queries

Creating a Query in Design View and Showing/ Hiding Query Columns

Being able to extract (pull out) specific data from a table is one of the most important functions of a database. Extracting data in Access is referred to as performing a query. The word *query* means "question" and to perform a query means to ask a question. Access provides several methods for designing a query. In this chapter, you will learn how to design your own query; use the Simple Query Wizard; create a calculated field; use aggregate functions in a query; and use the Crosstab Query Wizard, Find Duplicates Query Wizard, and Find Unmatched Query Wizard.

Hint The first step in designing a query is to choose the fields that you want to display in the query results datasheet.

Designing a query consists of identifying the table or tables containing the data to be extracted, the field or fields from which the data will be drawn, and the criteria for selecting the data.

Specifying Tables and Fields for a Query

Query Design

To design a query, open a database, click the Create tab, and then click the Query Design button in the Queries group. This displays a query window in the work area and also displays the Show Table dialog box, as shown in Figure 3.1.

Quick Steps

Design a Query
1. Click Create tab.
2. Click Query Design button.
3. Click table at Show Table dialog box.
4. Click Add button.
5. Add any additional tables.
6. In query design grid, click down arrow in field in *Field* row.
7. Click field at drop-down list.
8. Insert criterion.
9. Click Run button.
10. Save query.

Figure 3.1 Query Window with Show Table Dialog Box

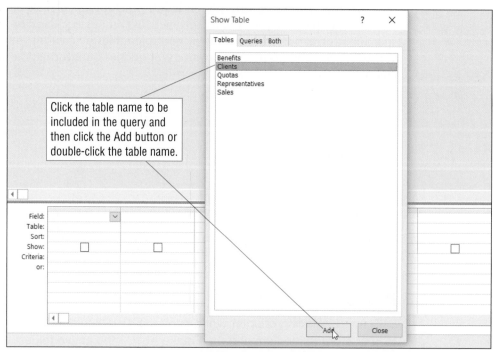

Click the table name to be included in the query and then click the Add button or double-click the table name.

Click the table name in the Show Table dialog box to be included in the query and then click the Add button or double-click the table. This inserts a field list box for the table. Add any other tables required for the query. When all tables have been added, click the Close button. Figure 3.2 displays a sample query window.

To insert a field in the query design grid, click the down arrow that displays in the field in the *Field* row and then click the specific field at the drop-down list. Or, double-click a field in a table field list box to insert the field in the first available field in the *Field* row in the query design grid.

A third method for inserting a field in the query design grid is to drag a field from the table field list box to the desired field in the query design grid. To do this, position the mouse pointer on the field in the table field list box, click and hold down the left mouse button, drag to the specific field in the *Field* row in the query design grid, and then release the mouse button.

Tutorial

Adding a Criteria
Statement to a
Query

Quick Steps

Establish a Query Criterion
1. At query window, click in field in the *Criteria* row in query design grid.
2. Type criterion and then press Enter key.
3. Click Run button.

 Run

Adding a Criteria Statement to a Query

Unless a criterion statement is added to a query in the *Criteria* row, the query will return (*return* is the term used for the query results) all records with the fields specified in the query design grid. While returning this information may be helpful, the information could easily be found in the table or tables. The value of performing a query is to extract specific information from a table or tables. To extract specific information, add a criterion statement to the query. To do this, click in the field in the *Criteria* row in the column containing the field name in the query design grid and then type the criterion. With the fields and criterion established, click the Run button in the Results group on the Query Tools Design tab. Access searches the specified tables for records that match the criterion and then displays those records in the query results datasheet.

Figure 3.2 Query Window

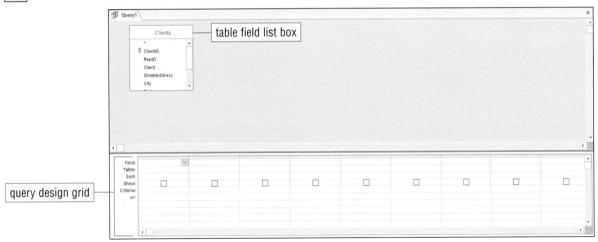

For example, to determine how many purchase orders were issued on a specific date, double-click the *PurchaseOrderID* field in the table field list box (which inserts *PurchaseOrderID* in the first field in the *Field* row in the query design grid) and then double-click the *OrderDate* field in the table field list box (which inserts *OrderDate* in the second field in the *Field* row in the query design grid). In this example, both fields are needed, so the purchase order ID is displayed along with the specific order date. After inserting the fields, add the criterion statement. The criterion statement for this example would be something like *#1/15/2018#*. After inserting the criterion, click the Run button in the Results group and the query returns only purchase orders for 1/15/2018 in the query results datasheet. If the criterion statement for the date was not added to the query, the query would return all purchase orders for all of the dates.

Access makes writing a criterion statement fairly simple by inserting the necessary symbols in the criterion. Type a city name, such as *Indianapolis*, in the *Criteria* row for a *City* field and then press the Enter key and Access changes the criterion to "*Indianapolis*". The quotation marks are inserted by Access and are necessary for the query to run properly. Let Access put the proper symbols around the criterion data in the field in the *Criteria* row or type the criterion with the symbols. Table 3.1 shows some examples of criteria statements, including what is typed and what is returned.

In the criteria examples, the asterisk is used as a wildcard character, which is a symbol that can be used to indicate any character. This is consistent with many other software applications. Two of the criteria examples in Table 3.1 use less-than and greater-than symbols. These symbols can be used for fields containing numbers, values, dates, amounts, and so forth. In the next several projects, you will design queries to extract specific information from different tables in databases.

Hint Insert fields in the *Field* row in the query design grid in the order in which you want the fields to display in the query results datasheet.

Hint Access inserts quotation marks around text criteria and pound symbols around date criteria.

Table 3.1 Criteria Examples

Typing This Criterion	Returns a Field Value Result That
"Smith"	matches *Smith*
"Smith" Or "Larson"	matches either *Smith* or *Larson*
Not "Smith"	is not *Smith* (anything but "Smith")
"s*"	begins with *S* or *s* and ends in anything
"*s"	begins with anything and ends in *S* or *s*
"[A-D]*"	begins with *A*, *B*, *C*, or *D* and ends in anything
#01/01/2018#	matches the date 01/01/2018
<#04/01/2018#	is less than (before) 04/01/2018
>#04/01/2018#	is greater than (after) 04/01/2018
Between #01/01/2018# And #03/31/2018#	is between 01/01/2018 and 03/31/2018

1. Open **3-Dearborn.accdb** from the AL1C3 folder on your storage medium and enable the content.
2. Create the following relationships and enforce referential integrity and cascade fields and records for each relationship:
   a. Create a one-to-many relationship with the *ClientID* field in the Clients table field list box the "one" and the *ClientID* field in the Sales table field list box the "many."
   b. Create a one-to-one relationship with the *RepID* field in the Representatives table field list box the "one" and the *RepID* field in the Benefits table field list box the "one."
   c. Create a one-to-many relationship with the *RepID* field in the Representatives table field list box the "one" and the *RepID* field in the Clients table field list box the "many."
   d. Create a one-to-many relationship with the *QuotaID* field in the Quotas table field list box the "one" and the *QuotaID* field in the Representatives table field list box the "many."
3. Click the Save button on the Quick Access Toolbar.
4. Print the relationships by completing the following steps:
   a. Click the Relationship Report button in the Tools group on the Relationship Tools Design tab.
   b. At the relationship report window, click the Landscape button in the Page Layout group on the Print Preview tab.
   c. Click the Print button at the left side of the Print Preview tab.
   d. At the Print dialog box, click OK.
5. Close the relationship report window without saving the report.
6. Close the Relationships window.
7. Extract records of those clients in Indianapolis by completing the following steps:
   a. Click the Create tab.
   b. Click the Query Design button in the Queries group.

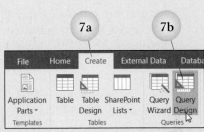

   c. At the Show Table dialog box with the Tables tab selected (see Figure 3.1 on page 62), click *Clients* in the list box, click the Add button, and then click the Close button.
   d. Insert fields from the Clients table field list box to the *Field* row in the query design grid by completing the following steps:

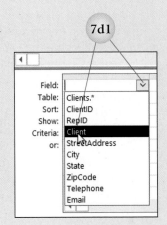

      1) Click the down arrow at the right of the first field in the *Field* row in the query design grid and then click *Client* at the drop-down list.
      2) Click in the next field in the *Field* row (to the right of *Client*) in the query design grid, click the down arrow, and then click *StreetAddress* at the drop-down list.
      3) Click in the next field in the *Field* row (to the right of *StreetAddress*), click the down arrow, and then click *City* at the drop-down list.
      4) Click in the next field in the *Field* row (to the right of *City*), click the down arrow, and then click *State* at the drop-down list.

5) Click in the next field in the *Field* row (to the right of *State*), click the down arrow, and then click *ZipCode* at the drop-down list.

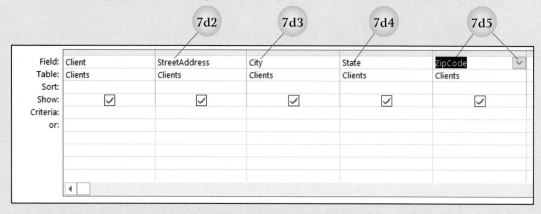

e. Insert the query criterion statement telling Access to display only those suppliers in Indianapolis by completing the following steps:
   1) Click in the *City* field in the *Criteria* row in the query design grid. (This positions the insertion point in the field.)
   2) Type Indianapolis and then press the Enter key. (This changes the criterion to "*Indianapolis*".)
f. Return the results of the query by clicking the Run button in the Results group on the Query Tools Design tab. (This displays the results in the query results datasheet.)

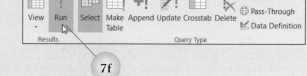

g. Save the results of the query by completing the following steps:
   1) Click the Save button on the Quick Access Toolbar.
   2) At the Save As dialog box, type ClientsIndianapolisQuery and then press the Enter key or click OK.
h. Print the query results datasheet by clicking the File tab, clicking the *Print* option, and then clicking the *Quick Print* option.
i. Close ClientsIndianapolisQuery.

8. Extract those records with quota identification numbers greater than 2 by completing the following steps:
   a. Click the Create tab and then click the Query Design button in the Queries group.
   b. Double-click *Representatives* in the Show Table dialog box and then click the Close button.
   c. In the query window, double-click *RepName*. (This inserts the field in the first field in the *Field* row in the query design grid.)
   d. Double-click *QuotaID*. (This inserts the field in the second field in the *Field* row in the query design grid.)

e. Insert the query criterion by completing the following steps:
   1) Click in the *QuotaID* field in the *Criteria* row in the query design grid.
   2) Type >2 and then press the Enter key. (Access will automatically insert quotation marks around *2* since the data type for the field is identified as *Short Text* [rather than *Number*].)

f. Return the results of the query by clicking the Run button in the Results group.

g. Save the query and name it *QuotaIDGreaterThanTwoQuery*.

h. Print and then close the query.

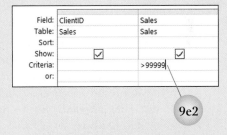

9. Extract those sales greater than $99,999 by completing the following steps:

   a. Click the Create tab and then click the Query Design button.

   b. Double-click *Sales* in the Show Table dialog box and then click the Close button.

   c. At the query window, double-click *ClientID*. (This inserts the field in the first field in the *Field* row in the query design grid.)

   d. Insert the *Sales* field in the second field in the *Field* row.

   e. Insert the query criterion by completing the following steps:
      1) Click in the *Sales* field in the *Criteria* row in the query design grid.
      2) Type >99999 and then press the Enter key. (Access will not insert quotation marks around *99999* since the field is identified as *Currency*.)

   f. Return the results of the query by clicking the Run button in the Results group.

   g. Save the query and name it *SalesOver$99999Query*.

   h. Print and then close the query.

10. Extract records of those representatives with a telephone number that begins with the 765 area code by completing the following steps:

    a. Click the Create tab and then click the Query Design button.

    b. Double-click *Representatives* in the Show Table dialog box and then click the Close button.

    c. Insert the *RepName* field in the first field in the *Field* row.

    d. Insert the *Telephone* field in the second field in the *Field* row.

    e. Insert the query criterion by completing the following steps:
       1) Click in the *Telephone* field in the *Criteria* row.
       2) Type "(765*" and then press the Enter key. (You need to type the quotation marks in this criterion because the criterion contains a left parenthesis.)

    f. Return the results of the query by clicking the Run button in the Results group.

    g. Save the query and name it *RepsWith765AreaCodeQuery*.

    h. Print and then close the query.

Check Your Work

In Project 1a, each query was performed on fields from one table. Queries can also be performed on fields from multiple tables. In Project 1b, queries will be performed on tables containing yes/no check boxes. When designing a query, both records that contain a check mark and records that do not contain a check mark can be extracted. To extract records that contain a check mark, click in the desired field in the *Criteria* row in the query design grid, type a *1*, press the Enter key, and Access changes the *1* to *True*. To extract records that do not contain a check mark, type *0* in the field in the *Criteria* row, press the Enter key, and Access changes the *0* to *False*.

The Zoom box can be used when entering a criterion in a query to provide a larger area for typing. To display the Zoom box, press Shift + F2 or right-click in the specific field in the *Criteria* row and then click *Zoom* at the shortcut menu. Type the criterion in the Zoom box and then click OK.

Project 1b Performing Queries on Related Tables

Part 2 of 8

1. With **3-Dearborn.accdb** open, extract information on representatives hired between January 2016 and June 2016 and include the representatives' names by completing the following steps:
   a. Click the Create tab and then click the Query Design button.
   b. Double-click *Representatives* in the Show Table dialog box.
   c. Double-click *Benefits* in the Show Table dialog box and then click the Close button.
   d. At the query window, double-click *RepName* in the Representatives table field list box.
   e. Double-click *HireDate* in the Benefits table field list box.
   f. Insert the query criterion in the Zoom box by completing the following steps:
      1) Click in the *HireDate* field in the *Criteria* row.
      2) Press Shift + F2 to display the Zoom box.
      3) Type Between 1/1/2016 And 6/30/2016.
      4) Click OK.
   g. Return the results of the query by clicking the Run button in the Results group.
   h. Save the query and name it *JanToJun2016HiresQuery*.
   i. Print and then close the query.

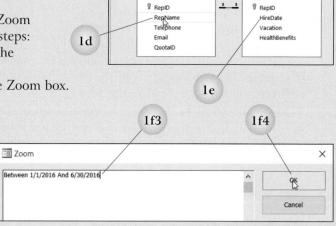

2. Extract records of those representatives who were hired in 2015 by completing the following steps:
   a. Click the Create tab and then click the Query Design button.
   b. Double-click *Representatives* in the Show Table dialog box.
   c. Double-click *Benefits* in the Show Table dialog box and then click the Close button.
   d. Double-click *RepID* in the Representatives table field list box.
   e. Double-click *RepName* in the Representatives table field list box.
   f. Double-click *HireDate* in the Benefits table field list box.

g. Insert the query criterion by completing the following steps:

    1) Click in the *HireDate* field in the *Criteria* row.

    2) Type *2015 and then press the Enter key.

h. Return the results of the query by clicking the Run button in the Results group.

i. Save the query and name it *RepsHiredIn2015Query*.

j. Print and then close the query.

3. Suppose you need to determine sales for a company but you can only remember that the company name begins with *Blue*. Create a query that finds the company and identifies the sales by completing the following steps:

a. Click the Create tab and then click the Query Design button.

b. Double-click *Clients* in the Show Table dialog box.

c. Double-click *Sales* in the Show Table dialog box and then click the Close button.

d. Insert the *ClientID* field from the Clients table field list box in the first field in the *Field* row in the query design grid.

e. Insert the *Client* field from the Clients table field list box in the second field in the *Field* row.

f. Insert the *Sales* field from the Sales table field list box in the third field in the *Field* row.

g. Insert the query criterion by completing the following steps:

    1) Click in the *Client* field in the *Criteria* row.

    2) Type Blue* and then press the Enter key.

h. Return the results of the query by clicking the Run button in the Results group.

i. Save the query and name it *BlueRidgeSalesQuery*.

j. Print and then close the query.

4. Close **3-Dearborn.accdb**.

5. Display the Open dialog box with the AL1C3 folder on your storage medium active.

6. Open **3-PacTrek.accdb** and enable the content.

7. Extract information on products ordered between February 1, 2018, and February 28, 2018, by completing the following steps:

a. Click the Create tab and then click the Query Design button.

b. Double-click *Products* in the Show Table dialog box.

c. Double-click *Orders* in the Show Table dialog box and then click the Close button.

d. Insert the *ProductID* field from the Products table field list box in the first field in the *Field* row.

e. Insert the *Product* field from the Products table field list box in the second field in the *Field* row.

f. Insert the *OrderDate* field from the Orders table field list box in the third field in the *Field* row.

g. Insert the query criterion by completing the following steps:

    1) Click in the *OrderDate* field in the *Criteria* row.

    2) Type Between 2/1/2018 And 2/28/2018 and then press the Enter key.

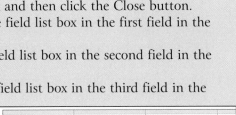

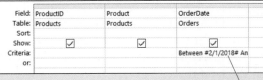

h. Return the results of the query by clicking the Run button in the Results group.

i. Save the query and name it *Feb1-28OrdersQuery*.

j. Print and then close the query.

8. Close **3-PacTrek.accdb**.

9. Open **3-CopperState.accdb** and enable the content.

10. Display the Relationships window and create the following additional relationships (enforce referential integrity and cascade fields and records):

a. Create a one-to-many relationship with the *AgentID* field in the Agents table field list box the "one" and the *AgentID* field in the Assignments table field list box the "many."

b. Create a one-to-many relationship with the *OfficeID* field in the Offices table field list box the "one" and the *OfficeID* field in the Assignments table field list box the "many."

c. Create a one-to-many relationship with the *OfficeID* field in the Offices table field list box the "one" and the *OfficeID* field in the Agents table field list box the "many."

11. Save and then print the relationships.

12. Close the relationship report without saving it and then close the Relationships window.

13. Extract records of clients that have uninsured motorist coverage by completing the following steps:

a. Click the Create tab and then click the Query Design button.

b. Double-click *Clients* in the Show Table dialog box.

c. Double-click *Coverage* in the Show Table dialog box and then click the Close button.

d. Insert the *ClientID* field from the Clients table field list box in the first field in the *Field* row.

e. Insert the *FirstName* field from the Clients table field list box in the second field in the *Field* row.

f. Insert the *LastName* field from the Clients table field list box in the third field in the *Field* row.

g. Insert the *UninsMotorist* field from the Coverage table field list box in the fourth field in the *Field* row. (You may need to scroll down the Coverage table field list box to display the *UninsMotorist* field.)

h. Insert the query criterion by clicking in the *UninsMotorist* field in the *Criteria* row, typing 1, and then pressing the Enter key. (Access changes the *1* to *True*.)

i. Click the Run button in the Results group.

j. Save the query and name it *UninsMotoristCoverageQuery*.

k. Print and then close the query.

14. Extract records of claims in January over $999 by completing the following steps:

a. Click the Create tab and then click the Query Design button.

b. Double-click *Clients* in the Show Table dialog box.

c. Double-click *Claims* in the Show Table dialog box and then click the Close button.

d. Insert the *ClientID* field from the *Clients* table field list box in the first field in the *Field* row.

e. Insert the *FirstName* field from the Clients table field list box in the second field in the *Field* row.

f. Insert the *LastName* field from the Clients table field list box in the third field in the *Field* row.

g. Insert the *ClaimID* field from the Claims table field list box in the fourth field in the *Field* row.

h. Insert the *DateOfClaim* field from the Claims table field list box in the fifth field in the *Field* row.

i. Insert the *AmountOfClaim* field from the Claims table field list box in the sixth field in the *Field* row.

j. Click in the *DateOfClaim* field in the *Criteria* row, type Between 1/1/2018 And 1/31/2018, and then press the Enter key.

k. With the insertion point positioned in the *AmountOfClaim* field in the *Criteria* row, type >999 and then press the Enter key.

Field:	ClientID	FirstName	LastName	ClaimID	DateOfClaim	AmountOfClaim
Table:	Clients	Clients	Clients	Claims	Claims	Claims
Sort:						
Show:	☑	☑	☑	☑	☑	☑
Criteria:					Between #1/1/2018# An	>999
or:						

14j   14k

l. Click the Run button in the Results group.

m. Save the query and name it *JanClaimsOver$999Query*.

n. Print and then close the query.

Check Your Work

Tutorial

Sorting Data and Hiding Fields in Query Results

Sorting in a Query

When designing a query, the sort order of a field or fields can be specified. Click in a field in the *Sort* row and a down arrow displays at the right of the field. Click this down arrow and a drop-down list displays with the choices *Ascending*, *Descending*, and *(not sorted)*. Click *Ascending* to sort from lowest to highest or click *Descending* to sort from highest to lowest.

Quick Steps

Sort Fields in a Query
1. At query window, click in field in *Sort* row in query design grid.
2. Click down arrow in field.
3. Click *Ascending* or *Descending*.

Hiding Fields in a Query

By default, each check box in the fields in the *Show* row in the query design grid contains a check mark, indicating that the column will be displayed in the query results datasheet. If a specific field is needed for the query but not needed when viewing the query results, remove the check mark from the field in the *Show* row to hide the field in the query results datasheet.

Arranging Fields in a Query

 Insert Columns

 Delete Columns

Use buttons in the Query Setup group on the Query Design Tools tab to insert a new field column in or delete an existing field column from the query design grid. To insert a field column, click in a field in the column that will display immediately to the right of the new column and then click the Insert Columns button in the Query Setup group on the Query Design Tools tab. To remove a column, click in a field in the column to be deleted and then click the Delete Columns button in the Query Setup group. Complete similar steps to insert or delete a row in the query design grid.

Columns in the query design grid can be rearranged by selecting the field column and then dragging the column to the desired position. To select a column in the query design grid, position the mouse pointer at the top of the column until the pointer turns into a small, black, down-pointing arrow and then click the left mouse button. Position the mouse pointer at the top of the selected column until the mouse displays as a pointer, click and hold down the left mouse button, drag to the desired position in the query design grid, and then release the mouse button. When dragging the column, a thick, black, vertical line displays identifying the location where the column will be inserted.

Project 1c Performing Queries on Related Tables and Sorting in Field Values

1. With **3-CopperState.accdb** open, extract information on clients with agents from the West Bell Road Glendale office and sort the information alphabetically by client last name by completing the following steps:
   a. Click the Create tab and then click the Query Design button.
   b. Double-click *Assignments* in the Show Table dialog box.
   c. Double-click *Clients* in the Show Table dialog box and then click the Close button.
   d. Insert the *OfficeID* field from the Assignments table field list box in the first field in the *Field* row.
   e. Insert the *AgentID* field from the Assignments table field list box in the second field in the *Field* row.
   f. Insert the *FirstName* field from the Clients table field list box in the third field in the *Field* row.
   g. Insert the *LastName* field from the Clients table field list box in the fourth field in the *Field* row.
   h. Click in the *OfficeID* field in the *Criteria* row, type GW, and then press the Enter key.
   i. Sort the *LastName* field column in ascending alphabetical order (A–Z) by completing the following steps:
       1) Click in the *LastName* field in the *Sort* row. (This causes a down arrow to display in the field.)
       2) Click the down arrow that displays in the field in the *Sort* row and then click *Ascending*.
   j. Specify that you do not want the *AgentID* field to show in the query results by clicking in the check box in the *AgentID* field in the *Show* row to remove the check mark.

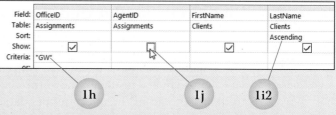

   k. Click the Run button in the Results group.
   l. Save the query and name it *GWClientsQuery*.
   m. Print and then close the query.
2. Close **3-CopperState.accdb**.
3. Open **3-PacTrek.accdb**.
4. Extract information on orders less than $1,500 by completing the following steps:
   a. Click the Create tab and then click the Query Design button.
   b. Double-click *Products* in the Show Table dialog box.
   c. Double-click *Orders* in the Show Table dialog box and then click the Close button.
   d. Insert the *ProductID* field from the Products table field list box in the first field in the *Field* row.
   e. Insert the *SupplierID* field from the Products table field list box in the second field in the *Field* row.

f. Insert the *UnitsOrdered* field from the Orders table field list box in the third field in the *Field* row.

g. Insert the *Amount* field from the Orders table field list box in the fourth field in the *Field* row.

h. Insert the query criterion by completing the following steps:

    1) Click in the *Amount* field in the *Criteria* row.

    2) Type <1500 and then press the Enter key.

Field:	ProductID	SupplierID	UnitsOrdered	Amount
Table:	Products	Products	Orders	Orders
Sort:				
Show:	☑	☑	☑	☑
Criteria:				<1500
or:				

4h2

i. Sort the *Amount* field column values from highest to lowest by completing the following steps:

    1) Click in the *Amount* field in the *Sort* row. (This causes a down arrow to display in the field.)

    2) Click the down arrow that displays in the field in the *Sort* row and then click *Descending*.

j. Return the results of the query by clicking the Run button in the Results group.

k. Save the query and name it *OrdersLessThan$1500Query*.

l. Print and then close the query.

UnitsOrdered	Amount
Orders	Orders
	⌄
☑	Ascending
	Descending
	(not sorted)

4i2

5. Close **3-PacTrek.accdb**.

6. Open **3-Dearborn.accdb**.

7. Design a query by completing the following steps:

    a. Click the Create tab and then click the Query Design button.

    b. Double-click *Representatives* in the Show Table dialog box.

    c. Double-click *Clients* in the Show Table dialog box.

    d. Double-click *Sales* in the Show Table dialog box and then click the Close button.

    e. Insert the *RepID* field from the Representatives table field list box in the first field in the *Field* row.

    f. Insert the *RepName* field from the Representatives table field list box in the second field in the *Field* row.

    g. Insert the *ClientID* field from the Clients table field list box in the third field in the *Field* row.

    h. Insert the *Sales* field from the Sales table field list box in the fourth field in the *Field* row.

8. Move the *RepName* field column by completing the following steps:

    a. Position the mouse pointer at the top of the *RepName* field column until the pointer turns into a small, black, down-pointing arrow and then click the left mouse button. (This selects the entire column.)

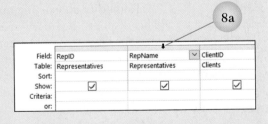

8a

Field:	RepID	RepName ⌄	ClientID
Table:	Representatives	Representatives	Clients
Sort:			
Show:	☑	☑	☑
Criteria:			
or:			

    b. Position the mouse pointer at the top of the selected column until the pointer turns into a white arrow.

    c. Click and hold down the left mouse button; drag to the right until a thick, black horizontal line displays between the *ClientID* field column and the *Sales* field column; and then release the mouse button.

8c

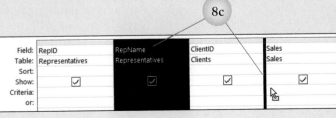

Field:	RepID	RepName	ClientID	Sales
Table:	Representatives	Representatives	Clients	Sales
Sort:				
Show:	☑	☑	☑	☑
Criteria:				
or:				

9. Delete the *RepID* field column by clicking in a field in the column and then clicking the Delete Columns button in the Query Setup group.
10. Insert a new field column and insert a new field in the column by completing the following steps:
    a. Click in a field in the *Sales* field column and then click the Insert Columns button in the Query Setup group.
    b. Click the down arrow that displays in the *Field* row in the new field column and then click *Clients.Client* at the drop-down list.
11. Hide the *ClientID* field so it does not display in the query results by clicking the *Show* check box in the *ClientID* field in the *Show* row to remove the check mark.
12. Insert the query criterion that extracts information on sales over $100,000 by completing the following steps:
    a. Click in the *Sales* field in the *Criteria* row.
    b. Type >100000 and then press the Enter key.
13. Sort the *Sales* field column values from highest to lowest by completing the following steps:
    a. Click in the *Sales* field in the *Sort* row.
    b. Click the down arrow that displays in the field in the *Sort* row and then click *Descending*.
14. Return the results of the query by clicking the Run button in the Results group.
15. Save the query and name it *SalesMoreThan$100000Query*.
16. Print and then close the query.

Check Your Work

Modifying a Query

A query can be modified and used for a new purpose rather than designing a new query. For example, if a query is designed that displays sales of more than $100,000, the query can be used to find sales that are less than $100,000. Rather than design a new query, open the existing query, make any needed changes, and then run the query.

To modify an existing query, double-click the query in the Navigation pane. (This displays the query in Datasheet view.) Click the View button to display the query in Design view. A query can also be opened in Design view by right-clicking the query in the Navigation pane and then clicking *Design View* at the shortcut menu. Make changes to the query and then click the Run button in the Results group. Click the Save button on the Quick Access Toolbar to save the query with the same name. To save the query with a new name, click the File tab, click the *Save As* option, click the *Save Object As* option, and then click the Save As button. At the Save As dialog box, type a name for the query and then press the Enter key.

If a database contains a number of queries, the queries can be grouped and displayed in the Navigation pane. To do this, click the down arrow in the Navigation pane menu bar and then click *Object Type* at the drop-down list. This displays objects grouped in categories, such as *Tables* and *Queries*.

Renaming and Deleting a Query

If a query has been modified, consider renaming it. To do this, right-click the query name in the Navigation pane, click *Rename* at the shortcut menu, type the new name, and then press the Enter key. If a query is no longer needed in the database, delete it by clicking the query name in the Navigation pane, clicking the Delete button in the Records group on the Home tab, and then clicking the Yes button at the deletion message. Another method is to right-click the query in the Navigation pane, click *Delete* at the shortcut menu, and then click Yes at the deletion message. If a query is being deleted from a file on the computer's hard drive, the deletion message will not display. This is because Access automatically sends the deleted query to the Recycle Bin, where it can be retrieved if necessary.

Project 1d Modifying Queries

Part 4 of 8

1. With **3-Dearborn.accdb** open, find sales less than $100,000 by completing the following steps:
   a. Double-click *SalesMoreThan$100000Query* in the Queries group in the Navigation pane.
   b. Click the View button in the Views group to switch to Design view.
   c. Click in the field in the *Criteria* row containing the text *>100000* and then edit the text so it displays as *<100000*.

   d. Click the Run button in the Results group.
2. Save the query with a new name by completing the following steps:
   a. Click the File tab, click the *Save As* option, click the *Save Object As* option, and then click the Save As button.
   b. At the Save As dialog box, type SalesLessThan$100000Query and then press the Enter key.
   c. Print and then close the query.

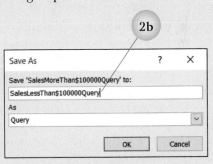

3. Modify an existing query and find employees with three weeks of vacation by completing the following steps:
   a. Right-click *JanToJun2016HiresQuery* in the Queries group in the Navigation pane and then click *Design View* at the shortcut menu.
   b. Click in the *HireDate* field in the *Field* row.
   c. Click the down arrow that displays in the field and then click *Vacation* at the drop-down list.
   d. Select the current text in the *Vacation* field in the *Criteria* row, type 3 weeks, and then press the Enter key.
   e. Click the Run button in the Results group.
   f. Save and then close the query.

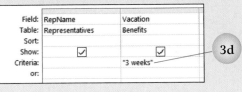

4. Rename the query by completing the following steps:
   a. Right-click *JanToJun2016HiresQuery* in the Navigation pane and then click *Rename* at the shortcut menu.
   b. Type RepsWith3WeekVacationsQuery and then press the Enter key.
   c. Open, print, and then close the query.
5. Delete the *SalesOver$99999Query* by right-clicking the query name in the Navigation pane and then clicking *Delete* at the shortcut menu. If a deletion message displays, click Yes.

Check Your Work

Tutorial

Designing a Query with *Or* Criteria

Tutorial

Designing a Query with *And* Criteria

💡 **Hint** A query can be designed that combines *And* and *Or* statements.

Designing Queries with *Or* and *And* Criteria

The query design grid contains an *or* row for designing a query that instructs Access to display records matching any of the criteria. Multiple criterion statements on different rows in a query become an *Or* statement, which means that any of the criterion can be met for a record to be displayed in the query results datasheet. For example, to display a list of employees with three weeks of vacation *or* four weeks of vacation, type *3 weeks* in the *Vacation* field in the *Criteria* row and then type *4 weeks* in the field immediately below *3 weeks* in the *or* row. Other examples include finding clients that live in *Muncie* or *Lafayette* and finding representatives with quotas of *1* or *2*.

When designing a query, criteria statements can be entered into more than one field in the *Criteria* row. Multiple criteria all entered in the same row become an *And* statement, for which each criterion must be met for Access to select the record. For example, a query can be designed that displays clients in the Indianapolis area with sales greater than $100,000.

Project 1e Designing Queries with *Or* and *And* Criteria

Part 5 of 8

1. With **3-Dearborn.accdb** open, modify an existing query and find employees with three weeks or four weeks of vacation by completing the following steps:
   a. Double-click the *RepsWith3WeekVacationsQuery*.
   b. Click the View button in the Views group to switch to Design view.
   c. Click in the empty field below "*3 weeks*" in the *or* row, type 4 weeks, and then press the Enter key.
   d. Click the Run button in the Results group.
2. Save the query with a new name by completing the following steps:
   a. Click the File tab, click the *Save As* option, click the *Save Object As* option, and then click the Save As button.
   b. At the Save As dialog box, type RepsWith3Or4WeekVacationsQuery and then press the Enter key.
   c. Print and then close the query.
3. Design a query that finds records of clients in the Indianapolis area with sales over $100,000 by completing the following steps:
   a. Click the Create tab and then click the Query Design button.
   b. Double-click *Clients* in the Show Table dialog box.

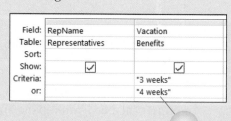

Field:	RepName	Vacation
Table:	Representatives	Benefits
Sort:		
Show:	☑	☑
Criteria:		"3 weeks"
or:		"4 weeks"

1c

c. Double-click *Sales* in the Show Table dialog box and then click the Close button.
d. Insert the *Client* field from the Clients table field list box in the first field in the *Field* row.
e. Insert the *City* field from the Clients table field list box in the second field in the *Field* row.
f. Insert the *Sales* field from the Sales table field list box in the third field in the *Field* row.
g. Insert the query criteria by completing the following steps:
   1) Click in the *City* field in the *Criteria* row.
   2) Type Indianapolis and then press the Enter key.
   3) With the insertion point positioned in the *Sales* field in the *Criteria* row, type >100000 and then press the Enter key.

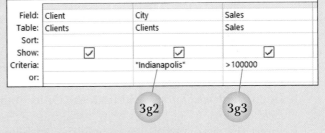

h. Click the Run button in the Results group.
i. Save the query and name it *SalesOver$100000IndianapolisQuery*.
j. Print and then close the query.
4. Close **3-Dearborn.accdb**.
5. Open **3-PacTrek.accdb**.
6. Design a query that finds products available from supplier numbers 25, 31, and 42 by completing the following steps:
   a. Click the Create tab and then click the Query Design button.
   b. Double-click *Suppliers* in the Show Table dialog box.
   c. Double-click *Products* in the Show Table dialog box and then click the Close button.
   d. Insert the *SupplierID* field from the Suppliers table field list box in the first field in the *Field* row.
   e. Insert the *SupplierName* field from the Suppliers table field list box in the second field in the *Field* row.
   f. Insert the *Product* field from the Products table field list box in the third field in the *Field* row.
   g. Insert the query criteria by completing the following steps:
      1) Click in the *SupplierID* field in the *Criteria* row.
      2) Type 25 and then press the Down Arrow key. (This makes the field below *25* active.)
      3) Type 31 and then press the Down Arrow key. (This makes the field below *31* active.)
      4) Type 42 and then press the Enter key.

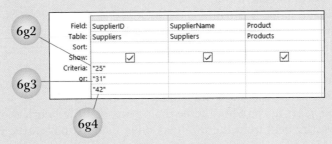

h. Click the Run button in the Results group.
i. Save the query and name it *Suppliers25-31-42Query*.
j. Print and then close the query.

7. Design a query that finds the number of ski hats or gloves on order by completing the following steps:
   a. Click the Create tab and then click the Query Design button.
   b. Double-click *Orders* in the Show Table dialog box.
   c. Double-click *Suppliers* in the Show Table dialog box.
   d. Double-click *Products* in the Show Table dialog box and then click the Close button.
   e. Insert the *OrderID* field from the Orders table field list box in the first field in the *Field* row.
   f. Insert the *SupplierName* field from the Suppliers table field list box in the second field in the *Field* row.
   g. Insert the *Product* field from the Products table field list box in the third field in the *Field* row.
   h. Insert the *UnitsOrdered* field from the Orders table field list box in the fourth field in the *Field* row.
   i. Insert the query criteria by completing the following steps:
      1) Click in the *Product* field in the *Criteria* row.
      2) Type *ski hat* and then press the Down Arrow key. (You need to type the asterisk before and after *ski hat* so the query will find any product that includes the words *ski hat* in the description, no matter what text comes before or after the words. When you press the Down Arrow key, Access changes the criteria to *Like "*ski hat*".*)
      3) Type *gloves* and then press the Enter key.

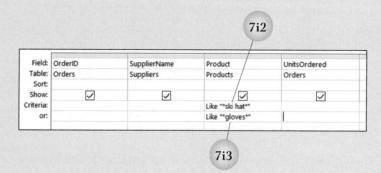

   j. Click the Run button in the Results group.
   k. Save the query and name it *SkiHatsGlovesOnOrderQuery*.
   l. Print and then close the query.
8. Design a query that finds boots, sleeping bags, or backpacks and the suppliers that produce them by completing the following steps:
   a. Click the Create tab and then click the Query Design button.
   b. Double-click *Products* in the Show Table dialog box.
   c. Double-click *Suppliers* in the Show Table dialog box and then click the Close button.
   d. Insert the *ProductID* field from the Products table field list box in the first field in the *Field* row.
   e. Insert the *Product* field from the Products table field list box in the second field in the *Field* row.
   f. Insert the *SupplierName* field from the Suppliers table field list box in the third field in the *Field* row.
   g. Insert the query criteria by completing the following steps:
      1) Click in the *Product* field in the *Criteria* row.

2) Type *boots* and then press the Down Arrow key on your keyboard.
3) Type *sleeping bag* and then press the Down Arrow key on your keyboard.
4) Type *backpack* and then press the Enter key.

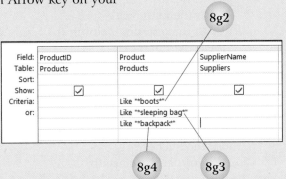

h. Click the Run button in the Results group.
i. Save the query and name it *BootsSleepingBagsBackpacksQuery*.
j. Print and then close the query.

9. Close **3-PacTrek.accdb**.
10. Open **3-CopperState.accdb**.
11. Design a query that finds clients who have only liability auto coverage by completing the following steps:
   a. Click the Create tab and then click the Query Design button.
   b. Double-click *Clients* in the Show Table dialog box.
   c. Double-click *Coverage* in the Show Table dialog box and then click the Close button.
   d. Insert the *ClientID* field from the Clients table field list box in the first field in the *Field* row.
   e. Insert the *FirstName* field from the Clients table field list box in the second field in the *Field* row.
   f. Insert the *LastName* field from the Clients table field list box in the third field in the *Field* row.
   g. Insert the *Medical* field from the Coverage table field list box in the fourth field in the *Field* row.
   h. Insert the *Liability* field from the Coverage table field list box in the fifth field in the *Field* row.
   i. Insert the *Comprehensive* field from the Coverage table field list box in the sixth field in the *Field* row.
   j. Insert the *UninsMotorist* field from the Coverage table field list box in the seventh field in the *Field* row. (You may need to scroll down the Coverage table field list box to display the *UninsMotorist* field.)
   k. Insert the *Collision* field from the Coverage table field list box in the eighth field in the *Field* row. (You may need to scroll down the Coverage table field list box to display the *Collision* field.)
   l. Insert the query criteria by completing the following steps:
      1) Click in the *Medical* field in the *Criteria* row, type 0, and then press the Enter key. (Access changes the *0* to *False*.)
      2) With the insertion point in the *Liability* field in the *Criteria* row, type 1 and then press the Enter key. (Access changes the *1* to *True*.)

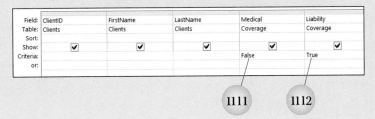

3) With the insertion point in the *Comprehensive* field in the *Criteria* row, type 0 and then press the Enter key.

4) With the insertion point in the *UninsMotorist* field in the *Criteria* row, type 0 and then press the Enter key.

5) With the insertion point in the *Collision* field in the *Criteria* row, type 0 and then press the Enter key.

   m. Click the Run button in the Results group.

   n. Save the query and name it *ClientsWithOnlyLiabilityQuery*.

   o. Print the query in landscape orientation.

   p. Close the query.

12. Close **3-CopperState.accdb**.

Check Your Work

Tutorial

Creating a Query
Using the Simple
Query Wizard

 Query Wizard

Quick Steps

Create a Query Using the Simple Query Wizard
1. Click Create tab.
2. Click Query Wizard button.
3. Make sure *Simple Query Wizard* is selected in list box and then click OK.
4. Follow query steps.
5. Click Finish button.

Creating a Query Using the Simple Query Wizard

The Simple Query Wizard provided by Access provides steps for preparing a query. To use this wizard, open the database, click the Create tab, and then click the Query Wizard button in the Queries group. At the New Query dialog box, make sure *Simple Query Wizard* is selected in the list box and then click the OK button. At the first Simple Query Wizard dialog box, shown in Figure 3.3, specify the table(s) in the *Tables/Queries* option box. After specifying the table(s), insert the fields to be included in the query in the *Selected Fields* list box and then click the Next button.

At the second Simple Query Wizard dialog box, specify a detail or summary query and then click the Next button. At the third (and last) Simple Query Wizard dialog box, shown in Figure 3.4, type a name for the completed query or accept the name provided by the wizard. The third Simple Query Wizard dialog box also includes options for choosing to open the query to view the information or to modify the query design. To extract specific information, be sure to choose the *Modify the query design* option. After making any necessary changes, click the Finish button.

If the query design is not modified in the last Simple Query Wizard dialog box, the query displays all records for the fields identified in the first Simple Query Wizard dialog box.

Figure 3.3 First Simple Query Wizard Dialog Box

Specify the table(s) in the *Tables/Queries* option box.

Click the One Field button to insert the selected field in the *Available Fields* list box into the *Selected Fields* list box.

Click the All Fields button to insert all of the fields in the *Available Fields* list box into the *Selected Fields* list box.

Insert in the *Selected Fields* list box the fields to be included in the query.

Figure 3.4 Last Simple Query Wizard Dialog Box

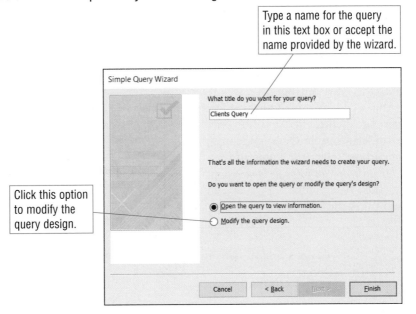

Type a name for the query in this text box or accept the name provided by the wizard.

Click this option to modify the query design.

Project 1f Creating Queries Using the Simple Query Wizard

1. Open **3-Dearborn.accdb** and then use the Simple Query Wizard to create a query that displays client names along with sales by completing the following steps:
   a. Click the Create tab and then click the Query Wizard button in the Queries group.
   b. At the New Query dialog box, make sure *Simple Query Wizard* is selected in the list box and then click OK.
   c. At the first Simple Query Wizard dialog box, click the *Tables/Queries* option box arrow and then click *Table: Clients*.
   d. With *ClientID* selected in the *Available Fields* list box, click the One Field button (the button containing the greater-than symbol, >). This inserts the *ClientID* field in the *Selected Fields* list box.
   e. Click *Client* in the *Available Fields* list box and then click the One Field button.

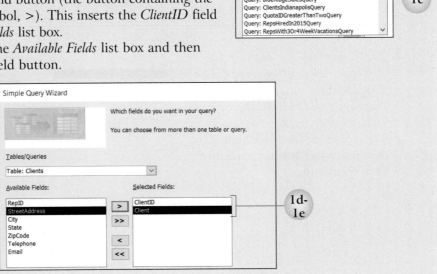

f. Click the *Tables/Queries* option box arrow and then click *Table: Sales*.

g. Click *Sales* in the *Available Fields* list box and then click the One Field button.

h. Click the Next button.

i. At the second Simple Query Wizard dialog box, click the Next button.

j. At the last Simple Query Wizard dialog box, select the name in the *What title do you want for your query?* text box, type ClientSalesQuery, and then press the Enter key.

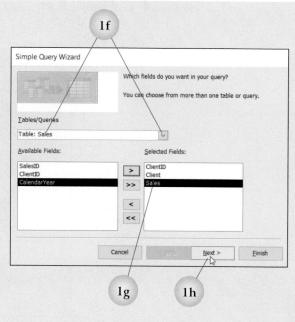

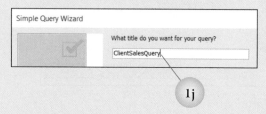

k. When the results of the query display, print the results.

2. Close the query.

3. Close **3-Dearborn.accdb**.

4. Open **3-PacTrek.accdb**.

5. Create a query that displays the products on order, order amounts, and supplier names by completing the following steps:

a. Click the Create tab and then click the Query Wizard button.

b. At the New Query dialog box, make sure *Simple Query Wizard* is selected in the list box and then click OK.

c. At the first Simple Query Wizard dialog box, click the *Tables/Queries* option box arrow and then click *Table: Suppliers*.

d. With *SupplierID* selected in the *Available Fields* list box, click the One Field button. (This inserts the *SupplierID* field in the *Selected Fields* list box.)

e. With *SupplierName* selected in the *Available Fields* list box, click the One Field button.

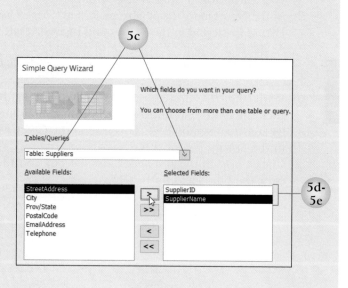

f. Click the *Tables/Queries* option box arrow and then click *Table: Orders*.
g. Click *ProductID* in the *Available Fields* list box and then click the One Field button.
h. Click *Amount* in the *Available Fields* list box and then click the One Field button.
i. Click the Next button.

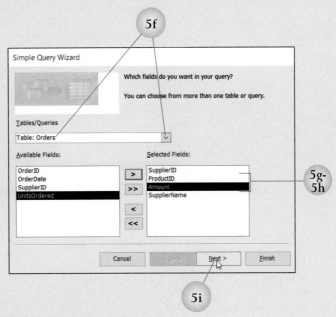

j. At the second Simple Query Wizard dialog box, click the Next button.
k. At the last Simple Query Wizard dialog box, select the text in the *What title do you want for your query?* text box, type ProductOrderAmountsQuery, and then press the Enter key.

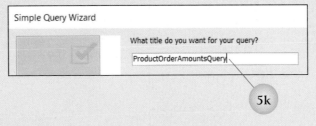

l. When the results of the query display, print the results.
m. Close the query.

Check Your Work

To extract specific information when using the Simple Query Wizard, tell the wizard that the query design is to be modified. This displays the query window with the query design grid, where query criteria can be entered.

1. With **3-PacTrek.accdb** open, use the Simple Query Wizard to create a query that displays suppliers outside British Columbia by completing the following steps:
    a. Click the Create tab and then click the Query Wizard button.
    b. At the New Query dialog box, make sure *Simple Query Wizard* is selected and then click OK.
    c. At the first Simple Query Wizard dialog box, click the *Tables/Queries* option box arrow and then click *Table: Suppliers*.
    d. Insert the following fields in the *Selected Fields* list box:

    SupplierName
    StreetAddress
    City
    Prov/State
    PostalCode

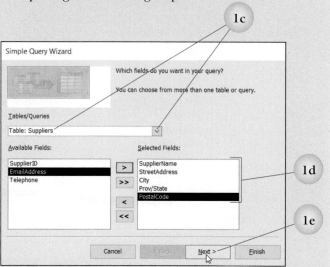

    e. Click the Next button.
    f. At the last Simple Query Wizard dialog box, select the current text in the *What title do you want for your query?* text box and then type SuppliersNotBCQuery.
    g. Click the *Modify the query design* option and then click the Finish button.
    h. At the query window, complete the following steps:
        1) Click in the *Prov/State field* field in the *Criteria* row in the query design grid.
        2) Type Not BC and then press the Enter key.
    i. Specify that the fields are to be sorted in descending order by postal code by completing the following steps:
        1) Click in the *PostalCode* field in the *Sort* row.
        2) Click the down arrow that displays in the field and then click *Descending*.

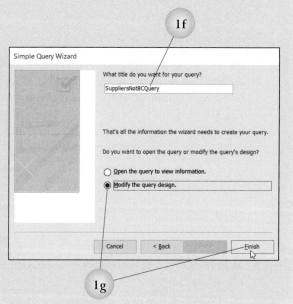

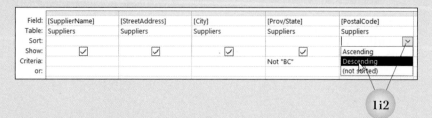

    j. Click the Run button in the Results group. (This displays suppliers that are not in British Columbia and displays the records sorted by postal code in descending order.)
    k. Save, print, and then close the query.

2. Close **3-PacTrek.accdb**.
3. Open **3-Dearborn.accdb**.
4. Use the Simple Query Wizard to create a query that displays clients in Muncie by completing the following steps:
   a. Click the Create tab and then click the Query Wizard button.
   b. At the New Query dialog box, make sure *Simple Query Wizard* is selected and then click OK.
   c. At the first Simple Query Wizard dialog box, click the *Tables/Queries* option box arrow and then click *Table: Clients*. (You may need to scroll up the list to display this table.)
   d. Insert the following fields in the *Selected Fields* list box:

      Client
      StreetAddress
      City
      State
      ZipCode

   e. Click the Next button.
   f. At the last Simple Query Wizard dialog box, select the current text in the *What title do you want for your query?* text box and then type ClientsMuncieQuery.
   g. Click the *Modify the query design* option and then click the Finish button.
   h. At the query window, complete the following steps:
      1) Click in the *City* field in the *Criteria* row in the query design grid.
      2) Type Muncie and then press the Enter key.

Field:	[Client]	[StreetAddress]	[City]	[State]	[ZipCode]
Table:	Clients	Clients	Clients	Clients	Clients
Sort:					
Show:	✓	✓	✓	✓	✓
Criteria:			"Muncie"		
or:					

4h2

   i. Click the Run button in the Results group. (This displays clients in Muncie.)
   j. Save, print, and then close the query.
5. Close **3-Dearborn.accdb**.
6. Open **3-CopperState.accdb**.
7. Use the Simple Query Wizard to display clients that live in Phoenix with claims over $500 by completing the following steps:
   a. Click the Create tab and then click the Query Wizard button in the Queries group.
   b. At the New Query dialog box, make sure *Simple Query Wizard* is selected in the list box and then click OK.
   c. At the first Simple Query Wizard dialog box, click the *Tables/Queries* option box arrow and then click *Table: Clients*.
   d. Insert the following fields in the *Selected Fields* list box:

      ClientID
      FirstName
      LastName
      StreetAddress
      City
      State
      ZIP

   e. Click the *Tables/Queries* option box arrow and then click *Table: Claims*.

f. With *ClaimID* selected in the *Available Fields* list box, click the One Field button.
g. Click *AmountOfClaim* in the *Available Fields* list box and then click the One Field button.
h. Click the Next button.
i. At the second Simple Query Wizard dialog box, click the Next button.
j. At the last Simple Query Wizard dialog box, select the current text in the *What title do you want for your query?* text box and then type PhoenixClientClaimsOver$500Query.
k. Click the *Modify the query design* option and then click the Finish button.
l. At the query window, complete the following steps:
   1) Click in the *City* field in the *Criteria* row in the query design grid.
   2) Type "Phoenix" and then press the Enter key. (Type the quotation marks to tell Access that this is a criterion, otherwise Access will insert the query name *PhoenixClientClaimsOver$500Query* in the field in the *Criteria* row.)
   3) Click in the *AmountOfClaim* field in the *Criteria* row. (You may need to scroll to the right to display this field.)
   4) Type >500 and then press the Enter key.

City	State	ZIP	ClaimID	AmountOfClaim
Clients	Clients	Clients	Claims	Claims
☑	☑	☑	☑	☑
"Phoenix"				>500

712   714

m. Click the Run button in the Results group. (This displays clients in Phoenix with claims greater than $500.)
n. Save the query, print the query in landscape orientation, and then close the query.
8. Close **3-CopperState.accdb**.

Check Your Work

Performing Calculations in a Query

In a query, values from a field can be calculated by inserting a calculated field in a field in the *Field* row in the query design grid. To insert a calculated field, click in a field in the *Field* row, type a field name followed by a colon, and then type the equation. For example, to determine pension contributions as 3% of an employee's annual salary, type *PensionContribution:[AnnualSalary]*0.03* in the field in the *Field* row. Use brackets to specify field names and use mathematical operators to perform the equation. Some basic operators include the plus (+) for addition, the hyphen (-) for subtraction, the asterisk (*) for multiplication, and the forward slash (/) for division.

Type a calculation in a field in the *Field* row or in the Expression Builder dialog box. To display the Expression Builder dialog box, display the query in Design view, click in the field where the calculated field expression is to be inserted, and then click the Builder button in the Query Setup group on the Query Tools Design tab. Type field names in the Expression Builder and click OK and the equation is inserted in the field with the correct symbols. For example, type *AnnualSalary*0.03* in the Expression Builder and *Expr1: [AnnualSalary]*0.03* is inserted in the field in the *Field* row when OK is clicked. If a name is not typed for the field, Access creates the alias *Expr1* for the field name. Provide a specific name for the field, such as *PensionContribution*, by typing the name in the Expression Builder, followed by a colon, and then typing the expression.

Builder

If the results of the calculation should display as currency, apply numeric formatting and define the number of digits past the decimal point using the Property Sheet task pane. In Design view, click the Property Sheet button in the Show/Hide group on the Query Tools Design tab and the Property Sheet task pane displays at the right side of the screen. Click in the *Format* property box, click the down arrow, and then click *Currency* at the drop-down list.

Project 1h Creating and Formatting a Calculated Field in a Query   Part 8 of 8

1. Open **3-MRInvestments.accdb** and enable the content.
2. Create a query that displays employer pension contributions at 3% of employees' annual salary by completing the following steps:
   a. Click the Create tab and then click the Query Design button.
   b. Double-click *Employees* in the Show Table dialog box and then click the Close button.
   c. Insert the *EmpID* field from the Employees table field list box in the first field in the *Field* row.
   d. Insert the *FirstName* field in the second field in the *Field* row.
   e. Insert the *LastName* field in the third field in the *Field* row.
   f. Insert the *AnnualSalary* field in the fourth field in the *Field* row.
   g. Click in the fifth field in the *Field* row.
   h. Type PensionContribution:[AnnualSalary]*0.03 and then press the Enter key.

   i. Click in the *PensionContribution* field and then click the Property Sheet button in the Show/Hide group.
   j. Click in the *Format* property box, click the down arrow, and then click *Currency* at the drop-down list.
   k. Click the Close button in the upper right corner of the Property Sheet task pane.
   l. Click the Run button in the Results group.
   m. Save the query and name it *PensionContributionsQuery*.
   n. Print and then close the query.
3. Modify *PensionContributionsQuery* and use the Expression Builder to write an equation finding the total amount of annual salary plus a 3% employer pension contribution by completing the following steps:
   a. Right-click *PensionContributionsQuery* in the Queries group in the Navigation pane and then click *Design View* at the shortcut menu.
   b. Click in the field in the *Field* row containing *PensionContribution:[AnnualSalary]*0.03*.
   c. Click the Builder button in the Query Setup group on the Query Tools Design tab.
   d. In the Expression Builder, select the existing expression *PensionContribution: [AnnualSalary]*0.03*.
   e. Type Salary&Pension:[AnnualSalary]*1.03 and then click OK.

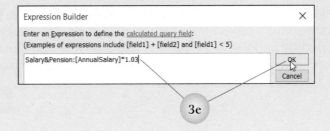

4. Click the Run button in the Results group.
5. Save the query by completing the following steps:
   a. Click the File tab, click the *Save As* option, click the *Save Object As* option, and then click the Save As button.
   b. At the Save As dialog box, type Salary&PensionQuery and then click OK.
6. Print and then close the query.
7. Close **3-MRInvestments.accdb**.
8. Open **3-PacTrek.accdb**.
9. Create a query that displays orders and total order amounts by completing the following steps:
   a. Click the Create tab and then click the Query Design button.
   b. Double-click *Products* in the Show Table dialog box.
   c. Double-click *Orders* in the Show Table dialog box and then click the Close button.
   d. Insert the *Product* field from the Products table field list box in the first field in the *Field* row.
   e. Insert the *OrderID* field from the Orders table field list box in the second field in the *Field* row.
   f. Insert the *UnitsOrdered* field from the Orders table field list box in the third field in the *Field* row.
   g. Insert the *Amount* field from the Orders table field list box in the fourth field in the *Field* row.
   h. Click in the fifth field in the *Field* row.
   i. Click the Builder button in the Query Setup group on the Query Tools Design tab.
   j. Type Total:Amount*UnitsOrdered in the Expression Builder and then click OK.
   k. Click the Run button in the Results group.
   l. Adjust the width of the columns to fit the longest entries.
   m. Save the query and name it *UnitsOrderedTotalQuery*.
   n. Print and then close the query.
10. Close **3-PacTrek.accdb**.

9j

Expression Builder   ×

Enter an Expression to define the calculated query field:
(Examples of expressions include [field1] + [field2] and [field1] < 5)

Total:Amount*UnitsOrdered

OK
Cancel

Check Your Work

Project 2 Create Aggregate Functions, Crosstab, Find Duplicates, and Find Unmatched Queries   6 Parts

You will create an aggregate functions query that determines the total, average, minimum, and maximum order amounts and then calculate total and average order amounts grouped by supplier. You will also use the Crosstab Query Wizard, Find Duplicates Query Wizard, and Find Unmatched Query Wizard to design queries.

Preview Finished Project

Designing Queries with Aggregate Functions

An *aggregate function*—such as Sum, Avg, Min, Max, or Count—can be included in a query to calculate statistics from numeric field values of all the records in the table. When an aggregate function is used, Access displays one row in the query results datasheet with the formula result for the function used. For example, in a table with a numeric field containing annual salary amounts, the Sum function can be used to calculate the total of all salary amount values.

 Totals

To use aggregate functions, click the Totals button in the Show/Hide group on the Query Tools Design tab. Access adds a *Total* row to the query design grid with a drop-down list of functions. Access also inserts the words *Group By* in the field in the *Total* row. Click the down arrow and then click an aggregate function at the drop-down list. In Project 2a, Step 1, you will create a query in Design view and use aggregate functions to find the total of all sales, average sales amount, maximum and minimum sales, and total number of sales. The completed query will display as shown in Figure 3.5. Access automatically determines the column heading names.

Quick Steps

Design a Query with an Aggregate Function
1. At query window, click Totals button.
2. Click down arrow in field in the *Total* row.
3. Click aggregate function.

Figure 3.5 Query Results for Project 2a, Step 1

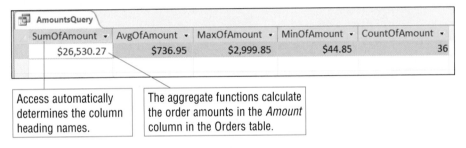

Access automatically determines the column heading names.

The aggregate functions calculate the order amounts in the *Amount* column in the Orders table.

Project 2a Using Aggregate Functions in Queries

Part 1 of 6

1. Open **3-PacTrek.accdb** and then create a query with aggregate functions that determines total, average, maximum, and minimum order amounts, as well as the total number of orders, by completing the following steps:
   a. Click the Create tab and then click the Query Design button.
   b. At the Show Table dialog box, make sure *Orders* is selected in the list box, click the Add button, and then click the Close button.
   c. Insert the *Amount* field in the first, second, third, fourth, and fifth fields in the *Field* row. (You may need to scroll down the Orders table field list box to display the *Amount* field.)

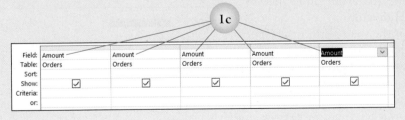

d. Click the Totals button in the Show/Hide group on the Query Tools Design tab. (This adds a *Total* row to the query design grid between *Table* and *Sort* with the default option of *Group By*.)

e. Specify a Sum function for the first field in the *Total* row by completing the following steps:
1) Click in the first field in the *Total* row.
2) Click the down arrow that displays in the field.
3) Click *Sum* at the drop-down list.

f. Complete steps similar to those in Step 1e to insert *Avg* in the second field in the *Total* row.

g. Complete steps similar to those in Step 1e to insert *Max* in the third field in the *Total* row.

h. Complete steps similar to those in Step 1e to insert *Min* in the fourth field in the *Total* row.

i. Complete steps similar to those in Step 1e to insert *Count* in the fifth field in the *Total* row.

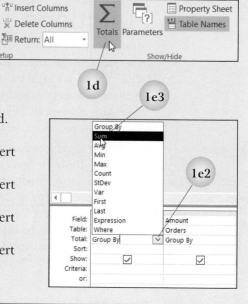

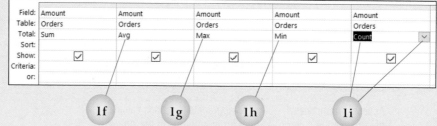

j. Click the Run button in the Results group. (Notice the headings that Access assigns to the columns.)

k. Automatically adjust the widths of the columns.

l. Save the query and name it *AmountsQuery*.

m. Print and then close the query.

2. Close **3-PacTrek.accdb**.

3. Open **3-CopperState.accdb**.

4. Create a query with aggregate functions that determines total, average, maximum, and minimum claim amounts by completing the following steps:

a. Click the Create tab and then click the Query Design button.

b. At the Show Table dialog box, double-click *Claims*.

c. Click the Close button to close the Show Table dialog box.

d. Insert the *AmountOfClaim* field in the first, second, third, and fourth fields in the *Field* row.

e. Click the Totals button in the Show/Hide group.

f. Click in the first field in the *Total* row, click the down arrow that displays in the field, and then click *Sum* at the drop-down list.

g. Click in the second field in the *Total* row, click the down arrow, and then click *Avg* at the drop-down list.

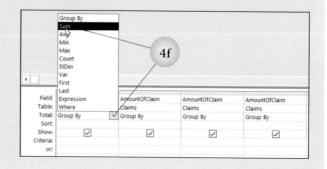

h. Click in the third field in the *Total* row, click the down arrow, and then click *Max* at the drop-down list.

i. Click in the fourth field in the *Total* row, click the down arrow, and then click *Min* at the drop-down list.

j. Click the Run button in the Results group. (Notice the headings that Access chooses for the columns.)

k. Automatically adjust the widths of the columns.

l. Save the query and name it *ClaimAmountsQuery*.

m. Print the query in landscape orientation and then close the query.

Check Your Work

Use the *Group By* field in the *Total* row to add a field to the query that groups records for statistical calculations. For example, to calculate the total of all orders for a specific supplier, add the *SupplierID* field to the query design grid with the *Total* row set to *Group By*. In Project 2b, Step 1, you will create a query in Design view and use aggregate functions to find the total of all order amounts and the average order amounts grouped by supplier number.

Project 2b Using Aggregate Functions and Grouping Records
Part 2 of 6

1. With **3-CopperState.accdb** open, determine the sum and average of client claims by completing the following steps:

   a. Click the Create tab and then click the Query Design button.

   b. At the Show Table dialog box, double-click *Clients* in the list box.

   c. Double-click *Claims* in the list box and then click the Close button.

   d. Insert the *ClientID* field from the Clients table field list box to the first field in the *Field* row.

   e. Insert the *AmountOfClaim* field from the Claims table field list box to the second field in the *Field* row.

   f. Insert the *AmountOfClaim* field from the Claims table field list box to the third field in the *Field* row.

   g. Click the Totals button in the Show/ Hide group.

   h. Click in the second field in the *Total* row, click the down arrow, and then click *Sum* at the drop-down list.

   i. Click in the third field in the *Total* row, click the down arrow, and then click *Avg* at the drop-down list.

   j. Make sure *Group By* displays in the first field in the *Total* row.

   k. Click the Run button in the Results group.

   l. Automatically adjust column widths.

   m. Save the query and name it *SumAvgClaimAmountsQuery*.

   n. Print and then close the query.

2. Close **3-CopperState.accdb**.

3. Open **3-PacTrek.accdb**.

4. Determine the total and average order amounts for each supplier by completing the following steps:

   a. Click the Create tab and then click the Query Design button.

b. At the Show Table dialog box, make sure *Orders* is selected in the list box and then click the Add button.

c. Click *Suppliers* in the list box, click the Add button, and then click the Close button.

d. Insert the *Amount* field from the Orders table field list box to the first field in the *Field* row. (You may need to scroll down the Orders table field list box to display the *Amount* field.)

e. Insert the *Amount* field from the Orders table field list box to the second field in the *Field* row.

f. Insert the *SupplierID* field from the Suppliers table field list box to the third field in the *Field* row.

g. Insert the *SupplierName* field from the Suppliers table field list box to the fourth field in the *Field* row.

h. Click the Totals button in the Show/Hide group.

i. Click in the first field in the *Total* row, click the down arrow, and then click *Sum* at the drop-down list.

j. Click in the second field in the *Total* row, click the down arrow, and then click *Avg* at the drop-down list.

k. Make sure *Group By* displays in the third and fourth fields in the *Total* row.

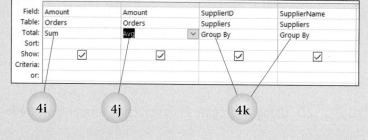

l. Click the Run button in the Results group.

m. Automatically adjust column widths.

n. Save the query and name it *SupplierAmountsQuery*.

o. Print and then close the query.

Check Your Work

Tutorial

Creating a Crosstab Query

Creating a
Crosstab Query

Quick Steps

Create a Crosstab Query
1. Click Create tab.
2. Click Query Wizard button.
3. Double-click *Crosstab Query Wizard*.
4. Complete wizard steps.

A crosstab query calculates aggregate functions, such as Sum and Avg, in which field values are grouped by two fields. A wizard is included that provides the steps to create the query. The first field selected causes one row to display in the query results datasheet for each group. The second field selected displays one column in the query results datasheet for each group. A third field is specified that is the numeric field to be summarized. The cell at the intersection of each row and column holds a value that is the result of the specified aggregate function for the designated row and column group.

Create a crosstab query from fields in one table. To include fields from more than one table, first create a query containing the fields, and then create the crosstab query. For example, in Project 2c, Step 2, you will create a new query that contains fields from each of the three tables in the Pacific Trek database. Using this query, you will use the Crosstab Query Wizard to create a query that summarizes the order amounts by supplier name and product ordered. Figure 3.6 displays the results of that crosstab query. The first column displays the supplier names, the second column displays the total amounts for each supplier, and the remaining columns display the amounts by suppliers for specific items.

Figure 3.6 Crosstab Query Results for Project 2c, Step 2

Order amounts are grouped by supplier name and individual product.

SupplierName	Total Of Amc ▾	Binoculars, 8 ▾	Cascade R4 jᵢ ▾	Cascade R4 jᵢ ▾	Cascade R4 jᵢ ▾	Cascade R4 jᵢ ▾	Deluxe map c ▾	Eight-piece sᵗ ▾
Bayside Supplies	$224.00							$99.75
Cascade Gear	$3,769.00		$1,285.00	$1,285.00	$599.50	$599.50		
Emerald City Products	$2,145.00	$2,145.00						
Fraser Valley Products	$3,892.75							
Freedom Corporation	$1,286.65							
Hopewell, Inc.	$348.60							
KL Distributions	$4,288.35							
Langley Corporation	$593.25							
Macadam, Inc.	$175.70						$129.75	
Manning, Inc.	$4,282.25							
Sound Supplies	$5,524.72							

OrdersBySupplierByProductQuery

Project 2c Creating Crosstab Queries

Part 3 of 6

1. With **3-PacTrek.accdb** open, create a query containing fields from the three tables by completing the following steps:
   a. Click the Create tab and then click the Query Design button.
   b. At the Show Table dialog box with *Orders* selected in the list box, click the Add button.
   c. Double-click *Products* in the list box.
   d. Double-click *Suppliers* in the list box and then click the Close button.
   e. Insert the following fields to the specified fields in the *Field* row:
      1) From the Orders table field list box, insert the *ProductID* field in the first field in the *Field* row.
      2) From the Products table field list box, insert the *Product* field in the second field in the *Field* row.
      3) From the Orders table field list box, insert the *UnitsOrdered* field in the third field in the *Field* row.
      4) From the Orders table field list box, insert the *Amount* field in the fourth field in the *Field* row.
      5) From the Suppliers table field list box, insert the *SupplierName* field in the fifth field in the *Field* row.
      6) From the Orders table field list box, insert the *OrderDate* field in the sixth field in the *Field* row.

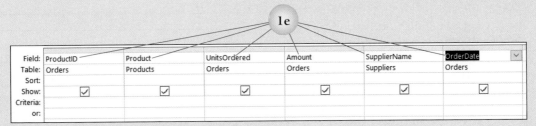

Field:	ProductID	Product	UnitsOrdered	Amount	SupplierName	OrderDate
Table:	Orders	Products	Orders	Orders	Suppliers	Orders
Sort:						
Show:	☑	☑	☑	☑	☑	☑
Criteria:						
or:						

   f. Click the Run button to run the query.
   g. Save the query and name it *ItemsOrderedQuery*.
   h. Close the query.

2. Create a crosstab query that summarizes the orders by supplier name and by product ordered by completing the following steps:

   a. Click the Create tab and then click the Query Wizard button.

   b. At the New Query dialog box, double-click *Crosstab Query Wizard* in the list box.

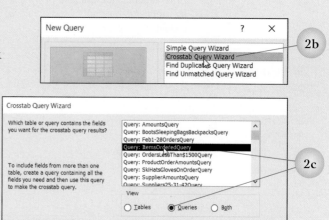

   c. At the first Crosstab Query Wizard dialog box, click the *Queries* option in the *View* section and then click *Query: ItemsOrderedQuery* in the list box.

   d. Click the Next button.

   e. At the second Crosstab Query Wizard dialog box, click *SupplierName* in the *Available Fields* list box and then click the One Field button. (This inserts *SupplierName* in the *Selected Fields* list box and specifies that you want the *SupplierName* field for the row headings.)

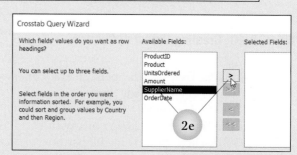

   f. Click the Next button.

   g. At the third Crosstab Query Wizard dialog box, click *Product* in the list box. (This specifies that you want the *Product* field for the column headings.)

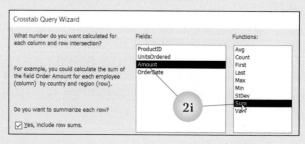

   h. Click the Next button.

   i. At the fourth Crosstab Query Wizard dialog box, click *Amount* in the *Fields* list box and then click *Sum* in the *Functions* list box.

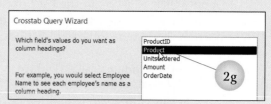

   j. Click the Next button.

   k. At the fifth Crosstab Query Wizard dialog box, select the current text in the *What do you want to name your query?* text box and then type OrdersBySupplierByProductQuery.

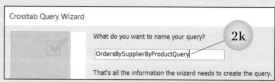

   l. Click the Finish button.

3. Display the query in Print Preview, change to landscape orientation, change the left margin to 0.4 inch and the right margin to 0.5 inch, and then print the query. (The query will print on four pages.)

4. Close the query.

5. Close **3-PacTrek.accdb**.

6. Open **3-CopperState.accdb**.
7. Create a crosstab query from fields in one table that summarizes clients' claims by completing the following steps:
   a. Click the Create tab and then click the Query Wizard button.
   b. At the New Query dialog box, double-click *Crosstab Query Wizard* in the list box.
   c. At the first Crosstab Query Wizard dialog box, click *Table: Claims* in the list box.
   d. Click the Next button.
   e. At the second Crosstab Query Wizard dialog box, click the One Field button. (This inserts the *ClaimID* field in the *Selected Fields* list box.)
   f. Click the Next button.
   g. At the third Crosstab Query Wizard dialog, make sure *ClientID* is selected in the list box and then click the Next button.
   h. At the fourth Crosstab Query Wizard dialog box, click *AmountOfClaim* in the *Fields* list box and click *Sum* in the *Functions* list box.
   i. Click the Next button.
   j. At the fifth Crosstab Query Wizard dialog box, select the current text in the *What do you want to name your query?* text box and then type ClaimsByClaimIDByClientIDQuery.
   k. Click the Finish button.
8. Change to landscape orientation and then print the query. The query will print on two pages.
9. Close the query.
10. Close **3-CopperState.accdb**.

> **Check Your Work**

Tutorial

Creating a Find
Duplicates Query

Quick Steps

**Create a Find
Duplicates Query**
1. Click Create tab.
2. Click Query Wizard button.
3. Double-click *Find Duplicates Query Wizard.*
4. Complete wizard steps.

Creating a Find Duplicates Query

Use a find duplicates query to search a specified table or query for duplicate field values within a designated field or fields. Create this type of query, for example, if a record (such as a product record) may have been entered two times inadvertently (perhaps under two different product numbers). A find duplicates query has many applications. Here are a few other examples of how to use a find duplicates query:

- In an orders table, find records with the same customer number to identify loyal customers.
- In a customers table, find records with the same last name and mailing address so only one mailing will be sent to a household to save on printing and postage costs.
- In an employee expenses table, find records with the same employee number to determine which employee is submitting the most claims.

Access provides the Find Duplicates Query Wizard to build the query based on the selections made in a series of dialog boxes. To use this wizard, open a database, click the Create tab, and then click the Query Wizard button. At the New Query dialog box, double-click *Find Duplicates Query Wizard* in the list box and then complete the steps provided by the wizard.

In Project 2d, you will assume that you have been asked to update the address for a supplier in the Pacific Trek database. Instead of updating the address, you create a new record. You will then use the Find Duplicates Query Wizard to find duplicate field values in the Suppliers table.

1. Open **3-PacTrek.accdb** and then open the Suppliers table.
2. Add the following record to the table:

    SupplierID#   29
    SupplierName   Langley Corporation
    StreetAddress   1248 Larson Avenue
    City   Burnaby
    Prov/State   BC
    PostalCode   V5V 9K2
    EmailAddress   lc@emcp.net
    Telephone   (604) 555-1200

3. Close the Suppliers table.
4. Use the Find Duplicates Query Wizard to find any duplicate supplier names by completing the following steps:
    a. Click the Create tab and then click the Query Wizard button.
    b. At the New Query dialog box, double-click *Find Duplicates Query Wizard*.
    c. At the first wizard dialog box, click *Table: Suppliers* in the list box.
    d. Click the Next button.
    e. At the second wizard dialog box, click *SupplierName* in the *Available fields* list box and then click the One Field button. (This moves the *SupplierName* field to the *Duplicate-value fields* list box.)

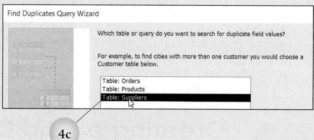

4c

    f. Click the Next button.
    g. At the third wizard dialog box, click the All Fields button (the button containing the two greater-than symbols, >>). This moves all the fields to the *Additional query fields* list box. You are doing this because if you find a duplicate supplier name, you want to view all the fields to determine which record is accurate.

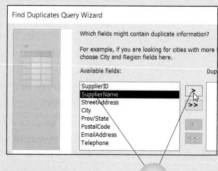

4e

    h. Click the Next button.
    i. At the fourth (and last) wizard dialog box, type DuplicateSuppliersQuery in the *What do you want to name your query?* text box.

4i

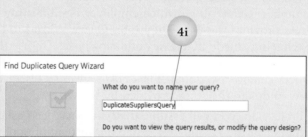

    j. Click the Finish button.
    k. Change to landscape orientation and then print the query.

5. As you look at the query results, you realize that an inaccurate record was entered for the Langley Corporation, so you decide to delete one of the records. To do this, complete the following steps:

   a. Select the row with a supplier ID of *29*.

   b. Click the Home tab and then click the Delete button in the Records group.

   c. At the message asking you to confirm the deletion, click Yes.

   d. Close the query.

6. Change the street address for Langley Corporation by completing the following steps:

   a. Open the Suppliers table in Datasheet view.

   b. Change the address for Langley Corporation from *805 First Avenue* to *1248 Larson Avenue*. Leave the other fields as displayed.

   c. Close the Suppliers table.

Check Your Work

In Project 2d, you used the Find Duplicates Query Wizard to find records containing the same field. In Project 2e, you will use the Find Duplicates Query Wizard to find information on the suppliers you order from the most. You could use this information to negotiate for better prices or to ask for discounts.

Project 2e Finding Duplicate Orders

Part 5 of 6

1. With **3-PacTrek.accdb** open, create a query with the following fields (in the order shown) from the specified tables:

SupplierID	Suppliers table
SupplierName	Suppliers table
ProductID	Orders table
Product	Products table

2. Run the query.

3. Save the query with the name *SupplierOrdersQuery* and then close the query.

4. Use the Find Duplicates Query Wizard to find the suppliers you order from the most by completing the following steps:

   a. Click the Create tab and then click the Query Wizard button.

   b. At the New Query dialog box, double-click *Find Duplicates Query Wizard*.

   c. At the first wizard dialog box, click the *Queries* option in the *View* section and then click *Query: SupplierOrdersQuery*. (You may need to scroll down the list to display this query.)

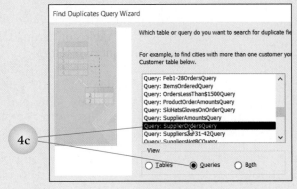

d. Click the Next button.

e. At the second wizard dialog box, click *SupplierName* in the *Available fields* list box and then click the One Field button.

f. Click the Next button.

g. At the third wizard dialog box, click the Next button.

h. At the fourth (and last) wizard dialog box, type SupplierOrdersCountQuery in the *What do you want to name your query?* text box.

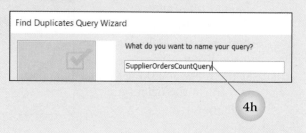

i. Click the Finish button.

j. Adjust the widths of the columns to fit the longest entries.

k. Save and then print the query.

5. Close the query.

Check Your Work

Tutorial

Creating a Find Unmatched Query

Quick Steps

Create a Find Unmatched Query
1. Click Create tab.
2. Click Query Wizard button.
3. Double-click *Find Unmatched Query Wizard.*
4. Complete wizard steps.

Creating a Find Unmatched Query

Create a find unmatched query to compare two tables and produce a list of the records in one table that have no matching record in the other table. This type of query is useful to produce lists such as customers who have never placed orders and invoices that have no records of payment. Access provides the Find Unmatched Query Wizard to build the query.

In Project 2f, you will use the Find Unmatched Query Wizard to find all of the products that have no units on order. This information is helpful in identifying which products are not selling and might need to be discontinued or returned. To use the Find Unmatched Query Wizard, click the Create tab and then click the Query Wizard button in the Queries group. At the New Query dialog box, double-click *Find Unmatched Query Wizard* in the list box and then follow the wizard steps.

Project 2f   Creating a Find Unmatched Query

Part 6 of 6

1. With **3-PacTrek.accdb** open, use the Find Unmatched Query Wizard to find all products that do not have units on order by completing the following steps:

a. Click the Create tab and then click the Query Wizard button.

b. At the New Query dialog box, double-click *Find Unmatched Query Wizard*.

c. At the first wizard dialog box, click *Table: Products* in the list box. (This is the table containing the fields you want to see in the query results.)

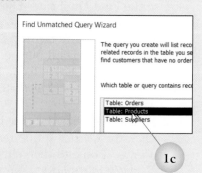

d. Click the Next button.

e. At the second wizard dialog box, make sure *Table: Orders* is selected in the list box. (This is the table containing the related records.)

f. Click the Next button.

g. At the third wizard dialog box, make sure *ProductID* is selected in both the *Fields in 'Products'* list box and in the *Fields in 'Orders'* list box.

h. Click the Next button.

i. At the fourth wizard dialog box, click the All Fields button to move all of the fields from the *Available fields* list box to the *Selected fields* list box.

j. Click the Next button.

k. At the fifth wizard dialog box, click the Finish button. (Let the wizard determine the query name: *Products Without Matching Orders*.)

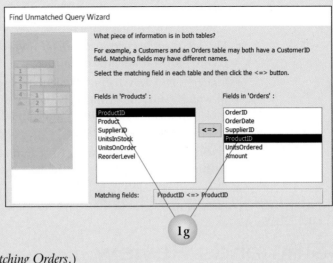

2. Print the query in landscape orientation and then close the query.

3. Close **3-PacTrek.accdb**.

Check Your Work

Chapter Summary

- One of the most important uses of a database is to select the information needed to answer questions and make decisions. Data can be extracted from an Access database by performing a query, which can be accomplished by designing a query or using a query wizard.

- Designing a query consists of identifying the table, the field or fields from which the data will be drawn, and the criterion or criteria for selecting the data.

- In designing a query, type the criterion (or criteria) statement for extracting the specific data. Access inserts any necessary symbols in the criterion when the Enter key is pressed.

- In a criterion, quotation marks surround field values and pound symbols (#) surround dates. Use the asterisk (*) as a wildcard character.

- A query can be performed on fields within one table or on fields from related tables.

- When designing a query, the sort order of a field or fields can be specified.

- An existing query can be modified and used for a new purpose rather than creating a new one from scratch.

- Enter a criterion in the *or* row in the query design grid to instruct Access to display records that match any of the criteria.

- Multiple criteria entered in the *Criteria* row in the query design grid become an *And* statement, where each criterion must be met for Access to select the record.

- The Simple Query Wizard provides the steps for preparing a query.

- A calculated field can be inserted in a field in the *Field* row when designing a query. If the results of the calculation should display as currency, apply numeric formatting and decimal places using the Format property box at the Property Sheet task pane. Display the task pane by clicking the Property Sheet button in the Show/Hide group on the Query Tools Design tab.

- Include an aggregate function (such as Sum, Avg, Min, Max, or Count) to calculate statistics from numeric field values. Click the Totals button in the Show/Hide group on the Query Tools Design tab to display the aggregate function list.
- Use a *Group By* field in the *Total* row to add a field to a query for grouping records for statistical calculations.
- Create a crosstab query to calculate aggregate functions (such as Sum and Avg), in which fields are grouped by two. Create a crosstab query from fields in one table. To include fields from more than one table, create a query first and then create the crosstab query.
- Use a find duplicates query to search a specified table for duplicate field values within a designated field or fields.
- Create a find unmatched query to compare two tables and produce a list of the records in one table that have no matching records in the other related table.

Commands Review

FEATURE	RIBBON TAB, GROUP	BUTTON, OPTION
add *Total* row to query design	Query Tools Design, Show/Hide	Σ
Crosstab Query Wizard	Create, Queries	, Crosstab Query Wizard
Expression Builder dialog box	Query Tools Design, Query Setup	
Find Duplicates Query Wizard	Create, Queries	, Find Duplicates Query Wizard
Find Unmatched Query Wizard	Create, Queries	, Find Unmatched Query Wizard
New Query dialog box	Create, Queries	
Property Sheet task pane	Query Tools Design, Show/Hide	
query results	Query Tools Design, Results	!
query window	Create, Queries	
Simple Query Wizard	Create, Queries	, Simple Query Wizard

Workbook

Chapter study tools and assessment activities are available in the *Workbook* ebook. These resources are designed to help you further develop and demonstrate mastery of the skills learned in this chapter.

Microsoft®

Access®

Creating and Modifying Tables in Design View

Performance Objectives

Precheck

Check your current skills to help focus your study.

Upon successful completion of Chapter 4, you will be able to:

1 Create a table in Design view

2 Assign a default value

3 Use the Input Mask Wizard and the Lookup Wizard

4 Validate field entries

5 Insert, move, and delete fields in Design view

6 Insert a *Total* row

7 Sort records in a table

8 Print selected records in a table

9 Complete a spelling check

10 Find and replace data in records in a table

11 Apply text formatting

12 Use the Help and Tell Me features

In Chapter 1, you learned how to create a table in Datasheet view. A table can also be created in Design view, where the table's structure and properties are established before entering data. In this chapter, you will learn how to create a table in Design view and use the Input Mask Wizard and Lookup Wizards; insert, move, and delete fields in Design view; sort records; check spelling in a table; find and replace data; apply text formatting to a table; and use the Help and Tell Me features.

SNAP

If you are a SNAP user, launch the Precheck and Tutorials from your Assignments page.

Data Files

Before beginning chapter work, copy the AL1C4 folder to your storage medium and then make AL1C4 the active folder.

You will open the Sun Properties database, create two new tables in Design view, modify existing tables, and sort data in tables. You will also complete a spelling check on data in tables, find data in a table and replace it with other data, create relationships and perform queries, and use the Help and Tell Me features.

Preview Finished Project

Tutorial

Creating a Table in Design View

Table

View

Ǫuick Steps

Create a Table in Design View

1. Open database.
2. Click Create tab.
3. Click Table button.
4. Click View button.
5. Type name for table.
6. Press Enter or click OK.
7. Type field names, specify data types, and include descriptions.
8. Click Save button.

Creating a Table in Design View

In Datasheet view, a table is created by assigning each column a data type and typing the field name. Once the columns are defined, the data is entered into records. A table can also be created in Design view, where field properties can be set before entering data.

To display a table in Design view, open the database, click the Create tab, and then click the Table button. This opens a new blank table in Datasheet view. Display the table in Design view by clicking the View button at the left side of the Table Tools Fields tab in the Views group. Click the View button in a new table and Access displays the Save As dialog box. Type a name for the table and then press the Enter key or click OK. Figure 4.1 displays the Properties table in Design view in the SunProperties database.

In Design view, each row in the top section of the work area represents one field in the table and is used to define the field name, the field data type, and a description. The *Field Properties* section in the lower half of the work area displays the properties for the active field. The properties vary depending on the active field. In the lower right corner of Design view, Help information displays about the active field or property in the Design window. In Figure 4.1, the *PropID* field name is active in Design view, so Access displays information on field names in the Help area.

Define each field in the table in the rows in the top section of Design view. When a table is created in Design view, Access automatically assigns the first field the name *ID* and assigns the AutoNumber data type. Leave this field name as *ID* or type a new name and accept the AutoNumber data type or change to a different data type. To create a new field in the table, click in a field in the *Field Name* column, type the field name, and then press the Tab key or Enter key. This makes the field in the *Data Type* column active. Click the down arrow in the field in the *Data Type* column and then click the data type at the drop-down list. In Chapter 1, you created tables in Datasheet view and assigned data types of Short Text, Date/Time, Currency, and Yes/No. The drop-down list in the *Data Type* column includes these data types plus additional types, as described in Table 4.1.

Click the specific data type at the drop-down list and then press the Tab key and the field in the *Description* column becomes active. In the field, type a description that provides useful information to someone entering data in the table. For example, consider identifying the field's purpose or contents or providing instructional information for data entry. The description typed in the field in the *Description* column displays in the Status bar when the table's field is active in the table in Datasheet view.

Figure 4.1 Properties Table in Design View

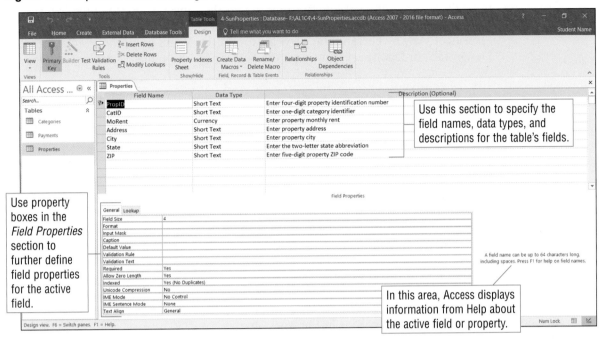

Table 4.1 Data Types

Data Type	Description
Short Text	Used for alphanumeric data up to 255 characters in length—for example, a name, address, or value (such as a telephone number or social security number) that is used as an identifier and not for calculating.
Long Text	Used for alphanumeric data up to 65,535 characters in length.
Number	Used for positive and negative values that can be used in calculations. Do not use for values that will calculate monetary amounts (see Currency).
Date/Time	Used to ensure dates and times are entered and sorted properly.
Currency	Used for values that involve money. Access will not round off during calculations.
AutoNumber	Used to automatically number records sequentially (increments of 1); each new record is numbered as it is typed.
Yes/No	Used for values of *Yes* or *No*, *True* or *False*, or *On* or *Off*.
OLE Object	Used to embed or link objects created in other Office applications.
Hyperlink	Used to store a hyperlink, such as a URL.
Attachment	Used to add file attachments to a record such as a Word document or Excel workbook.
Calculated	Used to display the Expression Builder dialog box, where an expression is entered to calculate the value of the calculated column.
Lookup Wizard	Used to enter data in the field from another existing table or to display a list of values in a drop-down list from which the user chooses.

Save

When creating the table, continue typing field names, assigning data types to fields, and typing field descriptions. When the table design is completed, save the table by clicking the Save button on the Quick Access Toolbar. Return to Datasheet view by clicking the View button in the Views group on the Table Tools Design tab. In Datasheet view, type the records for the table.

Project 1a Creating a Renters Table in Design View

Part 1 of 9

1. Open Access and then open **4-SunProperties.accdb** from the AL1C4 folder on your storage medium.
2. Click the Enable Content button in the message bar. (The message bar will display immediately below the ribbon.)
3. View the Properties table in Design view by completing the following steps:
   a. Open the Properties table.
   b. Click the View button in the Views group on the Home tab.
   c. Click each field name and then look at the information that displays in the *Field Properties* section.

   d. Click in various fields or properties in the work area and then read the information that displays in the Help area in the lower right corner of Design view.
   e. Click the View button to return the table to Datasheet view.
   f. Close the Properties table.
4. Create a new table in Design view, as shown in Figure 4.2, by completing the following steps:
   a. Click the Create tab and then click the Table button in the Tables group.
   b. Click the View button in the Views group on the Table Tools Fields tab.
   c. At the Save As dialog box, type Renters and then press the Enter key.
   d. Type RenterID in the first field in the *Field Name* column and then press the Tab key.
   e. Change to the Short Text data type by clicking the down arrow in the field in the *Data Type* column and then clicking *Short Text* at the drop-down list.
   f. Change the field size from the default of 255 characters to 3 characters by selecting *255* in the *Field Size* property box in the *Field Properties* section and then typing 3.

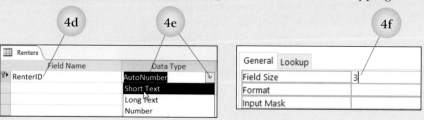

g. Click in the *Description* column for the *RenterID* field, type Enter three-digit renter identification number, and then press the Tab key.

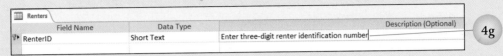

h. Type FirstName in the second field in the *Field Name* column and then press the Tab key.
i. Select *255* in the *Field Size* property box in the *Field Properties* section and then type 20.
j. Click in the *Description* column for the *FirstName* field, type Enter renter's first name, and then press the Tab key.
k. Type LastName in the third field in the *Field Name* column and then press the Tab key.
l. Change the field size to 30 characters (at the *Field Size* property box).
m. Click in the *Description* column for the *LastName* field, type Enter renter's last name, and then press the Tab key.
n. Enter the remaining field names, data types, and descriptions as shown in Figure 4.2. (Change the field size to 4 characters for the *PropID* field, 5 characters for the *EmpID* field, and 3 characters for the *CreditScore* field.)
o. After all of the fields are entered, click the Save button on the Quick Access Toolbar.
p. Make sure the *RenterID* field is identified as the primary key field. (A key icon displays in the *RenterID* field selector bar.)
q. Click the View button to return the table to Datasheet view.
5. Enter the records in the Renters table as shown in Figure 4.3.
6. After all of the records are entered, automatically adjust the column widths.
7. Save and then close the Renters table.

Check Your Work

Figure 4.2 Project 1a Renters Table in Design View

Field Name	Data Type	Des
RenterID	Short Text	Enter three-digit renter identification number
FirstName	Short Text	Enter renter's first name
LastName	Short Text	Enter renter's last name
PropID	Short Text	Enter four-digit property identification number
EmpID	Short Text	Enter five-digit employee identification number
CreditScore	Short Text	Enter renter's current credit score
LeaseBegDate	Date/Time	Enter beginning date of lease
LeaseEndDate	Date/Time	Enter ending date of lease

Figure 4.3 Project 1a Renters Table in Datasheet View

RenterID	FirstName	LastName	PropID	EmpID	CreditScore	LeaseBegDate	LeaseEndDate	Click t
110	Greg	Hamilton	1029	04-14	624	1/1/2018	12/31/2018	
111	Julia	Perez	1013	07-20	711	1/1/2018	12/31/2018	
115	Dana	Rozinski	1026	02-59	538	2/1/2018	1/31/2019	
117	Miguel	Villegas	1007	07-20	695	2/1/2018	1/31/2019	
118	Mason	Ahn	1004	07-23	538	3/1/2018	2/28/2019	
119	Michelle	Bertram	1001	03-23	621	3/1/2018	2/28/2019	
121	Travis	Jorgenson	1010	04-14	590	3/1/2018	2/28/2019	
123	Richard	Terrell	1014	07-20	687	3/1/2018	2/28/2019	
125	Rose	Wagoner	1015	07-23	734	4/1/2018	3/31/2019	
127	William	Young	1023	05-31	478	4/1/2018	3/31/2019	
129	Susan	Lowrey	1002	04-14	634	4/1/2018	3/31/2019	
130	Ross	Molaski	1027	03-23	588	5/1/2018	4/30/2019	
131	Danielle	Rubio	1020	07-20	722	5/1/2018	4/30/2019	
133	Katie	Smith	1018	07-23	596	5/1/2018	4/30/2019	
134	Carl	Weston	1009	03-23	655	6/1/2018	5/31/2019	
135	Marty	Lobdell	1006	04-14	510	6/1/2018	5/31/2019	
136	Nadine	Paschal	1022	05-31	702	6/1/2018	5/31/2019	

Assigning a Default Value

Chapter 1 covered how to specify a default value for a field in a table in Datasheet view using the Default Value button in the Properties group on the Table Tools Fields tab. In addition to this method, a default value for a field can be specified in Design view with the *Default Value* property box in the *Field Properties* section. Click in the *Default Value* property box and then type the field value.

In Project 1b, a health insurance field will be created with a Yes/No data type. Since most of the agents of Sun Properties have signed up for health insurance benefits, the default value for the field will be set to *Yes*. If a new field containing a default value is added to an existing table, the existing records do not reflect the default value. Only new records entered in the table reflect the default value.

Creating an Input Mask

To maintain consistency and control data entered in a field, consider using the *Input Mask* property box to set a pattern for how data is entered in the field. For example, a pattern can be set for a zip code field that requires that the nine-digit zip code is entered in the field rather than the five-digit zip code. Or, a pattern can be set for a telephone field that requires that the three-digit area code is entered with the telephone number. Use the *Input Mask* field property to set a pattern for how data is entered in a field. Access includes an Input Mask Wizard that provides the steps for creating an input mask. The Input Mask is available for fields with a data type of Short Text or Date/Time.

Use the Input Mask Wizard when assigning a data type to a field. In Design view, click in the *Input Mask* property box in the *Field Properties* section and then run the Input Mask Wizard by clicking the Build button (contains three black dots) that appears at the right side of the *Input Mask* property box. This displays the first Input Mask Wizard dialog box, as shown in Figure 4.4. In the *Input Mask*

Quick Steps

Use the Input Mask Wizard
1. Open table in Design view.
2. Type text in *Field Name* column.
3. Press Tab.
4. Change data type to *Short Text* or *Date/Time*.
5. Click Save button.
6. Click in *Input Mask* property box.
7. Click Build button.
8. Complete wizard steps.

list box, choose which input mask the data should look like and then click the Next button. At the second Input Mask Wizard dialog box, as shown in Figure 4.5, specify the appearance of the input mask and the placeholder character and then click the Next button. At the third Input Mask Wizard dialog box, specify if the data should be stored with or without the symbol in the mask and then click the Next button. At the fourth dialog box, click the Finish button.

The input mask controls how data is entered into a field. In some situations, such as establishing an input mask to enter the date in the Medium Date format, what is entered will not match what Access displays. An input mask with the Medium Date data type format will require that the date be entered as *12-Sep-18* but, after the date is entered, Access will change the display to *09/12/2018*. Use the *Format* property box to match how Access displays the date with the input mask. Click in the *Format* property box, click the down arrow in the property box and then click *Medium Date* at the drop-down list.

Figure 4.4 First Input Mask Wizard Dialog Box

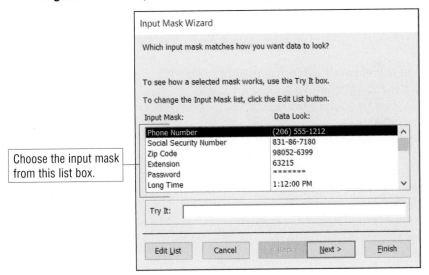

Choose the input mask from this list box.

Figure 4.5 Second Input Mask Wizard Dialog Box

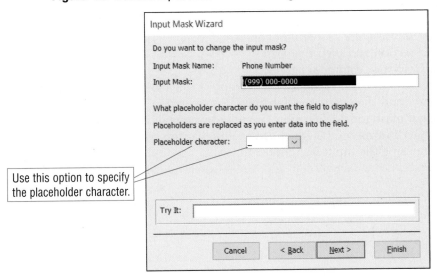

Use this option to specify the placeholder character.

1. With **4-SunProperties.accdb** open, create the Employees table in Design view as shown in Figure 4.6. Begin by clicking the Create tab and then clicking the Table button.
2. Click the View button to switch to Design view.
3. At the Save As dialog box, type Employees and then press the Enter key.
4. Type EmpID in the first field in the *Field Name* column and then press the Tab key.
5. Change to the Short Text data type by clicking the down arrow in the *Data Type* column and then clicking *Short Text* at the drop-down list.
6. Change the field size from the default of 255 characters to 5 characters by selecting *255* in the *Field Size* property box in the *Field Properties* section and then typing 5.
7. Click in the *Description* column for the *EmpID* field, type Enter five-digit employee identification number, and then press the Tab key.

8. Type FName in the second field in the *Field Name* column and then press the Tab key.
9. Select *255* in the *Field Size* property box in the *Field Properties* section and then type 20.
10. Click in the *Description* column for the *FName* field, type Enter employee's first name, and then press the Tab key.
11. Complete steps similar to those in Steps 8 through 10 to create the *LName*, *Address*, and *City* fields as shown in Figure 4.6. Change the field size for the *LName* field and *Address* field to 30 characters and change the *City* field to 20 characters.
12. Create the *State* field with a default value of *CA*, since all employees live in California, by completing the following steps:
    a. Type State in the field below the *City* field in the *Field Name* column and then press the Tab key.
    b. Click in the *Default Value* property box in the *Field Properties* section and then type CA.
    c. Click in the *Description* column for the *State* field, type CA automatically entered as state, and then press the Tab key.

13. Type ZIP and then press the Tab key.
14. Select *255* in the *Field Size* property box in the *Field Properties* section and then type 5.
15. Click in the *Description* column for the *ZIP* field, type Enter five-digit ZIP code, and then press the Tab key.
16. Type Telephone and then press the Tab key.
17. Create an input mask for the telephone number by completing the following steps:
    a. Click the Save button on the Quick Access Toolbar to save the table. (You must save the table before using the Input Mask Wizard.)

b. Click in the *Input Mask* property box in the *Field Properties* section.
c. Click the Build button (contains three black dots) that displays at the right side of the *Input Mask* property box.

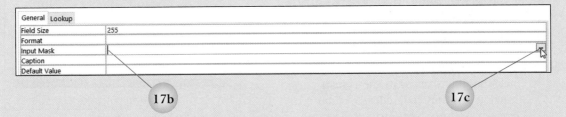

17b   17c

d. At the first Input Mask Wizard dialog box, make sure *Phone Number* is selected in the *Input Mask* list box and then click the Next button.
e. At the second Input Mask Wizard dialog box, click the *Placeholder character* option box arrow and then click # at the drop-down list.

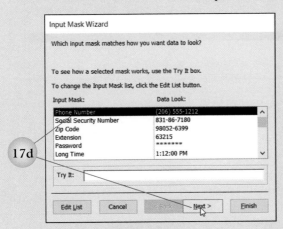

17d

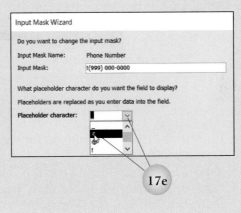

17e

f. Click the Next button.
g. At the third Input Mask Wizard dialog box, click the *With the symbols in the mask, like this* option.
h. Click the Next button.
i. At the fourth Input Mask Wizard dialog box, click the Finish button.

17g

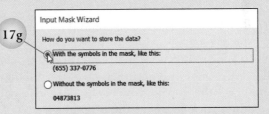

18. Click in the *Description* column for the *Telephone* field, type Enter employee's telephone number, and then press the Tab key.
19. Type HireDate and then press the Tab key.
20. Click the down arrow in the *Date Type* column and then click *Date/Time*.
21. Create an input mask for the date by completing the following steps:
    a. Click the Save button on the Quick Access Toolbar to save the table.
    b. Click in the *Input Mask* property box in the *Field Properties* section.
    c. Click the Build button (contains three black dots) at the right side of the *Input Mask* property box.

d. At the first Input Mask Wizard dialog box, click *Medium Date* in the list box and then click the Next button.

e. At the second Input Mask Wizard dialog box, click the Next button.

f. At the third Input Mask Wizard dialog box, click the Finish button.

g. Click in the *Format* property box.

h. Click the down arrow in the *Format* property box and then click *Medium Date* at the drop-down list.

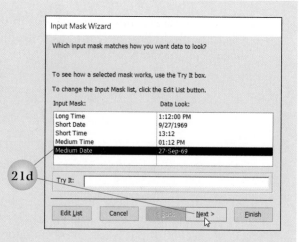

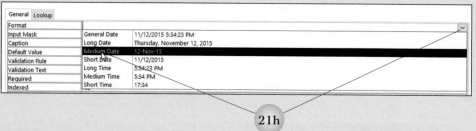

22. Click in the *Description* column for the *HireDate* field, type Enter employee's hire date and then press the Tab key.

23. Type HealthIns and then press the Tab key.

24. Click the down arrow in the *Data Type* column and then click *Yes/No* at the drop-down list.

25. Click in the *Default Value* property box in the *Field Properties* section, delete the text *No*, and then type Yes.

26. Click in the *Description* column for the *HealthIns* field, type Leave check mark if employee is signed up for health insurance, and then press the Tab key.

27. Type DentalIns and then press the Tab key.

28. Click the down arrow in the *Data Type* column and then click *Yes/No* at the drop-down list. (The text in the *Default Value* property box will remain as *No*.)

29. Click in the *Description* column for the *DentalIns* field, type Insert check mark if employee is signed up for dental insurance, and then press the Tab key.

30. After all of the fields are entered, click the Save button on the Quick Access Toolbar.

31. Click the View button to return the table to Datasheet view.

32. Enter the records in the Employees table as shown in Figure 4.7.

33. After all of the records are entered, automatically adjust the widths of the columns in the table as shown in Figure 4.7.

34. Save and then close the Employees table.

Check Your Work

Figure 4.6 Project 1b Employees Table in Design View

Field Name	Data Type	Description (Optional)
EmpID	Short Text	Enter five-digit employee identification number
FName	Short Text	Enter employee's first name
LName	Short Text	Enter employee's last name
Address	Short Text	Enter employee's address
City	Short Text	Enter employee's city
State	Short Text	CA automatically entered as state
ZIP	Short Text	Enter five-digit ZIP code
Telephone	Short Text	Enter employee's telephone number
HireDate	Date/Time	Enter employee's hire date
HealthIns	Yes/No	Leave check mark if employee is signed up for health insurance
DentalIns	Yes/No	Insert check mark if employee is signed up for dental insurance

Figure 4.7 Project 1b Employees Table in Datasheet View

EmpID	FName	LName	Address	City	State	ZIP	Telephone	HireDate	HealthIns	DentalIns
02-59	Christina	Solomon	12241 East 51st	Citrus Heights	CA	95611	(916) 555-8844	01-Feb-08	✓	✓
03-23	Douglas	Ricci	903 Mission Road	Roseville	CA	95678	(916) 555-4125	01-Mar-08	✓	
03-55	Tatiana	Kasadev	6558 Orchard Drive	Citrus Heights	CA	95610	(916) 555-8534	15-Nov-10	✓	
04-14	Brian	West	12232 142nd Avenue East	Citrus Heights	CA	95611	(916) 555-0967	01-Apr-12	✓	✓
04-32	Kathleen	Addison	21229 19th Street	Citrus Heights	CA	95621	(916) 555-3408	01-Feb-13	✓	✓
05-20	Teresa	Villanueva	19453 North 42nd Street	Citrus Heights	CA	95611	(916) 555-2302	15-Jul-14	✓	✓
05-31	Marcia	Griswold	211 Haven Road	North Highlands	CA	95660	(916) 555-1449	01-May-14		
06-24	Tiffany	Gentry	12312 North 20th	Roseville	CA	95661	(916) 555-0043	15-Apr-16	✓	✓
06-33	Joanna	Gallegos	6850 York Street	Roseville	CA	95747	(916) 555-7446	01-Jul-17		
07-20	Jesse	Scholtz	3412 South 21st Street	Fair Oaks	CA	95628	(916) 555-4204	15-Feb-17	✓	
07-23	Eugene	Bond	530 Laurel Road	Orangevale	CA	95662	(916) 555-9412	01-Mar-18	✓	
*					CA				✓	

Tutorial

Applying a Validation Rule in Design View

Hint Enter a validation rule in a field to control what is entered in the field. Create validation text that displays when someone enters invalid data.

Tutorial

Creating a Lookup Field

Validating Field Entries

Use the *Validation Rule* property box in the *Field Properties* section in Design view to enter a statement containing a conditional test that is checked each time data is entered into a field. If data is entered that fails to satisfy the conditional test, Access does not accept the entry and displays an error message. Entering a conditional statement in the *Validation Rule* property box that checks each entry against the acceptable range reduces errors. Customize the error message that will display if incorrect data is entered in the field by typing that message in the *Validation Text* property box.

Using the Lookup Wizard

Like the Input Mask Wizard, the Lookup Wizard can be used to control data entered in a field. Use the Lookup Wizard to confine data entered into a field to a specific list of items. For example, in Project 1c, the Lookup Wizard will be used to restrict the new *EmpCategory* field to one of three choices: *Salaried*, *Hourly*, and *Temporary*. When entering data, clicking in the field displays a down arrow. Click the down arrow and then click an option at the drop-down list.

Use the Lookup Wizard when assigning a data type to a field. Click in the field in the *Data Type* column, click the down arrow, and then click *Lookup Wizard* at the drop-down list. This displays the first Lookup Wizard dialog box, as shown in Figure 4.8. At this dialog box, indicate that specific field choices will be entered

Figure 4.8 First Lookup Wizard Dialog Box

1. Open table in Design view.
2. Type text in *Field Name* column.
3. Press Tab.
4. Click down arrow.
5. Click *Lookup Wizard*.
6. Complete wizard steps.

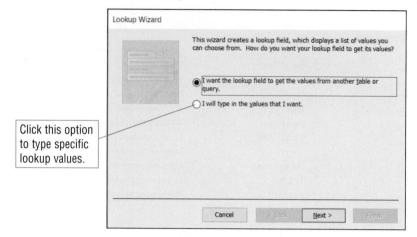

Click this option to type specific lookup values.

Figure 4.9 Second Lookup Wizard Dialog Box

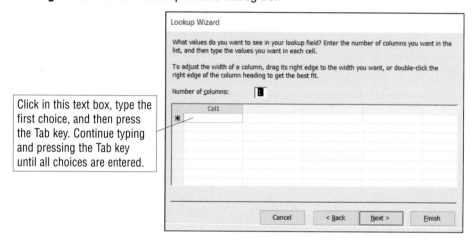

Click in this text box, type the first choice, and then press the Tab key. Continue typing and pressing the Tab key until all choices are entered.

by clicking the *I will type in the values that I want* option and then click the Next button. At the second Lookup Wizard dialog box, shown in Figure 4.9, click in the blank text box below *Col1* and then type the first choice. Press the Tab key and then type the second choice. Continue in this manner until all choices have been entered and then click the Next button. At the third Lookup Wizard dialog box, make sure the proper name displays in the *What label would you like for your lookup column?* text box and then click the Finish button.

Inserting, Moving, and Deleting Fields in Design View

Tutorial

Managing Fields in Design View

 Insert Rows

Quick Steps
Insert a Field in Design View
1. Open table in Design view.
2. Click in row that will follow new field.
3. Click Insert Rows button.

As shown in Chapter 1, field management tasks such as inserting, moving, and deleting fields can be completed in Datasheet view. These tasks can also be completed in Design view.

To insert a new field in a table in Design view, position the insertion point in a field in the row that will be immediately *below* the new field and then click the Insert Rows button in the Tools group on the Table Tools Design tab. Another option is to position the insertion point in text in the row that will display immediately *below* the new field, click the right mouse button, and then click *Insert Rows* at the shortcut menu. A row in the Design view creates a field in the table.

Quick Steps

Delete a Field in Design View
1. Open table in Design view.
2. Click in row to be deleted.
3. Click Delete Rows button.
4. Click Yes.

 Delete Rows

A field in a table can be moved to a different location in Datasheet view or Design view. To move a field in Design view, click the field selector bar at the left side of the row to be moved. With the row selected, position the arrow pointer in the field selector bar at the left side of the selected row, click and hold down the left mouse button, drag the arrow pointer with a gray square attached until a thick black line displays in the desired position, and then release the mouse button.

Delete a field in a table and all data entered in that field is also deleted. When a field is deleted, the deletion cannot be undone with the Undo button. Delete a field only if all data associated with it should be removed from the table. To delete a field in Design view, click in the field selector bar at the left side of the row to be deleted and then click the Delete Rows button in the Tools group. At the confirmation message, click Yes. A row can also be deleted by positioning the mouse pointer in the row to be deleted, clicking the right mouse button, and then clicking *Delete Rows* at the shortcut menu.

Tutorial

Inserting a *Total* Row

 Totals

Inserting a *Total* Row

A *Total* row can be added to a table in Datasheet view and then used to perform functions such as finding the sum, average, maximum, minimum, count, standard deviation, or variance results in a numeric column. To insert a *Total* row, click the Totals button in the Records group on the Home tab. Access adds a row to the bottom of the table with the label *Total*. Click in the *Total* row, click the down arrow that displays, and then click a specific function at the drop-down list.

Project 1c Validating Field Entries; Using the Lookup Wizard; and Inserting, Moving, and Deleting a Field

Part 3 of 9

1. With **4-SunProperties.accdb** open, open the Employees table.
2. Insert a new field in the Employees table and apply a validation rule by completing the following steps:
   a. Click the View button to switch to Design view.
   b. Click in the empty field immediately below the *DentalIns* field in the *Field Name* column and then type LifeIns.
   c. Press the Tab key.
   d. Click the down arrow in the field in the *Data Type* column and then click *Currency* at the drop-down list.
   e. Click in the *Validation Rule* property box, type <=100000, and then press the Enter key.
   f. With the insertion point positioned in the *Validation Text* property box, type Enter a value that is equal to or less than $100,000.

General	Lookup	
Format	Currency	
Decimal Places	Auto	
Input Mask		
Caption		
Default Value	0	
Validation Rule	<=100000	
Validation Text	Enter a value that is equal to or less than $100,000	
Required	No	
Indexed	No	
Text Align	General	

2e   2f

   g. Click in the *LifeIns* field in the *Description* column and then type Enter optional life insurance amount.
   h. Click the Save button on the Quick Access Toolbar. Since the validation rule was created *after* data was entered into the table, Access displays a warning message indicating that some data may not be valid. At this message, click No.
   i. Click the View button to switch to Datasheet view.

3. Click in the first empty field in the *LifeIns* column, type 200000, and then press the Down Arrow key on the keyboard.

4. Access displays the error message prompting you to enter an amount that is equal to or less than $100,000. At this error message, click OK.

5. Edit the amount in the field so it displays as *100000* and then press the Down Arrow key.

6. Type the following entries in the remaining fields in the *LifeIns* column:

Record 2	25000	Record 7	100000
Record 3	0	Record 8	50000
Record 4	50000	Record 9	25000
Record 5	50000	Record 10	0
Record 6	0	Record 11	100000

7. Insert the *EmpCategory* field in the Employees table and use the Lookup Wizard to specify field choices by completing the following steps:

a. Click the View button to change to Design view.

b. Click in the *FName* field in the *Field Name* column.

c. Click the Insert Rows button in the Tools group.

d. With the insertion point positioned in the new empty field in the *Field Name* column, type EmpCategory.

e. Press the Tab key. (This moves the insertion point to the *Data Type* column.)

f. Click the down arrow in the field in the *Data Type* column and then click *Lookup Wizard* at the drop-down list.

g. At the first Lookup Wizard dialog box, click the *I will type in the values that I want* option and then click the Next button.

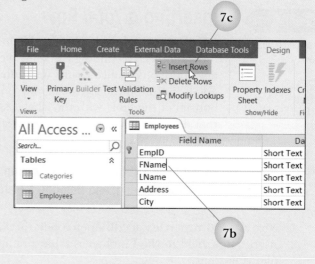

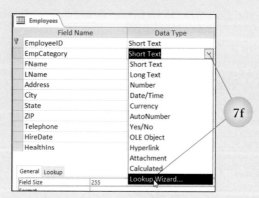

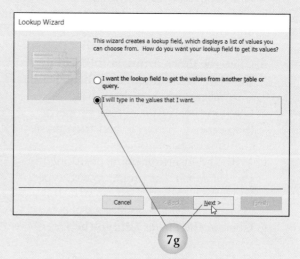

h. At the second Lookup Wizard dialog box, click in the blank text box below *Col1*, type Salaried, and then press the Tab key.

i. Type Hourly and then press the Tab key.

j. Type Temporary.

k. Click the Next button.

l. At the third Lookup Wizard dialog box, click the Finish button.

m. Press the Tab key and then type Click down arrow and then click employee category in the *Description* column.

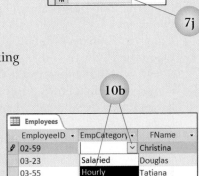

8. Click the Save button on the Quick Access Toolbar.

9. Click the View button to switch to Datasheet view.

10. Insert information in the *EmpCategory* column by completing the following steps:

a. Click in the first empty field in the new *EmpCategory* column.

b. Click the down arrow in the field and then click *Hourly* at the drop-down list.

c. Click in the next empty field in the *EmpCategory* column, click the down arrow, and then click *Salaried* at the drop-down list.

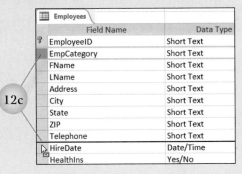

d. Continue entering information in the *EmpCategory* column by completing similar steps. Choose the following in the specified record:

> Third record: *Hourly*
> Fourth record: *Salaried*
> Fifth record: *Temporary*
> Sixth record: *Hourly*
> Seventh record: *Salaried*
> Eighth record: *Temporary*
> Ninth record: *Hourly*
> Tenth record: *Salaried*
> Eleventh record: *Salaried*

11. Print the Employees table. (The table will print on two pages.)

12. After looking at the printed table, you decide to move the *EmpCategory* field. Move the *EmpCatgory* field in Design view by completing the following steps:

a. With the Employees table open, click the View button to switch to Design view.

b. Click in the field selector bar at the left side of the *EmpCategory* field to select the row.

c. Position the arrow pointer in the *EmpCategory* field selector bar, click and hold down the left mouse button, drag down until a thick black line displays below the *Telephone* field, and then release the mouse button.

13. Delete the *DentalIns* field by completing the following steps:
    a. Click in the field selector bar at the left side of the *DentalIns* field. (This selects the row.)
    b. Click the Delete Rows button in the Tools group.
    c. At the message asking if you want to permanently delete the field and all of the data in the field, click Yes.
14. Click the Save button on the Quick Access Toolbar.
15. Click the View button to switch to Datasheet view.
16. Print the Employees table. (The table will print on two pages.)
17. Close the Employees table.
18. Open the Payments table and then insert a new field and apply a validation rule by completing the following steps:
    a. Click the View button to switch to Design view.
    b. Click in the empty field immediately below the *PymntAmount* field in the *Field Name* column and then type LateFee.
    c. Press the Tab key.
    d. Click the down arrow in the field in the *Data Type* column and then click *Currency* at the drop-down list.
    e. Click in the *Validation Rule* property box, type <=50, and then press the Enter key.
    f. With the insertion point positioned in the *Validation Text* property box, type Late fee must be $50 or less.
    g. Click in the box in the *Description* column for the *LateFee* field and then type Enter a late fee amount if applicable.

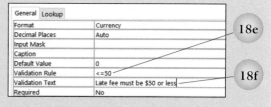

    h. Click the Save button on the Quick Access Toolbar. Since the validation rule was created *after* data was entered into the table, Access displays a warning message indicating that some data may not be valid. At this message, click No.
    i. Click the View button to switch to Datasheet view.
19. Insert late fees for the last three records by completing the following steps:
    a. Click in the *LateFee* field for record 15, type 25, and then press the Down Arrow key.
    b. With the *LateFee* field for record 16 active, type 25 and then press the Down Arrow key.
    c. With the *LateFee* field for record 17 active, type 50 and then press the Up Arrow key.

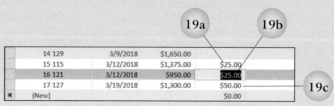

20. Insert a *Total* row by completing the following steps:
   a. In Datasheet view, click the Totals button in the Records group on the Home tab.
   b. Click in the empty field in the *PymntAmount* column in the *Total* row.
   c. Click the down arrow in the field and then click *Sum* at the drop-down list.
   d. Click in the empty field in the *LateFee* column in the *Total* row.
   e. Click the down arrow in the field and then click *Sum* at the drop-down list.
   f. Click in any other field.
21. Save, print, and then close the Payments table.

20a

20c

Check Your Work

Tutorial

Sorting Records in a Table

Sorting Records

The Sort & Filter group on the Home tab contains two buttons for sorting data in records. Click the Ascending button to sort data in the active field and text is sorted in alphabetical order from A to Z, numbers are sorted from lowest to highest, and dates are sorted from earliest to latest. Click the Descending button to sort data in the active field and text is sorted in alphabetical order from Z to A, numbers from highest to lowest, and dates from latest to earliest.

Quick Steps

Sort Records
1. Open table in Datasheet view.
2. Click field in specific column.
3. Click Ascending button or Descending button.

Quick Steps

Print Selected Records
1. Open table and select records.
2. Click File tab.
3. Click *Print* option.
4. Click next *Print* option.
5. Click *Selected Record(s)*.
6. Click OK.

Printing Specific Records

Specific records in a table can be printed by seleting the records and then displaying the Print dialog box. Display this dialog box by clicking the File tab, clicking the *Print* option, and then clicking the next *Print* option. At the Print dialog box, click the *Selected Record(s)* option in the *Print Range* section and then click OK.

To select specific records, display the table in Datasheet view, click the record selector for the first record, click and hold the left mouse button, drag to select the specific records, and then release the mouse button. The record selector is the light gray square at the left side of the record. When the mouse pointer is positioned on the record selector, the pointer turns into a right-pointing black arrow.

Formatting Table Data

A table in Datasheet view can be formatted with options available in the Text
Formatting group on the Home tab as shown in Figure 4.10 and described in
Table 4.2 (Some of the buttons in the Text Formatting group are dimmed and
unavailable. These buttons are only available for fields formatted as rich text.)
Alignment buttons such as Align Left, Center, or Align Right, apply formatting
to data in the currently active column. Click one of the other options or buttons
in the Text Formatting group and the formatting is applied to data in all columns
and rows.

Figure 4.10 Text Formatting Group on the Home Tab

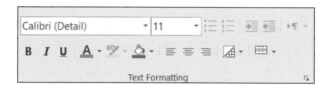

Table 4.2 Text Formatting Buttons and Option Boxes

Button/Option Box	Name	Description
Calibri (Detail)	*Font*	Change the text font.
11	*Font Size*	Change the text size.
B	Bold	Bold the text.
I	Italic	Italicize the text.
U	Underline	Underline the text.
A ▾	Font Color	Change the text color.
▾	Background Color	Apply a background color to all fields.
≣	Align Left	Align all text in the currently active column at the left side of the fields.
≣	Center	Center all text in the currently active column in the center of the fields.
≣	Align Right	Align all text in the currently active column at the right side of the fields.
▾	Gridlines	Specify whether to display vertical and/or horizontal gridlines.
▦ ▾	Alternate Row Color	Apply a specified color to alternating rows in the table.

When creating a table, a data type is specified for a field, such as the Short Text, Date/Time, or Currency data type. To format text in a field rather than all of the fields in a column or the entire table, choose the Long Text data type and then specify rich text formatting. For example, in Project 1d, specific credit scores will be formatted in the *CreditScore* column. To be able to format specific scores, the data type will be changed to Long Text with rich text formatting. Use the Long Text data type only for fields containing text—not for fields containing currency amounts, numbers, or dates.

By default, the Long Text data type uses plain text formatting. To change to rich text, click in the *Text Format* property box in the *Field Properties* section (displays with the text *Plain Text*), click the down arrow that displays at the right side of the property box, and then click *Rich Text* at the drop-down list.

Project 1d   Sorting, Printing, and Formatting Records and Fields in Tables   Part 4 of 9

1. With **4-SunProperties.accdb** open, open the Renters table.
2. With the table in Datasheet view, sort records in ascending alphabetical order by last name by completing the following steps:
   a. Click in any last name in the *LastName* column in the table.
   b. Click the Ascending button in the Sort & Filter group on the Home tab.
   c. Print the Renters table in landscape orientation.
3. Sort records in descending order (highest to lowest) by credit score number by completing the following steps:
   a. Click in any number in the *CreditScore* column.
   b. Click the Descending button in the Sort & Filter group.
   c. Print the Renters table in landscape orientation.
4. Close the Renters table without saving the changes.
5. Open the Properties table.
6. Sort and then print selected records with a specific apartment property type by completing the following steps:
   a. Click in any entry in the *CatID* column.
   b. Click the Ascending button in the Sort & Filter group.
   c. Position the mouse pointer on the record selector of the first record with a category ID of *A*, click and hold down the left mouse button, drag to select the four records with a category ID of *A*, and then release the mouse button.
   d. Click the File tab and then click the *Print* option.
   e. Click the next *Print* option.

f. At the Print dialog box, click the *Selected Record(s)* option in the *Print Range* section.

g. Click OK.

7. With the Properties table open, apply the following text formatting:

a. Click in any field in the *CatID* column and then click the Center button in the Text Formatting group on the Home tab.

6f

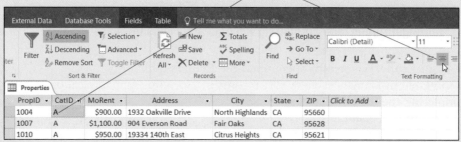

7a

b. Click in any field in the *PropID* column and then click the Center button in the Text Formatting group.

c. Click the Bold button in the Text Formatting group. (This applies bold to all text in the table.)

d. Click the Font Color button arrow and then click the *Dark Blue* color option (fourth column, first row in the *Standard Colors* section).

e. Adjust the column widths.

f. Save, print, and then close the Properties table.

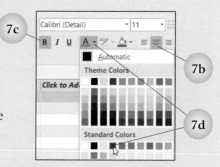

7c

7b

7d

8. Open the Payments table and apply the following text formatting:

a. With the first field active in the *PymntID* column, click the Center button in the Text Formatting group on the Home tab

b. Click in any field in the *RenterID* column and then click the Center button in the Text Formatting group.

c. Click the *Font* option box arrow, scroll down the drop-down list, and then click *Candara*. (Fonts are listed in alphabetical order in the drop-down list.)

d. Click the *Font Size* option box arrow and then click *12* at the drop-down list.

e. Click the Alternate Row Color button arrow and then click the *Green 2* color option (seventh column, third row in the *Standard Colors* section).

f. Adjust the column widths.

g. Save, print, and then close the Payments table.

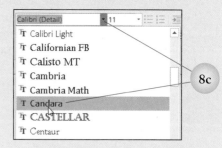

8c

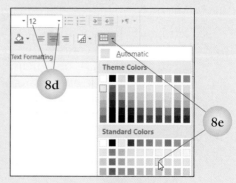

8d

8e

9. Open the Renters table and then apply the following formatting to columns in the table:
   a. With the first field active in the *RenterID* column, click the Center button in the Text Formatting group on the Home tab.
   b. Click in any field in the *PropID* column and then click the Center button.
   c. Click in any field in the *EmpID* column and then click the Center button
   d. Click in any field in the *CreditScore* column and then click the Center button.
10. Change the data type for the *CreditScore* field to Long Text with rich text formatting and apply formatting by completing the following steps:
    a. Click the View button to switch to Design view.
    b. Click in the *CreditScore* field in the *Data Type* column, click the down arrow that displays in the field, and then click *Long Text* at the drop-down list.
    c. Click in the *Text Format* property box in the *Field Properties* section (displays with the words *Plain Text*), click the down arrow that displays in the property box, and then click *Rich Text* at the drop-down list.

General	Lookup
Format	
Caption	
Default Value	
Validation Rule	
Validation Text	
Required	No
Allow Zero Length	Yes
Indexed	No
Unicode Compression	Yes
IME Mode	No Control
IME Sentence Mode	None
Text Format	Plain Text
Text Align	Plain Text
Append Only	Rich Text

10c

   d. At the message stating that the field will be converted to rich text, click the Yes button.
   e. Click the Save button on the Quick Access Toolbar.
   f. Click the View button to switch to Datasheet view.
   g. Double-click the field value *538* in the *CreditScore* column in the row for Dana Rozinski. (Double-clicking in the field selects the field value *538*.)
   h. With *538* selected, click the Font Color button in the Text Formatting group. (This changes the number to standard red. If the font color does not change to red, click the Font Color button arrow and then click the *Red* option [second column, bottom row in the *Standard Colors* section].)
   i. Change the font to standard red for any credit scores below 600.
   j. Save and print the Renters table in landscape orientation and then close the table.

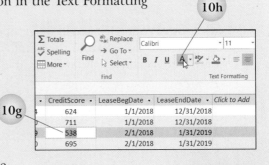

10h

10g

Check Your Work

Tutorial

Completing a Spelling Check

Completing a
Spelling Check

💡*Hint* Begin a
spelling check with the
keyboard shortcut F7.

 Spelling

Quick Steps

**Complete a Spelling
Check**
1. Open table in
   Datasheet view.
2. Click Spelling button.
3. Change or ignore
   spelling.
4. Click OK.

The spelling feature in Access finds misspelled words and suggests replacement words. It also finds duplicate words and irregular capitalizations. When checking the spelling of an object in a database, such as a table, the words in a table are compared with the words in the spelling dictionary. If a match is found, the word is passed over. If no match is found, then the word is selected and possible replacements are suggested.

To complete a spelling check, open a table in Datasheet view and then click the Spelling button in the Records group on the Home tab. If no match is found for a word in the table, the Spelling dialog box displays with replacement options. Figure 4.11 displays the Spelling dialog box with the word *Citruis* selected and possible replacements display in the *Suggestions* list box. Use options in the Spelling dialog box, to ignore the word (for example, if a proper name is selected), change to one of the replacement options, or add the word to the dictionary or AutoCorrect feature. A spelling check also can be completed on other objects in a database, such as a query, form, and report. (Forms and reports are covered in future chapters.)

Figure 4.11 Spelling Dialog Box

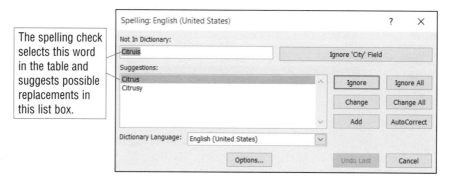

The spelling check selects this word in the table and suggests possible replacements in this list box.

Project 1e Checking Spelling in a Table

Part 5 of 9

1. With **4-SunProperties.accdb** open, open the Employees table.
2. Add the following record to the Employees table. (Type the misspelled words as shown below. You will correct the spelling in a later step.)

EmpID	02-72
FName	Roben
LName	Wildre
Address	9945 Valley Avenue
City	Citruis Heights
State	(CA automatically inserted)
ZIP	95610
Telephone	9165556522
EmpCategory	(choose *Salaried*)
HireDate	01may18
HealthIns	No (Remove check mark)
LifeIns	50000

3. Save the Employees table.

4. Click in the first field in the *EmpID* column.
5. Click the Spelling button in the Records group on the Home tab.
6. The name *Kasadev* is selected. This is a proper name, so click the Ignore button to leave the name as written.
7. The name *Scholtz* is selected. This is a proper name, so click the Ignore button to leave the name as written.
8. The name *Roben* is selected. Although this is a proper name, it is spelled incorrectly. Click *Robin* (the proper spelling) in the *Suggestions* list box and then click the Change button.
9. The name *Wildre* is selected. Although this is a proper name, it is spelled incorrectly. The proper spelling *(Wilder)* is selected in the *Suggestions* list box, so click the Change button.
10. The word *Citruis* is selected. The proper spelling *(Citrus)* is selected in the *Suggestions* list box, so click the Change button.
11. At the message stating that the spelling check is complete, click OK.
12. Print the Employees table and then close the table.

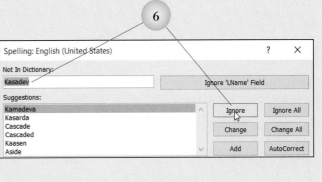

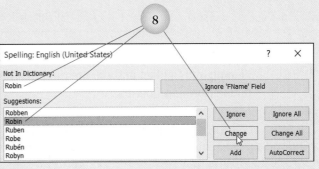

Check Your Work

Finding and Replacing Data

Tutorial

Finding Data

Tutorial

Finding and Replacing Data

Find

Quick Steps
Find Data in Table
1. Click Find button.
2. Type data in *Find What* text box.
3. Click Find Next button.

To find a specific entry in a field in a table, consider using options at the Find and Replace dialog box with the Find tab selected, as shown in Figure 4.12. Display this dialog box by clicking the Find button in the Find group on the Home tab or with the keyboard shortcut Ctrl + F. At the Find and Replace dialog box, enter the data to be found in the *Find What* text box. By default, Access looks only in the specific column where the insertion point is positioned. Click the Find Next button to find the next occurrence of the data or click the Cancel button to close the Find and Replace dialog box.

The *Look In* option defaults to the column where the insertion point is positioned. This can be changed to search the entire table by clicking the *Look In* option box arrow and then clicking the table name at the drop-down list. The *Match* option has a default setting of *Whole Field*. This can be changed to *Any Part of Field* or *Start of Field*. The *Search* option has a default setting of *All*, which means that Access will search all of the data in a specific column. This can be changed to *Up* or *Down*. To find data that contains specific uppercase and lowercase letters, insert a check mark in the *Match Case* check box and Access will return results that match the case formatting of the text entered in the *Find What* text box.

Use the Find and Replace dialog box with the Replace tab selected to search for specific data and replace it with other data. Display this dialog box by clicking the Replace button in the Find group on the Home tab or with the keyboard shortcut Ctrl + H.

Figure 4.12 Find and Replace Dialog Box with Find Tab Selected

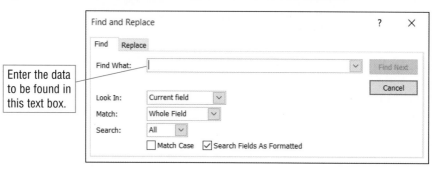

Project 1f Finding and Replacing Data, Creating Relationships, and Performing Queries

1. With **4-SunProperties.accdb** open, open the Properties table.
2. Find records containing the zip code *95610* by completing the following steps:
   a. Click in the first field in the *ZIP* column.
   b. Click the Find button in the Find group on the Home tab.
   c. At the Find and Replace dialog box with the Find tab selected, type *95610* in the *Find What* text box.
   d. Click the Find Next button. (Access finds and selects the first occurrence of *95610*. If the Find and Replace dialog box covers the data, position the mouse pointer on the dialog box title bar, click and hold down the left mouse button, and then drag the dialog box to a different location on the screen.)

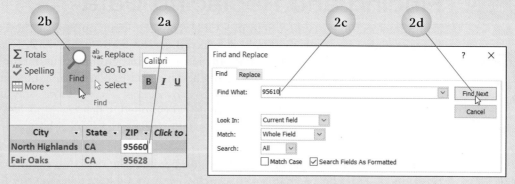

   e. Continue clicking the Find Next button until a message displays stating that Access has finished searching the records. At this message, click OK.
   f. Click the Cancel button to close the Find and Replace dialog box.
3. Suppose a new zip code has been added to the city of North Highlands and you need to change to this new zip code for some of the North Highlands properties. Complete the following steps to find *95660* and replace it with *95668*:
   a. Click in the first field in the *ZIP* column.
   b. Click the Replace button in the Find group.

c. At the Find and Replace dialog box with the Replace tab selected, delete the existing text in the *Find what* text box, and then type 95660 in the *Find What* text box.

d. Press the Tab key. (This moves the insertion point to the *Replace With* text box.)

e. Type 95668 in the *Replace With* text box.

f. Click the Find Next button.

g. When Access selects the first occurrence of *95660*, click the Replace button.

h. When Access selects the second occurrence of *95660*, click the Find Next button.

i. When Access selects the third occurrence of *95660*, click the Replace button.

j. When Access selects the fourth occurrence of *95660*, click the Find Next button.

k. When Access selects the fifth occurrence of *95660*, click the Find Next button.

l. When Access selects the sixth occurrence of *95660*, click the Replace button.

m. Access goes back and selects the first occurrence of *95660* (record 1003) in the table. Click the Cancel button to close the Find and Replace dialog box.

4. Print and then close the Properties table.

5. Display the Relationships window and then create the following relationships (enforce referential integrity and cascade fields and records):

a. Create a one-to-many relationship with the *CatID* field in the Categories table field list box the "one" and the *CatID* field in the Properties table field list box the "many."

b. Create a one-to-many relationship with the *EmpID* field in the Employees table field list box the "one" and the *EmpID* field in the Renters table field list box the "many."

c. Create a one-to-many relationship with the *PropID* field in the Properties table field list box the "one" and the *PropID* field in the Renters table field list box the "many."

d. Create a one-to-many relationship with the *RenterID* field in the Renters table field list box the "one" and the *RenterID* field in the Payments table field list box the "many."

e. Save the relationships and then print the relationships in landscape orientation.

f. Close the relationship report without saving it and then close the Relationships window.

6. Design a query that displays employees with health insurance benefits with the following specifications:

a. Insert the Employees table in the query window.

b. Insert the *EmpID* field in the first field in the *Field* row.

c. Insert the *FName* field in the second field in the *Field* row.

d. Insert the *LName* field in the third field in the *Field* row.

e. Insert the *HealthIns* field in the fourth field in the *Field* row.

f. Click in the check box in the *EmpID* field in the *Show* row to remove the check mark. (This hides the EmpID numbers in the query results.)

g. Extract those employees with health benefits. (Type 1 in the *HealthIns* field in the *Criteria* row.)

h. Run the query.

i. Save the query and name it *EmpsWithHealthInsQuery*.

j. Print and then close the query.

7. Design a query that displays all properties in the city of Citrus Heights with the following specifications:
   a. Insert the Properties table and the Categories table field list box in the query window.
   b. Insert the *PropID* field from the Properties table field list box in the first field in the *Field* row.
   c. Insert the *Category* field from the Categories table in the second field in the *Field* row.
   d. Insert the *Address*, *City*, *State*, and *ZIP* fields from the Properties table field list box to the third, fourth, fifth, and sixth fields in the *Field* row, respectively.
   e. Extract those properties in the city of Citrus Heights.
   f. Run the query.
   g. Save the query and name it *CitrusHeightsPropsQuery*.
   h. Print and then close the query.
8. Design a query that displays rent payments made between 3/1/2018 and 3/5/2018 with the following specifications:
   a. Insert the Payments table and the Renters table in the query window.
   b. Insert the *PymntID*, *PymntDate*, and *PymntAmount* fields from the Payments table field list box in the first, second, and third fields in the *Field* row fields, respectively.
   c. Insert the *FirstName* and *LastName* fields from the Renters table field list box in the fourth and fifth fields in the *Field* row, respectively.
   d. Extract those payments made between 3/1/2018 and 3/5/2018.
   e. Run the query.
   f. Save the query and name it *Pymnts3/1To3/5Query*.
   g. Print and then close the query.
9. Design a query that displays properties in Citrus Heights or Orangevale that rent for less than $1,501 a month as well as the type of property with the following specifications:
   a. Insert the Categories table and the Properties table in the query window.
   b. Insert the *Category* field from the Categories table field list box.
   c. Insert the *PropID*, *MoRent*, *Address*, *City*, *State*, and *ZIP* fields from the Properties table field list box.
   d. Extract those properties in Citrus Heights or Orangevale that rent for less than $1,501.
   e. Run the query.
   f. Save the query and name it *RentLessThan$1501InCHAndOVQuery*.
   g. Print the query in landscape orientation and then close the query.
10. Design a query that displays properties in Citrus Heights assigned to employee identification number *07-20* with the following specifications:
    a. Insert the Employees table and Properties table in the query window.
    b. Insert the *EmpID*, *FName*, and *LName* fields from the Employees table field list box.
    c. Insert the *Address*, *City*, *State*, and *ZIP* fields from the Properties table field list box.
    d. Extract those properties in Citrus Heights assigned to employee identification number 07-20.
    e. Run the query.
    f. Save the query and name it *Emp07-20CHPropsQuery*.
    g. Print and then close the query.

Check Your Work

Tutorial

Using the Help and Tell Me Features

Using the Help and Tell Me Features

Microsoft Access includes a Help feature that contains information about Access features and commands. This on-screen reference manual is similar to Windows Help and the Help features in Word, PowerPoint, and Excel. The Tell Me feature provides information and guidance on how to complete a function.

Getting Help at the Access Help Window

Hint Press the F1 function key to display the Access Help window.

Quick Steps

Use the Help Feature
1. Click Microsoft Access Help button.
2. Type topic or feature.
3. Press Enter.
4. Click article.

Click the Microsoft Access Help button (the question mark) in the upper right corner of the screen or press the keyboard shortcut F1 to display the Access Help window, as shown in Figure 4.13. In this window, type a topic, feature, or question in the search text box and then press the Enter key. Articles related to the search text display in the Access Help window. Open an article by clicking the article's hyperlink.

The Access Help window contains five buttons, which display above the search text box. Use the Back and Forward buttons to navigate within the window. Click the Home button to return to the Access Help window opening screen. Print information by clicking the Print button and then clicking the Print button at the Print dialog box. Click the Use Large Text button to increase the size of the text in the window.

Getting Help on a Button

Position the mouse pointer on a button and a ScreenTip displays with information about the button. Some button ScreenTips display with a Help icon and the text *Tell me more*. Click this hyperlinked text or press the F1 function key and the Access Help window opens with information about the button feature.

Figure 4.13 Access Help Window

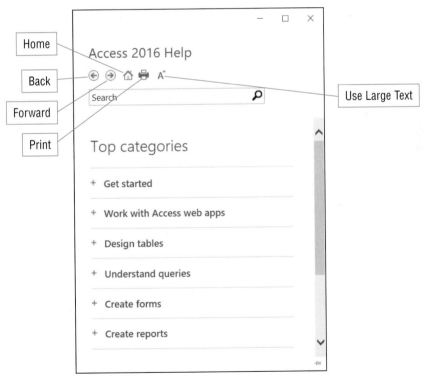

Chapter 4 | Creating and Modifying Tables in Design View

Project 1g Using the Help Feature

1. With **4-SunProperties.accdb** open, click the Microsoft Access Help button in the upper right corner of the screen.
2. At the Access Help window, type input mask in the search text box and then press the Enter key.
3. When the list of articles displays, click the Guide data entry in Access by using input masks hyperlink. (If this article is not available, choose a similar article.)
4. Read the information on creating an input mask. (If you want a printout of the information, click the Print button in the Access Help window and then click the Print button at the Print dialog box.)
5. Close the Access Help window by clicking the Close button in the upper right corner of the window.
6. Click the Create tab.
7. Hover the mouse over the Table button and then click the Tell me more hyperlink at the bottom of the ScreenTip.
8. At the Access Help window, read the information on tables and then click the Close button in the upper right corner of the Access Help window.

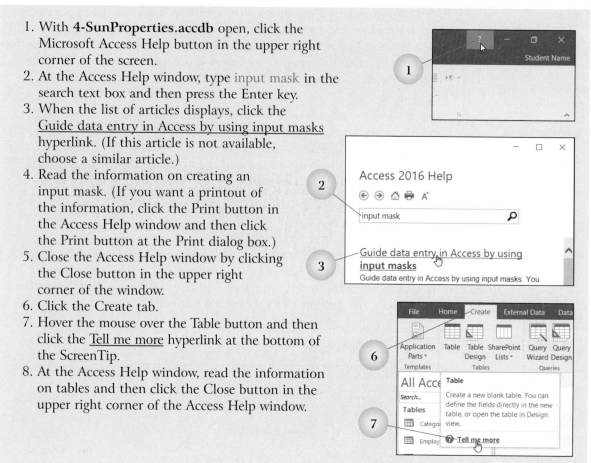

Getting Help in a Dialog Box or Backstage Area

Some dialog boxes and backstage areas provide a Help button that, when clicked, displays the Access Help window with specific information about the dialog box or backstage area. After reading and/or printing the information, close the dialog box by clicking the Close button in the upper right corner of the dialog box or close the backstage area by clicking the Back button or pressing the Esc key.

Project 1h Getting Help in a Dialog Box and Backstage Area

1. With **4-SunProperties.accdb** open, click the Database Tools tab.
2. Click the Relationships button. (Make sure the Show Table dialog box displays. If it does not, click the Show Table button in the Relationships group.)
3. Click the Help button in the upper right corner of the Show Table dialog box.
4. Click the Guide to table relationships hyperlink. (If this article is not available, choose a similar article.)

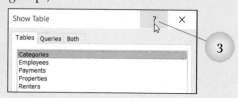

Chapter 4 | Creating and Modifying Tables in Design View

5. Read the information about table relationships and then close the Access Help window.
6. Close the Show Table dialog box and then close the Relationships window.
7. Click the File tab and then click the *Open* option.
8. At the Open backstage area, click the Microsoft Access Help button in the upper right corner.
9. Read the information in the Access Help window.
10. Close the Access Help window and then press the Esc key to return to the database.

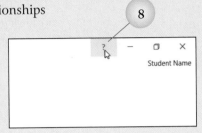

Using the Tell Me Feature

Hint Alt + Q is the keyboard shortcut to make the *Tell Me* text box active.

Access 2016 includes a Tell Me feature that provides information as well as guidance on how to complete a function. To use Tell Me, click in the *Tell Me* text box on the ribbon to the right of the View tab and then type the function. Type text in the *Tell Me* text box and a drop-down list displays with options that are refined as the text is typed, which is referred to as "word-wheeling." The drop-down list displays options for completing the function or for displaying information on the function in the Access Help window.

Project 1i Using the Tell Me Feature   Part 9 of 9

1. With **4-SunProperties.accdb** open, open the query named *CitrusHeightsPropsQuery*.
2. Use the Tell Me feature to display the Find and Replace dialog box with the Replace tab selected and apply vertical gridlines by completing the following steps:
   a. Click in the *Tell Me* text box.
   b. Type replace.
   c. Click the *Replace* option at the drop-down list. (This displays the Find and Replace dialog box with the Replace tab selected.)
   d. Click the Cancel button to close the Find and Replace dialog box.
   e. Click in the *Tell Me* text box.
   f. Type gridlines.
   g. Click the right arrow at the right side of the *Gridlines* option at the drop-down list.
   h. Click the *Gridlines: Vertical* option at the side menu.
3. Save, print, and then close the CitrusHeightsPropsQuery query.
4. Close the **4-SunProperties.accdb** database.

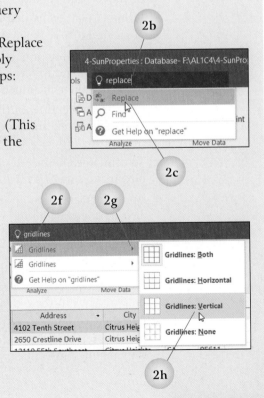

Check Your Work

Chapter Summary

- A table can be created in Datasheet view or Design view. Click the View button on the Table Tools Fields tab or the Home tab to switch between Datasheet view and Design view.

- Define each field in a table in the rows in the top section of Design view. Access automatically assigns the first field the name *ID* and assigns the AutoNumber data type.

- In Design view, specify a field name, data type, and description for each field.

- Assign a data type in Design view by clicking in a specific field in the *Data Type* column, clicking the down arrow at the right side of the field, and then clicking the data type at the drop-down list.

- Create a default value for a field in Design view with the *Default Value* property box in the *Field Properties* section.

- Use the Input Mask Wizard to set a pattern for how data is entered in a field. Use the *Format* property box to control what displays in a field.

- Use the *Validation Rule* property box in the *Field Properties* section in Design view to enter a statement containing a conditional test. Customize the error message that displays if the data entered violates the validation rule by typing that message in the *Validation Text* property box.

- Use the Lookup Wizard to confine data entered in a field to a specific list of items.

- Insert a field in Design view by clicking in the row immediately below where the new field is to be inserted and then clicking the Insert Rows button.

- Move a field in Design view by clicking in the field selector bar of the field to be moved and then dragging to the new position.

- Delete a field in Design view by clicking in the field selector bar at the left side of the field to be deleted and then clicking the Delete Rows button.

- Insert a *Total* row in a table in Datasheet view by clicking the Totals button in the Records group on the Home tab, clicking the down arrow in the *Total* row field, and then clicking a function at the drop-down list.

- Click the Ascending button in the Sort & Filter group on the Home tab to sort records in ascending order and click the Descending button to sort records in descending order.

- To print specific records in a table, select the records, display the Print dialog box, make sure *Selected Record(s)* is selected, and then click OK.

- Apply formatting to a table in Datasheet view with options and buttons in the Text Formatting group on the Home tab. Depending on the option or button selected, formatting is applied to all of the data in a table or data in a specific column in the table.

- To format text in a specific field, change the data type to Long Text and then specify rich text formatting. Do this in Design view with the *Text Format* property box in the *Field Properties* section.

- Use the spelling feature to find misspelled words in a table and consider possible replacement words. Begin checking the spelling in a table by clicking the Spelling button in the Records group on the Home tab.

- Use options at the Find and Replace dialog box with the Find tab selected to search for specific field entries in a table. Use options at the Find and Replace dialog box with the Replace tab selected to search for specific data and replace it with other data.
- Click the Microsoft Access Help button or press the F1 function key to display the Access Help window. At this window, type a topic in the search text box and then press the Enter key.
- The ScreenTip for some buttons displays with a Help icon and the text *Tell me more*. Click this hyperlinked text or press the F1 function key and the Access Help window opens with information about the button.
- Some dialog boxes and backstage areas contain a Help button that, when clicked, displays information specific to the dialog box or backstage area.
- The Tell Me feature provides information and guidance on how to complete a function. The *Tell Me* text box is on the ribbon to the right of the View tab.

Commands Review

FEATURE	RIBBON TAB, GROUP	BUTTON	KEYBOARD SHORTCUT
Access Help window		?	F1
align text left	Home, Text Formatting		
align text right	Home, Text Formatting		
alternate row color	Home, Text Formatting		
background color	Home, Text Formatting		
bold formatting	Home, Text Formatting	B	
center text	Home, Text Formatting		
delete field	Table Tools Design, Tools		
Design view	Home, Views OR Table Tools Fields, Views		
Find and Replace dialog box with Find tab selected	Home, Find		Ctrl + F
Find and Replace dialog box with Replace tab selected	Home, Find		Ctrl + H
font	Home, Text Formatting	Calibri (Detail)	
font color	Home, Text Formatting	A	
font size	Home, Text Formatting	11	
gridlines	Home, Text Formatting		
insert field	Table Tools Design, Tools		

FEATURE	RIBBON TAB, GROUP	BUTTON	KEYBOARD SHORTCUT
italic formatting	Home, Text Formatting	I	
sort records ascending	Home, Sort & Filter		
sort records descending	Home, Sort & Filter		
spelling check	Home, Records	ABC	F7
Tell Me feature			Alt + Q
Total row	Home, Records	Σ	
underline formatting	Home, Text Formatting	U	

Microsoft®

Access® Level 1

Unit 2

Creating Forms and Reports

Microsoft®

Access®

Creating Forms

Performance Objectives

Precheck

Check your current skills to help focus your study.

Upon successful completion of Chapter 5, you will be able to:

1　Create a form using the Form button

2　Change views in a form

3　Print a form

4　Navigate in a form

5　Delete a form

6　Add records to and delete records from a form

7　Sort records in a form

8　Create a form with a related table

9　Manage control objects in a form

10　Format a form

11　Apply conditional formatting to data in a form

12　Add an existing field to a form

13　Insert a calculation in a form

14　Create a split form and multiple items form

15　Create a form using the Form Wizard

In this chapter, you will learn how to create forms from database tables, improving the data display and making data entry easier. Access offers several methods for presenting data on the screen for easier data entry. You will create a form using the Form button, create a split form and multiple items form, and use the Form Wizard to create a form. You will also learn how to customize control objects, insert control objects and fields, and apply formatting to a form.

SNAP

If you are a SNAP user, launch the Precheck and Tutorials from your Assignments page.

Data Files

Before beginning chapter work, copy the AL1C5 folder to your storage medium and then make AL1C5 the active folder.

Preview Finished Project

Creating a Form

Hint A form allows you to focus on a single record at a time.

Access offers a variety of options for presenting data in a clear and attractive format. For instance, data can be viewed, added, or edited in a table in Datasheet view. When data is entered in a table in Datasheet view, multiple records display at the same time. If a record contains several fields, not all of the fields in the record may be visible at the same time. Create a form, however, and all of the fields for a record are generally visible on the screen.

Hint Save a form before making changes or applying formatting to it.

A form is an object used to enter and edit data in a table or query. It is a user-friendly interface for viewing, adding, editing, and deleting records. A form is also useful in helping to prevent incorrect data from being entered and it can be used to control access to specific data. Several methods are available for creating forms. This chapter covers creating forms using the Form, Split Form, and Multiple Items buttons, as well as the Form Wizard.

Tutorial

Creating a Form Using the Form Button

Creating a Form Using the Form Button

The simplest method for creating a form is to click a table in the Navigation pane, click the Create tab, and then click the Form button in the Forms groups. Figure 5.1 shows the form that will be created in Project 1a with the Sales table in 5-Dearborn.accdb. Access creates the form using all fields in the table in a vertical layout and displays the form in Layout view with the Form Layout Tools Design tab active.

Changing Views

 Form

 Form View

Layout View

Click the Form button to create a form and the form displays in Layout view. This is one of three views for working with forms. Use the Form view to enter and manage records. Use the Layout view to view the data and modify the appearance and contents of the form. Use the Design view to view the form's structure and modify it. Change views with the View button in the Views group on the Form Layout Tools Design tab or with buttons in the view area at the right side of the Status bar. An existing form can be opened in Layout view by right-clicking the form name in the Navigation pane and then clicking *Layout View* at the shortcut menu.

Quick Steps

Create a Form with the Form Button
1. Click table in Navigation pane.
2. Click Create tab.
3. Click Form button.

Printing a Form

Print all of the records in a form by clicking the File tab, clicking the *Print* option, and then clicking the *Quick Print* option. To print a specific record in a form, click the File tab, click the *Print* option, and then click the next *Print* option. At the Print dialog box, click the *Selected Record(s)* option and then click OK. Print a range of records by clicking the *Pages* option in the *Print Range* section of the Print dialog

Figure 5.1 Form Created with the Sales Table

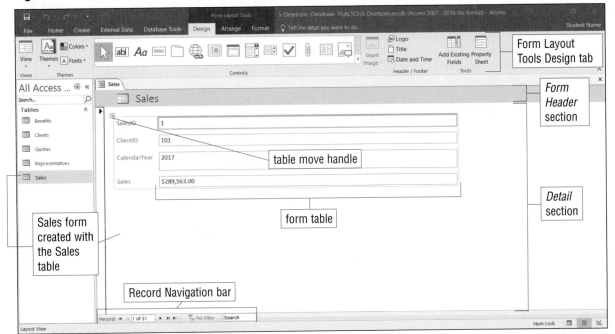

box and then entering the beginning record number in the *From* text box and the ending record number in the *To* text box.

Before printing a form, display the form in Print Preview. If column shading displays on the second page without any other data, decrease the width of the column. To do this, click the Columns button in the Page Layout group on the Print Preview tab. At the Page Setup dialog box with the Columns tab selected, decrease the measurement in the *Width* measurement box, and then click OK.

Deleting a Form

If a form is no longer needed in a database, delete the form. Delete a form by clicking the form name in the Navigation pane, clicking the Delete button in the Records group on the Home tab, and then clicking the Yes button at the confirmation message. Another method is to right-click the form name in the Navigation pane, click *Delete* at the shortcut menu, and then click Yes at the message. If a form is being deleted from a computer's hard drive, the confirmation message will not display. This is because Access automatically sends the deleted form to the Recycle Bin, where it can be retrieved if necessary.

Tutorial

Navigating in Objects

Navigating in a Form

When a form displays in Form view or Layout view, navigation buttons display along the bottom of the form in the Record Navigation bar, as identified in Figure 5.1. Use these navigation buttons to display the first, previous, next, or last record in the form or add a new record. Navigate to a specific record by clicking in the *Current Record* box, selecting the current number, typing the number of the record to view, and then pressing Enter. The keyboard also can be used to navigate in a form. Press the Page Down key to move forward or the Page Up key to move back a single record. Press Ctrl + Home to display the first record or press Ctrl + End to display the last record.

1. Display the Open dialog box with AL1C5 folder the active folder.
2. Open **5-Dearborn.accdb** and enable the content.
3. Create a form with the Sales table by completing the following steps:
   a. Click *Sales* in the Tables group in the Navigation pane.
   b. Click the Create tab.
   c. Click the Form button in the Forms group.

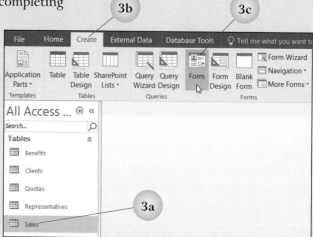

4. Switch to Form view by clicking the View button in the Views group on the Form Layout Tools Design tab.
5. Navigate in the form by completing the following steps:
   a. Click the Next record button in the Record Navigation bar to display the next record.
   b. Click in the *Current Record* box, select any numbers that display, type 15, and then press the Enter key.
   c. Click the First record button in the Record Navigation bar to display the first record.

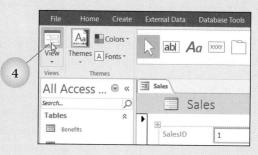

6. Save the form by completing the following steps:
   a. Click the Save button on the Quick Access Toolbar.
   b. At the Save As dialog box, with *Sales* inserted in the *Form Name* text box, click OK.
7. Print the current record in the form by completing the following steps:
   a. Click the File tab and then click the *Print* option.
   b. Click the next *Print* option.
   c. At the Print dialog box, click the *Selected Record(s)* option in the *Print Range* section and then click OK.
8. Close the Sales form.
9. Delete the RepBenefits form by right-clicking *RepBenefits* in the Navigation pane, clicking *Delete* at the shortcut menu, and then clicking Yes at the confirmation message.

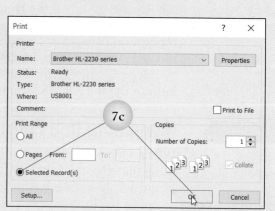

Check Your Work

New (blank)
record

Delete

Adding and Deleting Records

Add a new record to the form by clicking the New (blank) record button (contains a right-pointing arrow and a yellow asterisk) on the Record Navigation bar along the bottom of the form. A new record also can be added to a form by clicking the Home tab and then clicking the New button in the Records group.

To delete a record, display the record, click the Home tab, click the Delete button arrow in the Records group, and then click *Delete Record* at the drop-down list. At the confirmation message, click the Yes button. Add records to or delete records from the table from which the form was created and the form will reflect the additions or deletions. Also, if additions or deletions are made to the form, the changes are reflected in the table from which the form was created.

Quick Steps

Add a Record
Click New (blank)
record button on
Record Navigation bar.
OR
1. Click Home tab.
2. Click New button.

Delete a Record
1. Click Home tab.
2. Click Delete button
   arrow.
3. Click *Delete Record*.
4. Click Yes.

Sorting Records

Sort data in a form by clicking in the field containing data on which to sort and then clicking the Ascending button or Descending button in the Sort & Filter group on the Home tab. Click the Ascending button to sort text in alphabetic order from A to Z, numbers from lowest to highest, and dates from earliest to latest. Click the Descending button to sort text in alphabetic order from Z to A, numbers from highest to lowest, and dates from latest to earliest.

Project 1b Adding, Deleting, and Sorting Records in a Form   **Part 2 of 7**

1. With **5-Dearborn.accdb** open, open the Sales table (not the form) and add a new record by completing the following steps:
   a. Click the New (blank) record button in the Record Navigation bar.

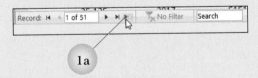

1a

   b. At the new blank record, type the following information in the specified fields. (Move to the next field by pressing the Tab key or the Enter key; move to the previous field by pressing Shift + Tab.)

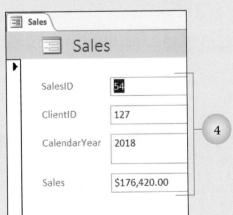

SalesID	(This is an AutoNumber field, so press the Tab key.)
ClientID	*127*
CalendarYear	*2018*
Sales	*176420*

2. Close the Sales table.
3. Open the Sales form.
4. Click the Last record button on the Record Navigation bar and notice that the new record you added to the table also has been added to the form.

5. Delete the second record (*SalesID 3*) in the form by completing the following steps:
   a. Click the First record button in the Record Navigation bar.
   b. Click the Next record button in the Record Navigation bar.
   c. With Record 2 active, click the Delete button arrow in the Records group on the Home tab and then click *Delete Record* at the drop-down list.

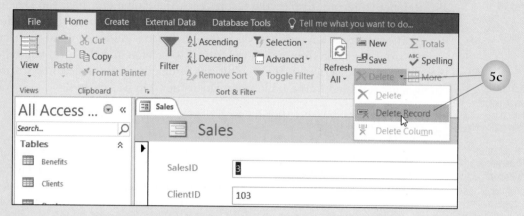

   d. At the confirmation message, click the Yes button.
6. Click the New (blank) record button in the Record Navigation bar and then type the following information in the specified fields:

SalesID	(Press the Tab key.)
ClientID	*103*
CalendarYear	*2018*
Sales	*110775*

7. Sort the records in the form by completing the following steps:
   a. Click in the field containing *103* and then click the Ascending button in the Sort & Filter group on the Home tab.
   b. Click in the field containing *$289,563.00* and then click the Descending button in the Sort & Filter group.
   c. Click in the field containing *36* and then click the Ascending button in the Sort & Filter group.
8. Close the Sales form.

Check Your Work

Creating a Form with a Related Table

Tutorial

Creating a Form with a Related Table

When the form was created with the Sales table, only the Sales table fields displayed in the form. If a form is created with a table that has a one-to-many relationship established, Access adds a datasheet to the form that is based on the related table.

For example, in Project 1c, a form will be created from the Representatives table and, since it is related to the Clients table by a one-to-many relationship, Access inserts a datasheet at the bottom of the form containing all of the records in the Clients table. Figure 5.2 displays the form that will be created in Project 1c. Notice the datasheet at the bottom of the form.

If only a single one-to-many relationship has been created in a database, the datasheet for the related table displays in the form. If multiple one-to-many relationships have been created in a table, Access will not display any datasheets when a form is created with that table.

Figure 5.2 Representatives Form with Clients Datasheet

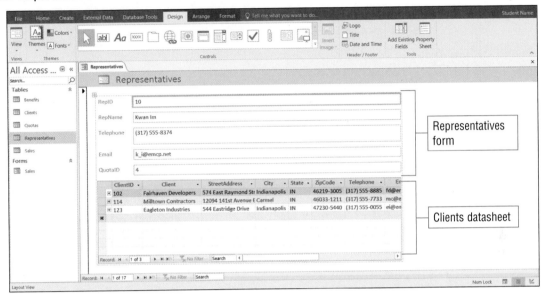

Project 1c Creating a Form with a Related Table

Part 3 of 7

1. With **5-Dearborn.accdb** open, create a form with the Representatives table by completing the following steps:
   a. Click *Representatives* in the Tables group in the Navigation pane.
   b. Click the Create tab.
   c. Click the Form button in the Forms group.
2. Insert a new record in the Clients table for representative *12* (Catherine Singleton) by completing the following steps:
   a. Click two times on the Next record button in the Record Navigation bar at the bottom of the form window (not the Record Navigation bar in the Clients datasheet) to display the record for Catherine Singleton.
   b. Click in the cell immediately below *127* in the *ClientID* field in the Clients datasheet.

c. Type the following information in the specified fields:

ClientID	*129*	*State*	*IN*
Client	*Dan-Built Construction*	*ZipCode*	*460339050*
StreetAddress	*903 James Street*	*Telephone*	*3175551122*
City	*Carmel*	*Email*	*dc@emcp.net*

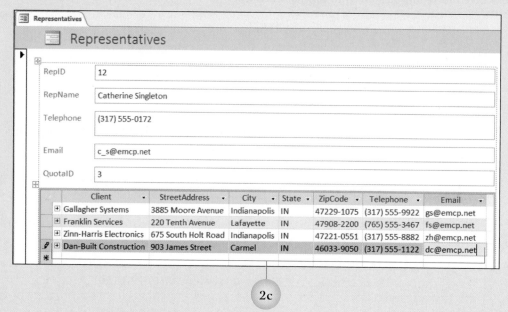

2c

3. Click the Save button on the Quick Access Toolbar and then, at the Save As dialog box with *Representatives* in the *Form Name* text box, click OK.
4. Print the current record in the form by completing the following steps:
   a. Click the File tab and then click the *Print* option.
   b. Click the next *Print* option.
   c. At the Print dialog box, click the *Selected Record(s)* option in the *Print Range* section and then click OK.
5. Close the Representatives form.

Check Your Work

Tutorial

Managing Control Objects in a Form

💡 *Hint* Almost all changes can be made to a form in Layout view.

Managing Control Objects

A form, like a table in a Word document, is made up of cells that are arranged in rows and columns. Each cell in a form can contain one control object, which is an object that displays a title or description, accepts data, or performs an action. For example, a cell can contain a label control object that displays a field name from the table used to create the form, a text box control that displays and accepts data, or a logo control object that will display a logo image. Control objects are contained in the *Form Header* and *Detail* sections of the form. (Refer to Figure 5.1 on page 137.) The control objects in the *Detail* section are contained within a form table.

Manage control objects with buttons on the Form Layout Tools ribbon with the Design tab, Arrange tab, or Format tab selected. When a form is opened in Layout view, the Form Layout Tools Design tab is active.

Inserting Data in a Control Object

Logo

Title

Date and Time

Use buttons in the Header/Footer group on the Form Layout Tools Design tab to insert a logo, form title, or date and time. Click the Logo button and the Insert Picture dialog box displays. Browse to the folder containing the image and then double-click the image file. Click the Title button and the current title is selected. Type the new title and then press the Enter key. Click the Date and Time button in the Header/Footer group and the Date and Time dialog box displays. At this dialog box, choose a date and time format and then click OK. The date and time are inserted at the right side of the *Form Header* section.

Resizing Control Objects

When Access creates a form from a table, the cells in the first column in the *Detail* section of the form contain the label control objects and displays the field names from the table. The second column of cells contains the text box control objects that display the field values entered in the table. The control objects in the *Form Header* section and the columns in the *Detail* section can be resized by dragging the border of a selected control object or with the *Width* property box on the Format tab in the Property Sheet task pane.

To resize a control object by dragging, select the object (displays with an orange border) and then position the mouse pointer on the left or right border of the object until the pointer displays as a left-and-right pointing arrow. Click and hold down the left mouse button, drag left or right to change the width of the column, and then release the mouse button. Complete similar steps to change the height of a control object. When dragging a border, a line and character count displays at the left side of the Status bar. Use the line and character count numbers to move the border to a precise location. When dragging the border of a label control or text box control object, the entire column width is resized.

In addition to dragging a control object border, the column width can be adjusted with the *Width* property box on the Format tab in the Property Sheet task pane and the height can be adjusted with the *Height* property box. Display this task pane by clicking the Property Sheet button in the Tools group. In the Property Sheet task pane with the Format tab selected, select the current measurement in the *Width* or *Height* property box, type the new measurement, and then press the Enter key. Close the Property Sheet task pane by clicking the Close button in the upper right corner of the task pane.

Deleting a Control Object

To delete a control object from the form, click the object and then press the Delete key. Or, right-click the object and then click *Delete* at the shortcut menu. To delete a form row, right-click an object in the row to be deleted and then click *Delete Row* at the shortcut menu. To delete a column, right-click one of the objects in the column to be deleted and then click *Delete Column* at the shortcut menu.

Tutorial

Inserting Control Objects

Inserting Control Objects

The Controls group on the Form Layout Tools Design tab contains a number of control objects that can be inserted in a form. By default, the Select button is active. With this button active, use the mouse pointer to select control objects.

Select	A new label control and text box control object can be inserted in a form by clicking the Text Box button in the Controls group and then clicking in the desired position in the form. Click the label control object, select the default text, and then type the label text.
abl Text Box	

Text can be entered in a label control object in Layout view, but not in a text box control object. In Form view, data can be entered in a text box control object but text in a label control object cannot be edited. The Controls group contains a number of additional buttons for inserting control objects in a form, such as a hyperlink, combo box, or image.

Project 1d Creating a Form and Customizing the Design of a Form

Part 4 of 7

1. With **5-Dearborn.accdb** open, create a form with the Clients table and delete the accompanying datasheet by completing the following steps:

   a. Click *Clients* in the Tables group in the Navigation pane.

   b. Click the Create tab.

   c. Click the Form button in the Forms group.

   d. Click in the *SalesID* field in the datasheet that displays below the form.

   e. Click the table move handle in the upper left corner of the datasheet (see image at right).

   f. Press the Delete key.

2. Insert a logo image in the *Form Header* section by completing the following steps:

   a. Right-click the logo object that displays in the *Form Header* section (to the left of the title *Clients*) and then click *Delete* at the shortcut menu.

   b. Click the Logo button in the Header/Footer group.

   c. At the Insert Picture dialog box, navigate to the AL1C5 folder on your storage medium and then double-click the file named ***DearbornLogo.jpg***.

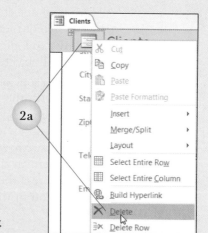

3. Change the title by completing the following steps:

   a. Click the Title button in the Header/Footer group. (This selects *Clients* in the *Form Header* section.)

   b. Type Dearborn Clients Form and then press the Enter key.

4. Insert the date and time in the *Form Header* section by completing the following steps:

   a. Click the Date and Time button in the Header/Footer group.

   b. At the Date and Time dialog box, click OK.

5. Size the control object containing the title by completing the following steps:

   a. Click any field outside the title and then click the title to select the control object.

   b. Position the mouse pointer on the right border of the selected object until the pointer displays as a black left-and-right-pointing arrow.

c. Click and hold down the left mouse button, drag to the left until the right border is immediately right of the title, and then release the mouse button.

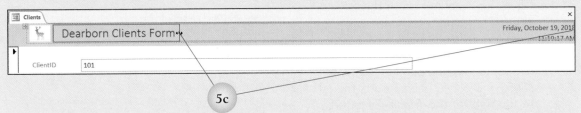

5c

6. Size and move the control objects containing the date and time by completing the following steps:
   a. Click the date to select the control object.
   b. Press and hold down the Shift key, click the time, and then release the Shift key. (Both control objects should be selected.)
   c. Position the mouse pointer on the left border of the selected objects until the pointer displays as a black left-and-right-pointing arrow.

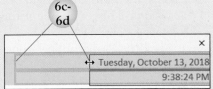

   6c-6d

   d. Click and hold down the left mouse button, drag to the right until the border is immediately left of the date, and then release the mouse button.
   e. Position the mouse pointer in the selected objects until the pointer displays with a four-headed arrow attached.
   f. Click and hold down the left mouse button, drag the outline of the date and time objects to the left until the outline displays near the title, and then release the mouse button.
7. Decrease the size of the second column of cells containing control objects in the *Detail* section by completing the following steps:
   a. Click the text box control object containing the client number *101*. (This selects and inserts an orange border around the object.)
   b. Position the mouse pointer on the right border of the selected object until the pointer displays as a black left-and-right-pointing arrow.
   c. Click and hold down the left mouse button, drag to the left until *Lines: 1 Characters: 30* displays at the left side of the Status bar, and then release the mouse button.

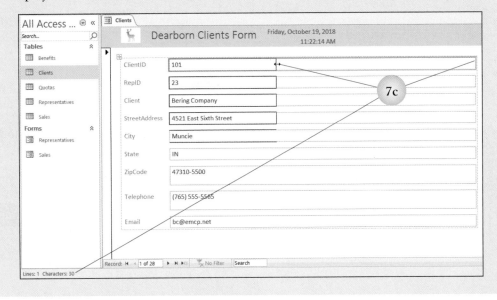

7c

8. Insert a label control object by completing the following steps:
   a. Click the Label button in the Controls group.
   b. Click immediately right of the text box control object containing the telephone number *(765) 555-5565*. (This inserts the label to the right of the *Telephone* text box control object.)
   c. With the insertion point positioned inside the label, type Type the telephone number without symbols or spaces and then press the Enter key.
9. Change the width and height of the new label control object by completing the following steps:
   a. Click the Property Sheet button in the Tools group.
   b. In the Property Sheet task pane that displays, if necessary, click the Format tab.
   c. Select the current measurement in the *Width* property box, type 2, and then press the Enter key.
   d. With the current measurement selected in the *Height* property box, type 0.4.
   e. Close the Property Sheet task pane by clicking the Close button in the upper right corner of the task pane.

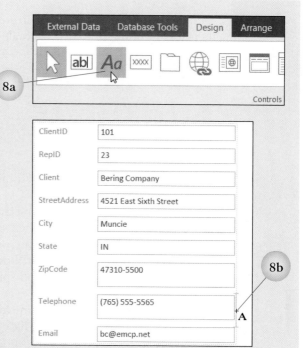

10. Delete the control object containing the time by clicking the time to select the object and then pressing the Delete key.
11. Click the Save button on the Quick Access Toolbar.
12. At the Save As dialog box with *Clients* in the *Form Name* text box, click OK.

Check Your Work

Moving a Form Table

The control objects in the *Detail* section in a form in Layout view are contained in cells within the form table. Click in a control object and the table move handle is visible. The table move handle is a small square with a four-headed arrow inside that displays in the upper left corner of the table. (Refer to Figure 5.1 on page 137.) To move the table, position the mouse pointer on the table move handle, click and hold down the left mouse button, drag the table to the new position, and then release the mouse button.

Arranging a Control Object

The Form Layout Tools Arrange tab contains options for selecting, inserting, deleting, arranging, merging, and splitting cells. When a label control object was inserted to the right of the *Telephone* text box control object in Project 1d, empty cells were inserted in the form above and below the new label control object. Select a control object or cell by clicking in the object or cell. Select adjacent control objects or cells by pressing and holding down the Shift key while clicking in each of the objects or cells. To select nonadjacent control objects or cells, press and hold down the Ctrl key while clicking in each of the objects or cells.

 Select Row

 Select Column

Select a row of cells by clicking the Select Row button in the Rows & Columns group or by right-clicking in a cell and then clicking *Select Entire Row* at the shortcut menu. To select a column of cells, click the Select Column button in the Rows & Columns group or right-click an object or cell and then click *Select Entire Column* at the shortcut menu. A column of cells can also be selected by positioning the mouse pointer at the top of the column until the pointer displays as a small black arrow that points down and then clicking the left mouse button.

The Rows & Columns group contains buttons for inserting a row or column of blank cells. To insert a new row, select a cell in a row and then click the Insert Above button to insert a row of blank cells above the current row or click the Insert Below button to insert a row of blank cells below the current row. Complete similar steps to insert a new column of blank cells to the left or right of the current column.

 Insert Above

 Insert Below

Merge adjacent selected cells by clicking the Merge button in the Merge/Split group on the Form Layout Tools Arrange tab. A cell can contain only one control object. So, merging two cells, each containing a control object, is not possible. A cell containing a control object can be merged with an empty cell or cells. Split a cell by clicking in the cell to make it active and then clicking the Split Vertically button or Split Horizontally button in the Merge/Split group. When a cell is split, an empty cell is created to the right of the cell or below the cell.

 Merge

 Split Vertically

 Split Horizontally

A row of cells can be moved up or down by selecting the row and then clicking the Move Up button in the Move group or the Move Down button. Use the Control Margins button in the Position group to increase or decrease margins within cells. The Position group also contains a Control Padding button for increasing or decreasing spacing between cells.

 Control Margins

 Control Padding

The Table group at the left side of the Form Layout Tools Arrange tab contains buttons for applying gridlines to cells and changing the layout of the cells to a stacked or columnar layout.

1. With the Clients form in **5-Dearborn.accdb** open in Design view, select and merge cells by completing the following steps:
   a. Click to the right of the text box control object containing the text *101*. (This selects the empty cell.)
   b. Press and hold down the Shift key, click to the right of the text box control object containing the text *Muncie*, and then release the Shift key. (This selects five adjacent cells.)
   c. Click the Form Layout Tools Arrange tab.
   d. Click the Merge button in the Merge/Split group.

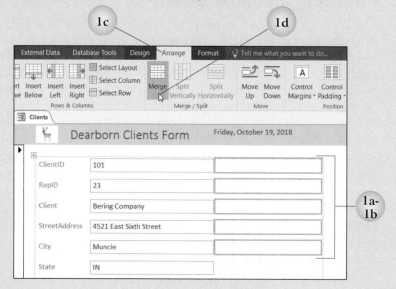

2. With the cells merged, insert an image control object and then insert an image by completing the following steps:
   a. Click the Form Layout Tools Design tab.
   b. Click the Image button in the Controls group.
   c. Move the mouse pointer (which displays as crosshairs with an image icon next to the crosshairs) to the location of the merged cell until the cell displays with pink fill color and then click the left mouse button.

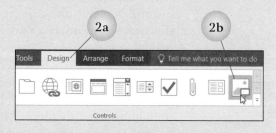

   d. At the Insert Picture dialog box, navigate to the AL1C5 folder on your storage medium and then double-click **Dearborn.jpg**.

3. Move down a row of cells by completing the following steps:
   a. Click the Form Layout Tools Arrange tab.
   b. Click in the control object containing the text *Telephone*.
   c. Click the Select Row button in the Rows & Columns group.
   d. Click the Move Down button in the Move group.
4. Decrease the margins within cells, increase the spacing (padding) between cells in the form, and apply gridlines by completing the following steps:
   a. If necessary, click the Form Layout Tools Arrange tab.
   b. Click the Select Layout button in the Rows & Columns group. (This selects all cells in the form table.)
   c. Click the Control Margins button in the Position group and then click *Narrow* at the drop-down list.

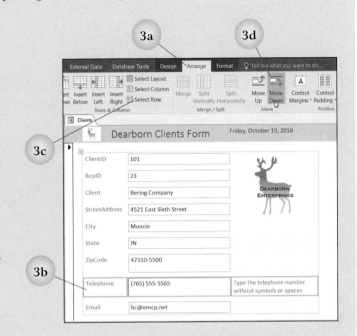

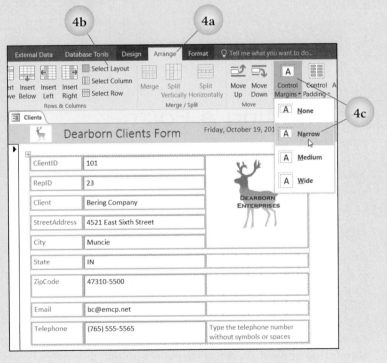

d. Click the Control Padding button in the Position group and then click *Medium* at the drop-down list.

e. Click the Gridlines button in the Table group and then click *Top* at the drop-down list.

f. Click the Gridlines button in the Table group, point to *Color*, and then click the *Orange, Accent 2, Darker 50%* option (sixth column, bottom row in the *Theme Colors* section).

5. Move the form table by completing the following steps:

a. Position the mouse pointer on the table move handle (which displays as a small square with a four-headed arrow inside in the upper left corner of the table).

b. Click and hold down the left mouse button, drag the form table up and to the left so it is positioned close to the top left border of the *Detail* section, and then release the mouse button.

6. Click in the control object containing the field name *ClientID*.

7. Save the Clients form.

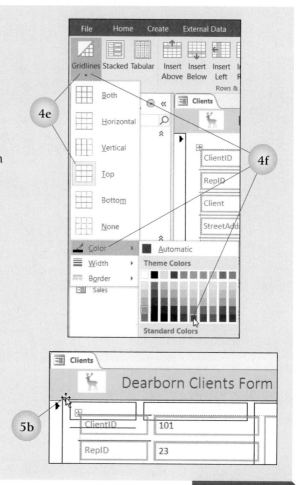

Check Your Work

Tutorial

Formatting a Form

Formatting a Form

Apply formatting to enhance the appearance of a form. Format a form by applying a theme, theme colors, and theme fonts; applying formatting with options on the Form Layout Tools Format tab; and applying conditional formatting that meets a specific criterion.

Hint Themes available in Access are the same as the themes available in Word, Excel, and PowerPoint.

Applying Themes

Access provides a number of themes for formatting objects in a database. A theme is a set of formatting choices that include a color theme (a set of colors) and a font theme (a set of heading and body text fonts). To apply a theme to a form, click the Themes button in the Themes group on the Form Layout Tools Design tab and then click a theme at the drop-down gallery. Position the mouse pointer over a theme and the live preview feature will display the form with the theme formatting applied. When a theme is applied, any new objects created in the database will be formatted with that theme.

 Themes

 Colors

 Fonts

Further customize the formatting of a form with the Colors button and the Fonts button in the Themes group on the Form Layout Tools Design tab. To customize the theme colors, click the Colors button in the Themes group and then click an option at the drop-down list. Change the theme fonts by clicking the Fonts button in the Themes group and then clicking an option at the drop-down list.

Formatting with the Form Layout Tools Format Tab

Click the Form Layout Tools Format tab and buttons and options display for applying formatting to a form or specific cells in a form. To apply formatting to a specific cell, click the cell in the form or click the Object button arrow in the Selection group and then click the control object at the drop-down list. To format all cells in the form, click the Select All button in the Selection group. This selects all cells in the form, including cells in the *Form Header* section. To select all of the cells in the *Detail* section (and not the *Form Header* section), click in a cell in the *Detail* section and then click the table move handle.

 Object

 Select All

Use buttons in the Font, Number, Background, and Control Formatting groups to apply formatting to a cell or selected cells in a form. Use options and buttons in the Font group to change the font, change the font size, apply text effects (such as bold and underline), and change the alignment of data in cells. If the form contains data with a Number or Currency data type, use buttons in the Number group to apply specific formatting to numbers. Insert a background image in the form using the Background Image button and apply formatting to cells with buttons in the Control Formatting group. Depending on what is selected in the form, some of the buttons may not be active.

Background Image

Project 1f Formatting a Form

Part 6 of 7

1. With the Clients form in **5-Dearborn.accdb** open and in Layout view, apply a theme by completing the following steps:
   a. Click the Form Layout Tools Design tab.
   b. Click the Themes button and then click the *Facet* option (second column, first row in the *Office* section).
2. Change the theme fonts by clicking the Fonts button in the Themes group and then clicking *Gill Sans MT* at the drop-down gallery. (You will need to scroll down the list to display *Gill Sans MT*.)
3. Change the theme colors by clicking the Colors button in the Themes group and then clicking *Orange* at the drop-down gallery.

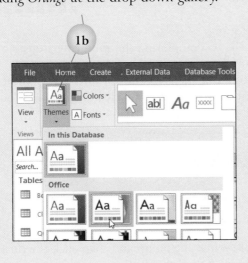

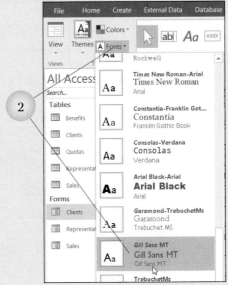

4. Change the font and font size of text in the form table by completing the following steps:
   a. Click in any cell containing a control object in the form table.
   b. Select all cells in the form table by clicking the table move handle in the upper left corner of the *Detail* section.
   c. Click the Form Layout Tools Format tab.
   d. Click the *Font* option box arrow, scroll down the drop-down list, and then click *Tahoma*. (Fonts are alphabetized in the drop-down list.)
   e. Click the *Font Size* option box arrow and then click *10* at the drop-down list.

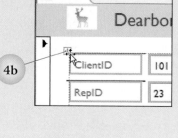

5. Apply formatting and change the alignment of the first column of cells by completing the following steps:
   a. Click in the control object containing the field name *ClientID*, press and hold down the Shift key, click in the bottom control object containing the field name *Telephone*, and then release the Shift key.
   b. Click the Bold button in the Font group.
   c. Click the Shape Fill button in the Control Formatting group and then click the *Brown, Accent 3, Lighter 60%* option (seventh column, third row in the *Theme Colors* section).
   d. Click the Shape Outline button in the Control Formatting group and then click the *Brown, Accent 3, Darker 50%* option (seventh column, bottom row in the *Theme Colors* section).
   e. Click the Align Right button in the Font group.
6. Apply shape fill to the second column of cells by completing the following steps:
   a. Click in the text box control object containing the text *101*.
   b. Position the mouse pointer at the top border of the selected cell until the pointer displays as a small black arrow that points down and then click the left mouse button. (Make sure all of the cells in the second column are selected.)

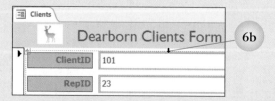

   c. Click the Shape Fill button in the Control Formatting group and then click the *Brown, Accent 3, Lighter 80%* option (seventh column, second row in the *Theme Colors* section).

7. Remove the gridlines by completing the following steps:
   a. Click the Form Layout Tools Arrange tab.
   b. Click the Select Layout button in the Rows & Columns group.
   c. Click the Gridlines button in the Table group and then click *None* at the drop-down list.
8. Click the Save button on the Quick Access Toolbar to save the Clients form.
9. Insert a background image by completing the following steps:
   a. Click the Form Layout Tools Format tab.
   b. Click the Background Image button in the Background group and then click *Browse* at the drop-down list.
   c. Navigate to the AL1C5 folder on your storage medium and then double-click **Mountain.jpg**.
   d. View the form and background image in Print Preview. (To display Print Preview, click the File tab, click the *Print* option, and then click the *Print Preview* option.)
   e. After viewing the form in Print Preview, return to the form by clicking the Close Print Preview button.
10. Click the Undo button on the Quick Access Toolbar to remove the background image. (If this does not remove the image, close the form without saving it and then reopen the form.)
11. Save the Clients form.

Check Your Work

Tutorial

Applying Conditional Formatting to a Form

Conditional Formatting

Quick Steps

Apply Conditional Formatting
1. Click Form Layout Tools Format tab.
2. Click Conditional Formatting button.
3. Click New Rule button.
4. Specify formatting.
5. Click OK.
6. Click OK.

Applying Conditional Formatting

Use the Conditional Formatting button in the Control Formatting group on the Form Layout Tools Format tab to apply formatting to data that meets a specific criterion. For example, conditional formatting can be applied to display sales amounts higher than a certain number in a different color, or to display certain state names in a specific color. Conditional formatting also can be applied that inserts data bars that visually compare data among records. The data bars provide a visual representation of the comparison. For example, in Project 1g, data bars will be inserted in the *Sales* field that provide a visual representation of how the sales amount in one record compares to the sales amounts in other records.

To apply conditional formatting, click the Conditional Formatting button in the Control Formatting group and the Conditional Formatting Rules Manager dialog box displays. At this dialog box, click the New Rule button and the New Formatting Rule dialog box displays, as shown in Figure 5.3. In the *Select a rule type* list box, choose the *Check values in the current record or use an expression* option if the conditional formatting is applied to a field in the record that matches a specific condition. Click the *Compare to other records* option to insert data bars in a field in all records that compare the data among the records.

Apply conditional formatting to a field by specifying the field and field condition with options in the *Edit the rule description* section of the dialog box. Specify the type of formatting to be applied to data in a field that meets the specific criterion. For example, in Project 1g, conditional formatting will be applied that changes the shape fill to a light green for all *City* fields containing the text *Indianapolis*. When all changes have been made at the dialog box, click OK to close the dialog box and then click OK to close the Conditional Formatting Rules Manager dialog box.

To insert data bars in a field, click the Conditional Formatting button, click the New Rule button at the Conditional Formatting Rules Manager dialog box, and then click the *Compare to other records* option in the *Select a rule type* list box. This changes the options in the dialog box, as shown in Figure 5.4. Make specific changes in the *Edit the rule description* section.

Figure 5.3 New Formatting Rule Dialog Box with the *Check values in the current record or use an expression* Option Selected

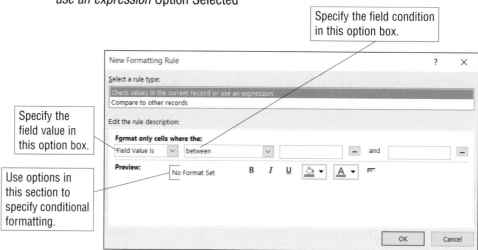

Figure 5.4 New Formatting Rule Dialog Box with the *Compare to other records* Option Selected

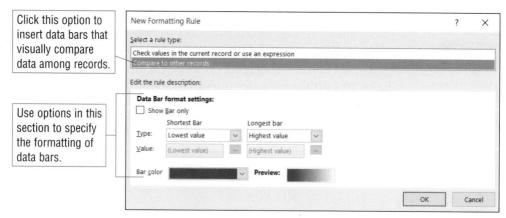

1. With the Clients form in **5-Dearborn.accdb** open and in Layout view, apply conditional formatting so that the *City* field displays all Indianapolis entries with a light green shape fill by completing the following steps:
   a. Click in the text box control object containing the text *Muncie*.
   b. Click the Form Layout Tools Format tab.
   c. Click the Conditional Formatting button in the Control Formatting group.
   d. At the Conditional Formatting Rules Manager dialog box, click the New Rule button.

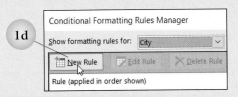

   e. At the New Formatting Rule dialog box, click the option box arrow for the option box containing the word *between* and then click *equal to* at the drop-down list.
   f. Click in the text box to the right of the *equal to* option box and then type Indianapolis.
   g. Click the Background color button arrow and then click the *Green 3* option (seventh column, fourth row).
   h. Click OK to close the New Formatting Rule dialog box.
   i. Click OK to close the Conditional Formatting Rules Manager dialog box.

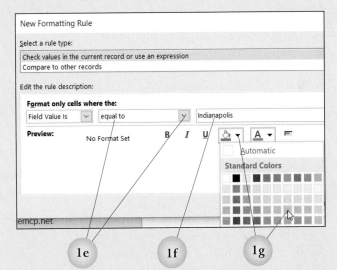

2. Click the Home tab and then click the View button to switch to Form view.
3. Click the Next record button to display the next record in the form. Continue clicking the Next record button to view records and notice that *Indianapolis* entries display with a light green shape fill.
4. Click the First record button in the Record Navigation bar.
5. Click the Save button on the Quick Access Toolbar.
6. Print page 1 of the form by completing the following steps:
   a. Click the File tab and then click the *Print* option.
   b. Click the next *Print* option.
   c. At the Print dialog box, click the *Pages* option in the *Print Range* section, type 1 in the *From* text box, press the Tab key, and then type 1 in the *To* text box.
   d. Click OK.
7. Close the Clients form.
8. Open the Sales form and switch to Layout View by clicking the View button in the Views group on the Home tab.

9. With the text box control object containing the sales ID number *1* selected, drag the right border to the left until *Lines: 1 Characters: 21* displays at the left side of the Status bar.

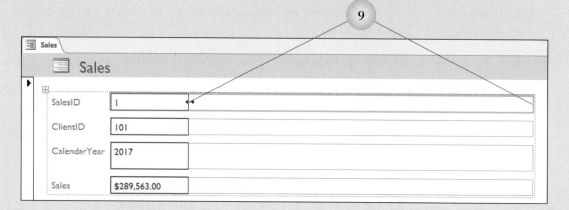

10. Change the alignment of text by completing the following steps:
    a. Right-click the selected text box control object (the object containing *1*) and then click *Select Entire Column* at the shortcut menu.
    b. Click the Form Layout Tools Format tab.
    c. Click the Align Right button in the Font group.
11. Apply data bars to the *Sales* field by completing the following steps:
    a. Click in the text box control object containing the amount *$289,563.00*.
    b. Make sure the Form Layout Tools Format tab is active.
    c. Click the Conditional Formatting button.
    d. At the Conditional Formatting Rules Manager dialog box, click the New Rule button.
    e. At the New Formatting Rule dialog box, click the *Compare to other records* option in the *Select a rule type* list box.
    f. Click the *Bar color* option box arrow and then click the *Green 4* option (seventh column, fifth row).
    g. Click OK to close the New Formatting Rule dialog box and then click OK to close the Conditional Formatting Rules Manager dialog box.

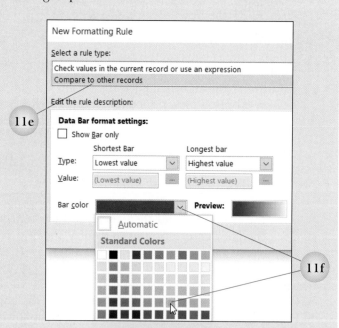

12. Click the Next record button in the Record Navigation bar to display the next record. Continue clicking the Next record button and notice the data bars that display in the *Sales* field.
13. Click the First record button in the Record Navigation bar.
14. Click the Save button on the Quick Access Toolbar.

15. Print page 1 of the form by completing the following steps:
    a. Click the File tab and then click the *Print* option.
    b. Click the next *Print* option.
    c. At the Print dialog box, click the *Selected Record(s)* option in the *Print Range* section and then click OK.
16. Close the Sales form.
17. Close **5-Dearborn.accdb**.

Check Your Work

Project 2 Add Fields, Create a Split Form and Multiple Items Form, and Use the Form Wizard   6 Parts

You will open the Skyline database, create a form and add related fields and a calculation to the form, create a split and multiple items form, and create a form using the Form Wizard.

Preview Finished Project

Tutorial

Adding an
Existing Field to
a Form

 Add Existing
Fields

Hint Alt + F8 is the keyboard shortcut to display the Field List task pane.

Hint Use the Field List task pane to add fields from a table or query to a form.

Quick Steps

Add Existing Field to Form
1. Click Add Existing Fields button on Form Layout Tools Design tab.
2. Drag field from Field List task pane to specific location in form.

Adding an Existing Field

A field can be inserted into an existing form by opening the form in Layout view and then clicking the Add Existing Fields button in the Tools group on the Form Layout Tools Design tab. Clicking the Add Existing Field button displays the Field List task pane at the right side of the screen. This task pane displays the fields available in the current view, fields available in related tables, and fields available in other tables. Figure 5.5 displays the Field List task pane that will be opened in Project 2a.

In the *Fields available for this view* section, Access displays all fields in any tables used to create the form. So far, forms in projects have been created using all fields in one table. In the *Fields available in related tables* section, Access displays tables that are related to the table(s) used to create the form. To display the fields in the related table, click the expand button (plus symbol in a square) that displays before the table name in the Field List task pane and the list expands to display all of the field names.

To add a field to the form, double-click the field in the Field List task pane. This inserts the field below the active control object in the form. Another method for inserting a field is to drag the field from the Field List task pane into the form. To do this, position the mouse pointer on the field in the Field List task pane, click and hold down the left mouse button, drag into the form, and then release the mouse button. A pink insert indicator bar displays when dragging the field into the existing fields in the form. Drag over an empty cell and the cell displays with pink fill. When the pink insert indicator bar is in the desired position or the cell is selected, release the mouse button.

Multiple fields can be inserted in a form from the Field List task pane. To do this, press and hold down the Ctrl key while clicking specific fields and then drag the fields into the form. Trying to drag a field from a table in the *Fields available in other tables* section will cause the Specify Relationship dialog box to display. To move a field from the Field List task pane to the form, the field must be in a table that is related to the table(s) used to create the form.

Figure 5.5 Field List Task Pane

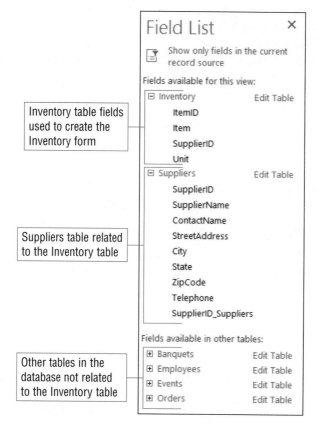

Inventory table fields used to create the Inventory form

Suppliers table related to the Inventory table

Other tables in the database not related to the Inventory table

Project 2a Adding Existing Fields to a Form

Part 1 of 6

1. Open **5-Skyline.accdb** from the AL1C5 folder on your storage medium and enable the content.
2. Create a form with the Inventory table by clicking *Inventory* in the Tables group in the Navigation pane, clicking the Create tab, and then clicking the Form button in the Forms group.
3. With the text box control object containing the text *001* selected, drag the right border to the left until the selected object is approximately one-half the original width.

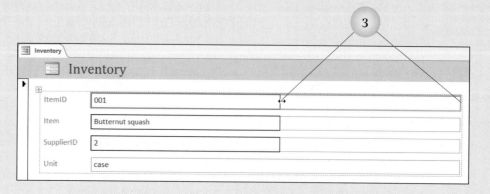

4. With the text box control object still selected, click the Form Layout Tools Arrange tab and then click the Split Horizontally button in the Merge/Split group. (This splits the text box control object into one object and one empty cell.)
5. You decide that you want to add the supplier name to the form so the name displays when entering data in the form. Add the *SupplierName* field by completing the following steps:
   a. Click the Form Layout Tools Design tab.
   b. Click the Add Existing Fields button in the Tools group.
   c. Click the <u>Show all tables</u> hyperlink that displays in the Field List task pane.
   d. Click the expand button immediately left of the Suppliers table name in the *Fields available in related tables* section of the Field List task pane.

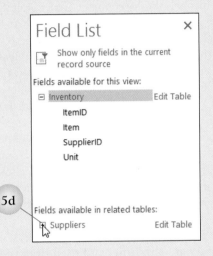

e. Position the mouse pointer on the *SupplierName* field, click and hold down the left mouse button, drag into the form until the pink insert indicator bar displays immediately right of the text box control containing the *2* (the text box control at the right side of the *SupplierID* label control), and then release the mouse button. Access inserts the field as a Lookup field (a down arrow displays at the right side of the field).

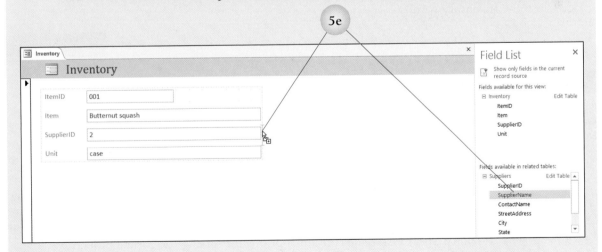

f. Change the *SupplierName* field from a Lookup field to a text box by clicking the Options button that displays below the field and then clicking *Change to Text Box* at the drop-down list. (This removes the down arrow at the right side of the field.)

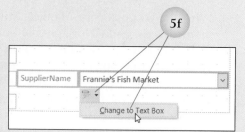

g. Close the Field List task pane by clicking the Close button in the upper right corner of the task pane.

6. Insert a logo image in the *Form Header* section by completing the following steps:
   a. Right-click the logo object that displays in the *Form Header* section (to the left of the title *Inventory*) and then click *Delete* at the shortcut menu.
   b. Click the Logo button in the Header/Footer group.
   c. At the Insert Picture dialog box, navigate to the AL1C5 folder on your storage medium and then double-click the file named ***Cityscape.jpg***.

7. Change the title by completing the following steps:
   a. Click the Title button in the Header/Footer group. (This selects *Inventory* in the *Form Header* section.)
   b. Type Skyline Inventory Input Form and then press the Enter key.

8. Insert the date and time in the *Form Header* section by clicking the Date and Time button in the Header/Footer group and then clicking OK at the Date and Time dialog box.

9. Click in any field outside the title, click the title to select the control object, and then drag the right border of the title control object to the left until the border displays near the title.

10. Select the date and time control objects, drag in the left border until the border displays near the date and time, and then drag the objects so they are positioned near the title.

11. Scroll through the records in the form.

12. Click the First record button in the Record Navigation bar.

13. Click the Save button on the Quick Access Toolbar and save the form with the name *Inventory*.

14. Print the current record.

15. Close the Inventory form.

Check Your Work

Tutorial

Inserting a Calculation in a Form

Inserting a Calculation in a Form

A calculation can be inserted in a form in a text box control object. To insert a text box control object as well as a label control object, click the Text Box button in the gallery in the Controls group on the Form Layout Tools Design tab, and then click in the location in the form where the two objects are to display. Click in the label control box and then type a label for the calculated field.

Insert a calculation by clicking in the text box control object and then clicking the Property Sheet button in the Tools group on the Form Layout Tools Design tab. This displays the Property Sheet task pane at the right side of the screen. The Property Sheet task pane contains options for setting the form's properties. To insert a calculation in the text box, click the Data tab in the Property Sheet task pane, click in the *Control Source* property box, and then type the calculation.

Quick Steps

Insert Calculation in Form

1. Click Text Box button on Form Layout Tools Design tab.
2. Click in form to insert label and text box control objects.
3. Click in text box control object.
4. Click Property Sheet button in Tools group.
5. Click Data tab.
6. Click in *Control Source* property box.
7. Type calculation.
8. Click Close button.

Type a calculation in the *Control Source* property box using mathematical operators such as the plus symbol (+) for addition, hyphen (-) for subtraction, the asterisk (*) for multiplication, and the forward slash symbol (/) for division. Type field names in the calculation inside square brackets. A field name must be typed in the calculation as it appears in the source object. For example, in Project 2b the calculation =*[AmountTotal]-[AmountPaid]* will be inserted in a text box control object to determine the amount due on banquet reservations. Notice that the calculation begins with the equals sign, the field names are typed inside brackets, and the hyphen is used to indicate subtraction. This calculation will subtract the amount paid for a banquet event from the banquet event total amount.

If a calculation result is currency, apply currency formatting to the text box control object. Apply currency formatting by clicking the Form Layout Tools Format tab and then clicking the Apply Currency Format button in the Number group.

Project 2b Inserting a Calculation in a Form

1. With **5-Skyline.accdb** open, create a form with the AmountDue query using the Form button in the Forms group on the Create tab.
2. With the form open in Layout view, insert a text box control by completing the following steps:
   a. Click the Text Box button in the gallery in the Controls group on the Form Layout Tools Design tab.
   b. Position the crosshair below the *AmountPaid* field (the pink insert indicator bar displays below the field) and then click the left mouse button. (This inserts a label control object and a text box control object in the form.)

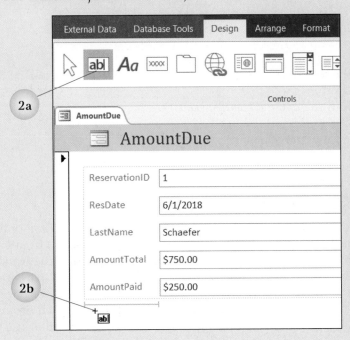

3. Name the new field by clicking in the label control object, double-clicking the text in the label control object, and then typing AmountDue.

4. Click in the text box control object and then insert a calculation by completing the following steps:
   a. Click the Property Sheet button in the Tools group on the Form Layout Tools Design tab.
   b. At the Property Sheet task pane, click the Data tab.
   c. Click in the *Control Source* property box.
   d. Type =[AmountTotal]-[AmountPaid] and then press the Enter key.
   e. Close the Property Sheet task pane by clicking the Close button in the upper right corner of the task pane.

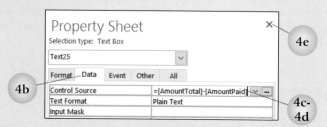

5. With the text box control object still selected, apply currency formatting by completing the following steps:
   a. Click the Form Layout Tools Format tab.
   b. Click the Apply Currency Format button in the Number group.

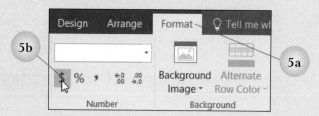

6. Scroll through the records in the form by clicking the Next record button and then click the First record button.
7. Save the form with the name *BanquetAmountsDue*.
8. Print the first page of the form.
9. Close the BanquetAmountsDue form.

Check Your Work

Tutorial

Creating a Split Form and Multiple Items Form

 More Forms

Quick Steps

Create a Split Form
1. Click table.
2. Click Create tab.
3. Click More Forms button.
4. Click *Split Form.*

Creating a Split Form

Another method for creating a form is to use the *Split Form* option at the More Forms button drop-down list in the Forms group on the Create tab. Use this option to create a form and Access splits the screen in the work area and provides two views of the form. The top half of the work area displays the form in Layout view and the bottom half of the work area displays the form in Datasheet view. The two views are connected and are synchronous, which means that displaying or modifying a specific field in the Layout view portion will cause the same action to occur in the field in the Datasheet view portion. Figure 5.6 displays the split form that will be created in Project 2c.

Figure 5.6 Split Form

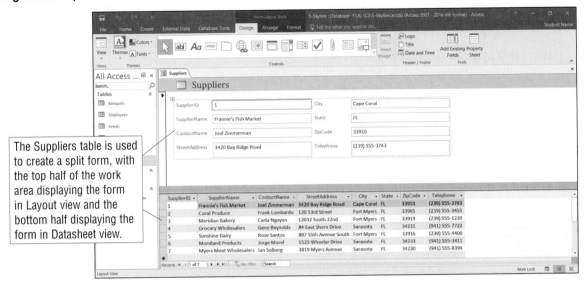

The Suppliers table is used to create a split form, with the top half of the work area displaying the form in Layout view and the bottom half displaying the form in Datasheet view.

Project 2c Creating a Split Form

Part 3 of 6

1. With **5-Skyline.accdb** open, create a split form with the Suppliers table by completing the following steps:
   a. Click *Suppliers* in the Tables group in the Navigation pane.
   b. Click the Create tab.
   c. Click the More Forms button in the Forms group and then click *Split Form* at the drop-down list.

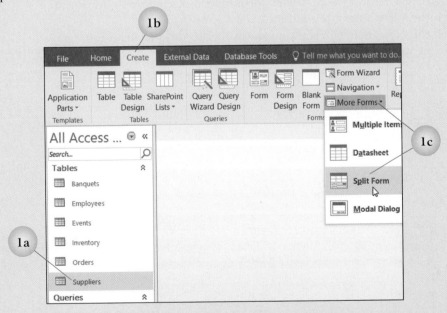

   d. Click several times on the Next record button in the Record Navigation bar. (As you display records, notice that the current record in the Form view in the top portion of the window is the same record selected in Datasheet view in the lower portion of the window.)
   e. Click the First record button.

2. Apply a theme by clicking the Themes button in the Themes group on the Form Layout Tools Design tab and then clicking *Integral* at the drop-down gallery (fourth column, first row in the *Office* section).

3. Insert a logo image in the *Form Header* section by completing the following steps:
   a. Right-click the logo object that displays in the *Form Header* section (to the left of the title *Suppliers*) and then click *Delete* at the shortcut menu.
   b. Click the Logo button in the Header/Footer group.
   c. At the Insert Picture dialog box, navigate to the AL1C5 folder on your storage medium and then double-click *Cityscape.jpg*.

4. Change the title by completing the following steps:
   a. Click the Title button in the Header/Footer group. (This selects *Suppliers* in the *Form Header* section.)
   b. Type Skyline Suppliers Input Form and then press the Enter key.
   c. Click in any field outside the title, click the title again to select the control object, and then drag the right border to the left until the border displays near the title.

5. Click the text box control object containing the supplier identification number *1*, and then drag the right border of the text box control object to the left until *Lines: 1 Characters: 25* displays at the left side of the Status bar.

6. Click the text box control object containing the city *Cape Coral* and drag the right border of the text box control object to the left until *Lines: 1 Characters: 25* displays at the left side of the Status bar.

7. Insert a new record in the Suppliers form by completing the following steps:
   a. Click the View button to switch to Form view.
   b. Click the New (blank) record button in the Record Navigation bar.
   c. Click in the *SupplierID* field in the Form view portion of the window and then type the following information in the specified fields:

SupplierID	8
SupplierName	Jackson Produce
ContactName	Marshall Jackson
StreetAddress	5790 Cypress Avenue
City	Fort Myers
State	FL
ZipCode	33917
Telephone	2395555002

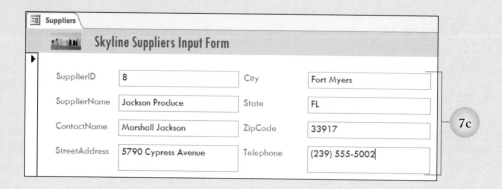

8. Click the Save button on the Quick Access Toolbar and save the form with the name *Suppliers*.
9. Print the current form by completing the following steps:
   a. Click the File tab and then click the *Print* option.
   b. Click the next *Print* option.
   c. At the Print dialog box, click the Setup button.
   d. At the Page Setup dialog box, click the *Print Form Only* option in the *Split Form* section of the dialog box and then click OK.
   e. At the Print dialog box, click the *Selected Record(s)* option and then click OK.
10. Close the Suppliers form.

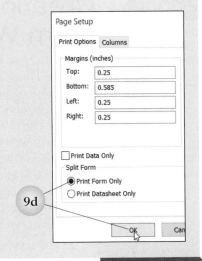

Check Your Work

Creating a Multiple Items Form

Create a Multiple Items Form
1. Click table.
2. Click Create tab.
3. Click More Forms button.
4. Click *Multiple Items.*

When a form is created with the Form button, a single record displays. Use the *Multiple Items* option at the More Forms button drop-down list to create a form that displays multiple records. The advantage to creating a multiple items form over displaying the table in Datasheet view is that the form can be customized using buttons on the Form Layout Tools ribbon with the Design, Arrange, or Format tab selected.

Project 2d Creating a Multiple Items Form

Part 4 of 6

1. With **5-Skyline.accdb** open, create a multiple items form by completing the following steps:
   a. Click *Orders* in the Tables group in the Navigation pane.
   b. Click the Create tab.
   c. Click the More Forms button in the Forms group and then click *Multiple Items* at the drop-down list.
2. Delete the existing logo and then insert the **Cityscape.jpg** image as the logo.
3. Type Skyline Orders as the title.
4. Click in any field outside the title, click the title again to select the control object, and then drag the right border to the left until the border displays near the title.
5. Save the form with the name *Orders*.
6. Print the first page of the form by completing the following steps:
   a. Click the File tab and then click the *Print* option.
   b. Click the next *Print* option.
   c. At the Print dialog box, click the *Pages* option in the *Print Range* section.
   d. Type 1 in the *From* text box, press the Tab key, and then type 1 in the *To* text box.
   e. Click OK.
7. Close the Orders form.

Check Your Work

Access Level 1 | Unit 2

Chapter 5 | Creating Forms **165**

Creating a Form Using the Form Wizard

Access offers a Form Wizard that provides steps for creating a form. To create a form using the Form Wizard, click the Create tab and then click the Form Wizard button in the Forms group. At the first Form Wizard dialog box, shown in Figure 5.7, specify the table or query and then the fields to be included in the form. To select the table or query, click the *Table/Queries* option box arrow and then click the table or query at the drop-down list. Select a field in the *Available Fields* list box and then click the One Field button (the button containing the greater-than [>] symbol). This inserts the field in the *Selected Fields* list box. Continue in this manner until all of the fields have been inserted in the *Selected Fields* list box. To insert all of the fields into the *Selected Fields* list box at one time, click the All Fields button (the button containing two greater-than symbols). After specifying the fields, click the Next button.

At the second Form Wizard dialog box, specify the layout for the records. Choose from these layout type options: *Columnar, Tabular, Datasheet,* and *Justified.* Click the Next button and the third and final Form Wizard dialog box displays. It offers a title for the form and also provides the option *Open the form to view or enter information.* Make any necessary changes in this dialog box and then click the Finish button.

Figure 5.7 First Form Wizard Dialog Box

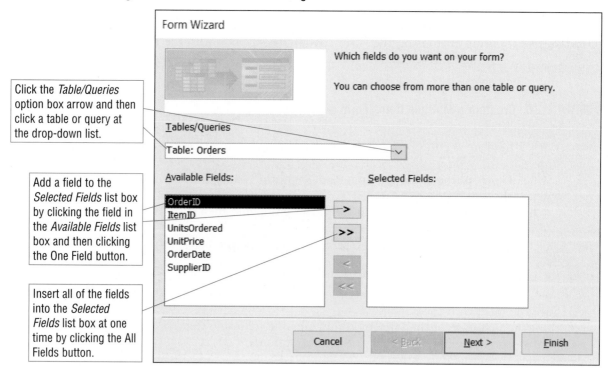

Click the *Table/Queries* option box arrow and then click a table or query at the drop-down list.

Add a field to the *Selected Fields* list box by clicking the field in the *Available Fields* list box and then clicking the One Field button.

Insert all of the fields into the *Selected Fields* list box at one time by clicking the All Fields button.

1. With **5-Skyline.accdb** open, create a form with the Form Wizard by completing the following steps:
   a. Click the Create tab.
   b. Click the Form Wizard button in the Forms group.
   c. At the first Form Wizard dialog box, click the *Tables/Queries* option box arrow and then click *Table: Employees* at the drop-down list.
   d. Specify that you want all of the fields included in the form by clicking the All Fields button (the button containing the two greater-than symbols).

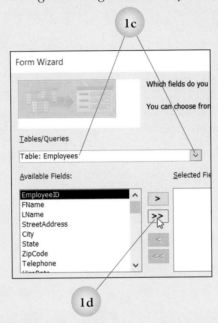

   e. Click the Next button.
   f. At the second Form Wizard dialog box, click the *Justified* option and then click the Next button.
   g. At the third and final Form Wizard dialog box, click the Finish button.
2. Format the field headings by completing the following steps:
   a. Click the View button to switch to Layout view.
   b. Click the *EmployeeID* label control object. (This selects the object.)

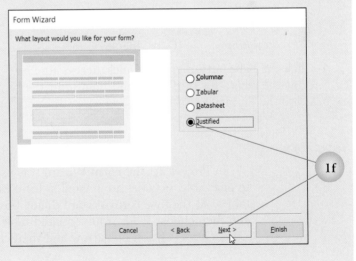

c. Press and hold down the Ctrl key and then click each of the following label control objects: *FName*, *LName*, *StreetAddress*, *City*, *State*, *ZipCode*, *Telephone*, *HireDate*, and *HealthIns*.

d. With all of the label control objects selected, release the Ctrl key.

e. Click the Form Layout Tools Format tab.

f. Click the Shape Fill button and then click the *Aqua Blue 2* option (ninth column, third row in the *Standard Colors* section).

g. Click the Form Layout Tools Design tab and then click the View button to switch to Form view.

3. In Form view, click the New (blank) record button and then add the following records:

EmployeeID	13
FName	Carol
LName	Thompson
StreetAddress	6554 Willow Drive, Apt. B
City	Fort Myers
State	FL
ZipCode	33915
Telephone	2395553719
HireDate	10/1/2018
HealthIns	(Click the check box to insert a check mark.)

EmployeeID	14
FName	Eric
LName	Hahn
StreetAddress	331 South 152nd Street
City	Cape Coral
State	FL
ZipCode	33906
Telephone	2395558107
HireDate	10/1/2018
HealthIns	(Leave blank.)

4. Click the Save button on the Quick Access Toolbar.

5. Print the record for Eric Hahn and then print the record for Carol Thompson.

6. Close the Employees form.

Check Your Work

In Project 2e, the Form Wizard was used to create a form with all of the fields in one table. If tables are related, a form can be created using fields from related tables. At the first Form Wizard dialog box, choose fields from the selected table and then choose fields from a related table. To change to a related table, click the *Tables/Queries* option box arrow and then click the name of the related table.

1. With **5-Skyline.accdb** open, create a form with related tables by completing the following steps:

   a. Click the Create tab.

   b. Click the Form Wizard button in the Forms group.

   c. At the first Form Wizard dialog box, click the *Tables/ Queries* option box arrow and then click *Table: Banquets*.

   d. Click *ResDate* in the *Available Fields* list box and then click the One Field button. (This inserts *ResDate* in the *Selected Fields* list box.)

   e. Click *AmountTotal* in the *Available Fields* list box and then click the One Field button.

   f. With *AmountPaid* selected in the *Available Fields* list box, click the One Field button.

   g. Click the *Tables/Queries* option box arrow and then click *Table: Events* at the drop-down list.

   h. Click *Event* in the *Available Fields* list box and then click the One Field button.

   i. Click the *Tables/Queries* option box arrow and then click *Table: Employees* at the drop-down list.

   j. Click *LName* in the *Available Fields* list box and then click the One Field button.

   k. Click the Next button.

   l. At the second Form Wizard dialog box, click the Next button.

   m. At the third Form Wizard dialog box, click the Next button.

   n. At the fourth Form Wizard dialog box, select the text in the *What title do you want for your form?* text box, type Upcoming Banquets, and then click the Finish button.

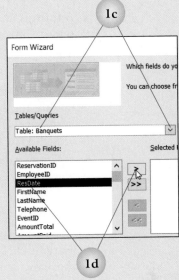

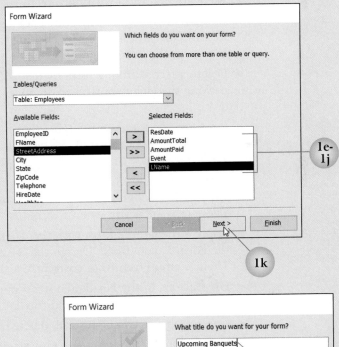

2. When the first record displays, print the record.

3. Save and then close the form.

4. Close **5-Skyline.accdb**.

Check Your Work

Chapter Summary

- Creating a form generally improves the ease of entering data into a table. Some methods for creating a form include using the Form, Split Form, and Multiple Items buttons or the Form Wizard.

- A form is an object used to enter and edit data in a table or query and to help prevent incorrect data from being entered in a database.

- The simplest method for creating a form is to click a table in the Navigation pane, click the Create button, and then click the Form button in the Forms group.

- Create a form and it displays in Layout view. Use this view to display data and modify the appearance and contents of the form. Other form views include Form view and Design view. Use Form view to enter and manage records and use Design view to view and modify the structure of the form.

- Open an existing form in Layout view by right-clicking the form in the Navigation pane and then clicking *Layout View* at the shortcut menu.

- Print a form with options at the Print dialog box. To print an individual record, display the Print dialog box, click the *Selected Record(s)* option, and then click OK.

- Delete a form with the Delete button in the Records group on the Home tab or by right-clicking the form in the Navigation pane and then clicking *Delete* at the shortcut menu. A message may display asking to confirm the deletion.

- Navigate in a form with buttons in the Record Navigation bar.

- Add a new record to a form by clicking the New (blank) record button in the Record Navigation bar or by clicking the Home tab and then clicking the New button in the Records group.

- Delete a record from a form by displaying the record, clicking the Home tab, clicking the Delete button arrow, and then clicking *Delete Record* at the drop-down list.

- If a form is created with a table that has a one-to-many relationship established, Access adds a datasheet at the bottom of the form.

- A form is made up of cells arranged in rows and columns and each cell can contain one control object. Customize control objects with buttons on the Form Layout Tools ribbon with the Design tab, Arrange tab, or Format tab selected. These tabs are active when a form displays in Layout view.

- Apply a theme to a form with the Themes button in the Themes group on the Form Layout Tools Design tab. Use the Colors and Fonts buttons in the Themes group to further customize a theme.

- Use buttons in the Header/Footer group on the Form Layout Tools Design tab to insert a logo, form title, and the date and time.

- Control objects can be resized, deleted, and inserted in Layout view.

- Use buttons in the Rows & Columns group on the Form Layout Tools Arrange tab to select or insert rows or columns of cells.

- The Controls group on the Form Layout Tools Design tab contains control objects that can be inserted in a form.

- Merge cells in a form by selecting cells and then clicking the Merge button in the Merge/Split group on the Form Layout Tools Arrange tab. Split selected cells by clicking the Split Vertically or Split Horizontally button.

- Format cells in a form with buttons on the Form Layout Tools Format tab.
- Use the Conditional Formatting button in the Control Formatting group on the Form Layout Tools Format tab to apply formatting to data that matches a specific criterion.
- Click the Add Existing Fields button in the Tools group on the Form Layout Tools Design tab to display the Field List task pane. Add fields to the form by double-clicking a field or dragging the field from the task pane to the form.
- Insert a calculation in a form by inserting a text box control object, displaying the Property Sheet task pane with the Data tab selected, and then typing the calculation in the *Control Source* property box. If a calculation result is currency, apply currency formatting with the Apply Currency Format button on the Form Layout Tools Format tab.
- Create a split form by clicking the More Forms button on the Create tab and then clicking *Split Form* in the drop-down list. Access displays the form in Layout view in the top portion of the work area and in Datasheet view in the bottom portion of the work area. The two views are connected and synchronous.
- Create a Multiple Items form by clicking the More Forms button on the Create tab and then clicking *Multiple Items* in the drop-down list.
- The Form Wizard provides steps for creating a form such as specifying the fields to be included in the form, a layout for the records, and a name for the form.
- A form can be created with the Form Wizard that contains fields from tables connected by a one-to-many relationship.

Commands Review

FEATURE	RIBBON TAB, GROUP	BUTTON, OPTION	KEYBOARD SHORTCUT
Conditional Formatting Rules Manager dialog box	Form Layout Tools Format, Control Formatting		
Field List task pane	Form Layout Tools Design, Tools		
form	Create, Forms		
Form Wizard	Create, Forms		
multiple items form	Create, Forms	, *Multiple Items*	
Property Sheet task pane	Form Layout Tools Design, Tools		Alt + Enter
split form	Create, Forms	, *Split Form*	

Microsoft®

Access®

Creating Reports and Mailing Labels

Performance Objectives

Precheck

Check your current skills to help focus your study.

Upon successful completion of Chapter 6, you will be able to:

1. Create a report using the Report button
2. Modify the record source
3. Select, edit, size, move, and delete control objects
4. Sort records
5. Find data
6. Display and customize a report in Print Preview
7. Delete a report
8. Format a report
9. Apply conditional formatting to data in a report
10. Group and sort records in a report
11. Insert a calculation in a report
12. Create a report using the Report Wizard
13. Create mailing labels using the Label Wizard

In this chapter, you will learn how to prepare reports from data in a table or query using the Report button in the Reports group on the Create tab and using the Report Wizard. You will also learn how to manage control objects, format, and insert a calculation in a report and create mailing labels using the Label Wizard.

Data Files

Before beginning chapter work, copy the AL1C6 folder to your storage medium and then make AL1C6 the active folder.

S
SNAP

If you are a SNAP user, launch the Precheck and Tutorials from your Assignments page.

Preview Finished Project

Creating a Report

Create a report in a database to control what data appears on the page when printed and how the data is formatted. Reports generally answer specific questions (queries). For example, a report could answer the question *What customers have submitted claims?* or *What products do we currently have on order?* The record source for a report can be a table or query. Create a report with the Report button in the Reports group or use the Report Wizard that provides steps for creating a report.

 Report

Creating a Report with the Report Button

To create a report with the Report button, click a table or query in the Navigation pane, click the Create tab, and then click the Report button in the Reports group. This displays the report in columnar style in Layout view with the Report Layout Tools Design tab active, as shown in Figure 6.1. Access creates the report using all of the fields in the table or query.

Figure 6.1 Report Created with Sales Table

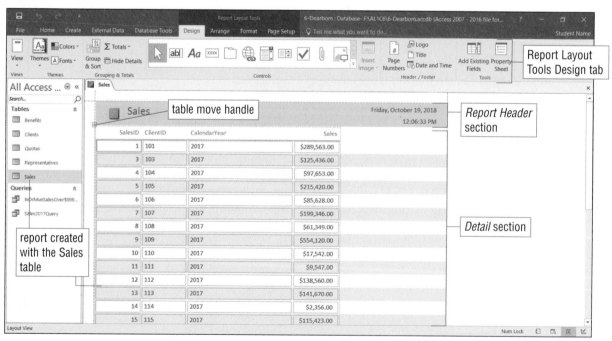

Modifying the Record Source

The record source for a report is the table or query used to create the report. If changes are made to the record source, such as adding or deleting records, those changes are reflected in the report. For example, in Project 1a, a report will be created based on the Sales table. A record will be added to the Sales table (the record source for the report) and the added record will display in the Sales report.

Project 1a **Creating a Report with the Report Button** Part 1 of 5

1. Open **6-Dearborn.accdb** from the AL1C6 folder on your storage medium and enable the content.
2. Create a report based on the Sales table by completing the following steps:
   a. Click *Sales* in the Tables group in the Navigation pane.
   b. Click the Create tab.
   c. Click the Report button in the Reports group.

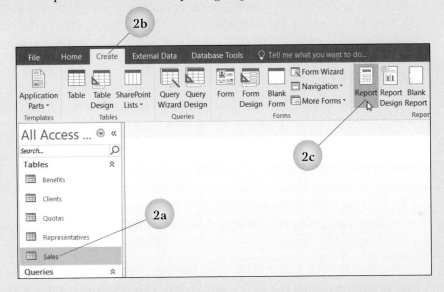

   d. Save the report by clicking the Save button on the Quick Access Toolbar and then clicking OK at the Save As dialog box. (This saves the report with the default name *Sales*.)
   e. Close the Sales report.
3. Add a record to the Sales table by completing the following steps:
   a. Double-click *Sales* in the Tables group in the Navigation pane. (Make sure you open the Sales table and not the Sales report.)
   b. Click the New button in the Records group on the Home tab.
   c. Press the Tab key to accept the default number in the *SalesID* field.
   d. Type 127 in the *ClientID* field and then press the Tab key.
   e. Type 2018 in the *CalendarYear* field and then press the Tab key.
   f. Type 176420 in the *Sales* field.
   g. Close the Sales table.
4. Open the Sales report and then scroll down to the bottom. Notice that the new record you added to the Sales table displays in the report.
5. Close the Sales report.

6. Use the Sales2017Query query to create a report by completing the following steps:
   a. Click *Sales2017Query* in the Queries group in the Navigation pane.
   b. Click the Create tab.
   c. Click the Report button in the Reports group.
7. Access automatically inserted a total amount for the *Sales* column of the report. Delete this amount by scrolling down to the bottom of the report, clicking the total amount at the bottom of the *Sales* column, and then pressing the Delete key. (This deletes the total amount but not the underline above the amount.)
8. Save the report by clicking the Save button on the Quick Access Toolbar, typing 2017Sales in the *Report Name* text box in the Save As dialog box, and then clicking OK.

> Check Your Work

Modifying a Report

Make modifications to a report as needed to address specific needs. For example, select, size, move, edit, or delete control objects in a report; sort records in ascending or descending order, and find data in a report. Use options in Print Preview to customize a report and, if the report is no longer needed, delete the report.

> Tutorial
>
> Managing Control Objects in a Report

Managing Control Objects

A report, like a form, is comprised of control objects, such as logos, titles, labels, and text boxes. Select a control object in a report by clicking the object and the object displays with an orange border. Click in a cell in the report and Access selects all of the objects in the column except the column heading. Select adjacent control objects by pressing and holding down the Shift key and then clicking objects or select nonadjacent control objects by pressing and holding down the Ctrl key and then clicking objects.

Like a form, a report contains a *Header* section and a *Detail* section. Select all of the control objects in the report in both the *Header* and *Detail* sections by pressing Ctrl + A. Control objects in the *Detail* section are contained in a report table. To select the control objects in the report table, click in any cell in the report and then click the table move handle. The table move handle is a small square with a four-headed arrow inside that displays in the upper left corner of the table (see Figure 6.1). Move the table and all of the control objects within the table by dragging the table move handle using the mouse.

Change the size of control objects by dragging the border of a selected control object or with the *Width* and *Height* property boxes in the Property Sheet task pane with the Data tab selected. To change the size of a control object by dragging, select the object (displays with an orange border) and then, using the mouse, drag a left or right border to increase or decrease the width or drag a top or bottom border to increase or decrease the height of the control object. When dragging the border of a control object, a line and character count displays at the left side of the Status bar. Use the line and character count numbers to adjust the width and/or height of the object by a precise line and character count number.

The width and height of a control object or column of control objects can be adjusted with the *Width* and *Height* property boxes in the Property Sheet task pane. Display this task pane by clicking the Property Sheet button in the Tools group. In the Property Sheet task pane, click the Data tab, select the current measurement in the *Width* or *Height* property box, type the new measurement, and then press the Enter key.

A selected control object can be moved by positioning the mouse pointer in the object until the pointer displays with a four-headed arrow attached. Click and hold down the left mouse button, drag to the new location, and then release the mouse button. To move a column of selected control objects, position the mouse pointer in the column heading until the pointer displays with a four-headed arrow attached and then click and drag to the new location. While dragging a control object(s), a pink insert indicator bar displays indicating where the control object(s) will be positioned when the mouse button is released.

Some control objects in a report, such as a column heading or title, are label control objects. Edit a label control by double-clicking in the label control object and then making the specific changes. For example, to rename a label control, double-click in the label control and then type the new name.

Sorting Records

 Ascending

 Descending

Sort data in a report by clicking in the field containing the data to be sorted and then clicking the Ascending button or the Descending button in the Sort & Filter group on the Home tab. Click the Ascending button to sort text in alphabetic order from A to Z, numbers from lowest to highest, and dates from earliest to latest. Click the Descending button to sort text in alphabetic order from Z to A, numbers from highest to lowest, and dates from latest to earliest.

Quick Steps

Sort Records
1. Click in field containing data.
2. Click Ascending button or Descending button.

 Find

Finding Data in a Report

Find specific data in a report with options at the Find dialog box. Display this dialog box by clicking the Find button in the Find group on the Home tab. At the Find dialog box, enter the search data in the *Find What* text box.

The *Match* option at the Find dialog box is set at *Whole Field* by default. At this setting, the data entered must match the entire entry in a field. To search for partial data in a field, change the *Match* option to *Any Part of Field* or *Start of Field*. If the text entered in the *Find What* text box needs to match the case in a field entry, click the *Match Case* check box to insert a check mark.

Access searches the entire report by default. This can be changed to *Up* to tell Access to search from the currently active field to the beginning of the report or *Down* to search from the currently active field to the end of the report. Click the Find Next button to find data that matches the data in the *Find What* text box.

Tutorial

Customizing a Report in Print Preview

 Print Preview

Displaying and Customizing a Report in Print Preview

When a report is created, the report displays in the work area in Layout view. In addition to Layout view, three other views are available: Report, Print Preview, and Design. Use Print Preview to display the report as it will appear when printed. To change to Print Preview, click the Print Preview button in the view area at the right side of the Status bar. Another method for displaying the report in Print Preview is to click the View button arrow in the Views group on the Home tab or Report Layout Tools Design tab and then click *Print Preview* at the drop-down list.

In Print Preview, send the report to the printer by clicking the Print button on the Print Preview tab. Use options in the Page Size group to change the page size and margins. To print only the report data and not the column headings, report title, shading, and gridlines, insert a check mark in the *Print Data Only* check box. Use options in the Page Layout group to specify the page orientation, specify the number and size of columns, and display the Page Setup dialog box. Click the Page Setup button and the Page Setup dialog box displays with options for customizing margins, orientation, size, and columns. The Zoom group contains options and buttons for specifying a zoom percentage and for displaying one, two, or multiples pages of the report.

Deleting a Report

Quick Steps

Delete a Report
1. Click report name in Navigation pane.
2. Click Delete button on Home tab.
3. Click Yes.
OR
1. Right-click report name in Navigation pane.
2. Click *Delete.*
3. Click Yes.

If a report is no longer needed in a database, delete the report. Delete a report by clicking the report name in the Navigation pane, clicking the Delete button in the Records group on the Home tab, and then clicking the Yes button at the confirmation message. Another method is to right-click the report in the Navigation pane, click *Delete* at the shortcut menu, and then click the Yes at the message. If a report is being deleted from the computer's hard drive, the confirmation message will not display. This is because Access automatically sends the deleted report to the Recycle Bin, where it can be retrieved at a later time, if necessary.

Project 1b **Adjusting Control Objects, Renaming Labels, Finding and Sorting**
Data, Displaying a Report in Print Preview, and Deleting a Report   **Part 2 of 5**

1. With the 2017Sales report open, reverse the order of the *RepName* and *Client* columns by completing the following steps:
   a. Make sure the report displays in Layout view.
   b. Click the *RepName* column heading.
   c. Press and hold down the Shift key, click in the first control object below the *RepName* column heading (the control object containing *Linda Foster*), and then release the Shift key.
   d. Position the mouse pointer inside the *RepName* column heading until the pointer displays with a four-headed arrow attached.
   e. Click and hold down the left mouse button, drag to the left until the vertical pink insert indicator bar displays to the left of the *Client* column, and then release the mouse button.
2. Sort the data in the *Sales* column in descending order by completing the following steps:
   a. Click the Home tab.
   b. Click in any field in the *Sales* column.
   c. Click the Descending button in the Sort & Filter group.
3. Rename the *RepName* label control as *Representative* by double-clicking in the label control object containing the text *RepName*, selecting *RepName*, and then typing Representative.

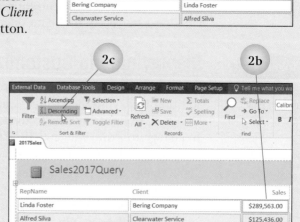

4. Double-click in the *Sales* label control and then rename it *Sales 2017*.
5. Move the report table by completing the following steps:
   a. Click in a cell in the report.
   b. Position the mouse pointer on the table move handle (a small square with a four-headed arrow inside that displays in the upper left corner of the table).
   c. Click and hold down the left mouse button, drag the report table to the right until it is centered between the left and right sides of the *Detail* section, and then release the mouse button. (When you drag with the mouse, you will see only outlines of some of the control objects.)

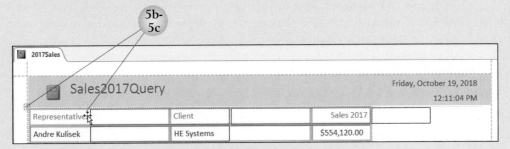

6. Display the report in Print Preview by clicking the Print Preview button in the view area at the right side of the Status bar.

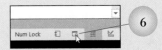

7. Click the One Page button (already active) in the Zoom group to display the entire page.
8. Click the Zoom button arrow in the Zoom group and then click *50%* at the drop-down list.
9. Click the One Page button in the Zoom group.

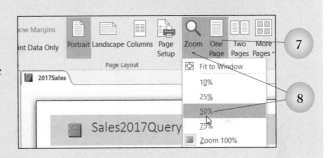

10. Print the report by clicking the Print button on the Print Preview tab and then clicking OK at the Print dialog box.
11. Close Print Preview by clicking the Close Print Preview button at the right side of the Print Preview tab.
12. Save and then close the 2017Sales report.
13. Create a report with the Representatives table by completing the following steps:
    a. Click *Representatives* in the Tables group in the Navigation pane.
    b. Click the Create tab.
    c. Click the Report button in the Reports group.
14. Adjust the width of the second column by completing the following steps:
    a. Click in the *RepName* column heading.
    b. Drag the right border of the selected column heading to the left until *Lines: 1 Characters: 16* displays at the left side of the Status bar, and then release the mouse button.
15. Complete steps similar to those in Step 14 to decrease the width of the third column (*Telephone*) to *Lines: 1 Characters: 12* and the fourth column (*Email*) to *Lines: 1 Characters: 13*.

16. Adjust the width of the *QuotaID* column and the width and height of the title control object by completing the following steps:
   a. Click in the *QuotaID* column heading.
   b. Click the Property Sheet button in the Tools group and, if necessary, click the Format tab.
   c. Select the current measurement in the *Width* property box, type 0.8, and then press the Enter key.
   d. Click *Representatives* in the title control object.
   e. Select the current measurement in the *Width* property box, type 2, and then press the Enter key.
   f. With the current measurement selected in the *Height* property box, type 0.6.
   g. Close the Property Sheet task pane by clicking the Close button in the upper right corner of the task pane.
17. Search for fields containing a quota of *2* by completing the following steps:
   a. Click in the *RepID* column heading.
   b. Click the Home tab and then click the Find button in the Find group.
   c. At the Find dialog box, type 2 in the *Find What* text box.
   d. Make sure the *Match* option is set to *Whole Field*. (If not, click the *Match* option box arrow and then click *Whole Field* at the drop-down list.)
   e. Click the Find Next button.
   f. Continue clicking the Find Next button until a message displays stating that Access has finished searching the records. Click OK at the message.
   g. Click the Cancel button to close the Find dialog box.

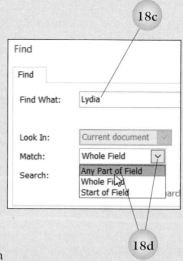

18. Suppose you want to find information on a representative and you remember the first name but not the last name. Search for a field containing the first name *Lydia* by completing the following steps:
   a. Click in the *RepID* column heading.
   b. Click the Find button in the Find group.
   c. At the Find dialog box, type Lydia in the *Find What* text box.
   d. Click the *Match* option box arrow and then click *Any Part of Field* at the drop-down list.
   e. Click the Find Next button. (Access will find and select the representative name *Lydia Alvarado*.)
   f. Click the Cancel button to close the Find dialog box.
19. Click the control object at the bottom of the *RepID* column containing the number *17* and then press the Delete key. (This does not delete the underline above the amount.)

20. Switch to Print Preview by clicking the View button arrow in the Views group on the Home tab and then clicking *Print Preview* at the drop-down list.
21. Click the Margins button in the Page Size group and then click *Normal* at the drop-down list.

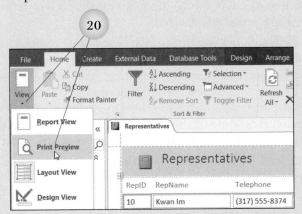

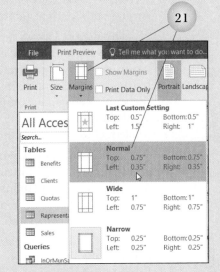

22. Decrease column width (so gray shading does not print on a second page) by completing the following steps:
    a. Click the Columns button in the Page Layout group on the Print Preview tab.
    b. Select the current measurement in the *Width* measurement box in the *Column Size* section of the dialog box and then type 8.
    c. Click OK to close the dialog box.

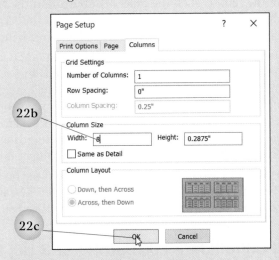

23. Print the report by clicking the Print button at the left side of the Print Preview tab and then clicking OK at the Print dialog box.
24. Close Print Preview by clicking the Close Print Preview button.
25. Save the report with the name *Representatives*.
26. Close the Representatives report.
27. Delete the Sales report by right-clicking *Sales* in the Reports group in the Navigation pane, clicking *Delete* at the shortcut menu, and then cicking Yes at the confirmation message.

Check Your Work

Formatting a Report

Customize a report in much the same manner as customizing a form. When a report is created, the report displays in Layout view and the Report Layout Tools Design tab is active. Customize control objects in the *Detail* section and the *Header* section with buttons on the Report Layout Tools ribbon with the Design tab, Arrange tab, Format tab, or Page Setup tab selected.

 Totals

The Report Layout Tools Design tab contains many of the same options as the Form Layout Tools Design tab. Use options on this tab to apply a theme, insert controls, insert header or footer data, and add existing fields. Use the Totals button in the Grouping & Totals group to perform calculations, such as finding the sum, average, maximum, or minimum of the numbers in a column. To use the Totals button, click in the column heading of the column containing the data to be totaled, click the Totals button, and then click a function at the drop-down list.

Hint The themes available in Access are the same as the themes available in Word, Excel, and PowerPoint.

Click the Report Layout Tools Arrange tab and options display for inserting and selecting rows, splitting cells horizontally and vertically, moving data up or down, controlling margins, and changing the padding between cells. The options on the Report Layout Tools Arrange tab are the same as the options on the Form Layout Tools Arrange tab.

Select and format data in a report with options on the Report Layout Tools Format tab. The options on this tab are the same as the options on the Form Layout Tools Format tab. Use options to apply formatting to a report or specific objects in a report. To apply formatting to a specific object, click the object in the report or click the Object button arrow in the Selection group on the Report Layout Tools Format tab and then click the object at the drop-down list. To format all objects in the report, click the Select All button in the Selection group. This selects all objects in the report, including objects in the *Header* section. To select all of the objects in the report table, click the table move handle.

 Background

Use buttons in the Font, Number, Background, and Control Formatting groups to apply formatting to a cell or selected cells in a report. Use buttons in the Font group to change the font, apply a different font size, apply text effects (such as bold and underline), and change the alignment of data in objects. Insert a background image in the report using the Background button and apply formatting to cells with buttons in the Control Formatting group. Depending on what is selected in the report, some of the buttons may not be active.

Click the Report Layout Tools Page Setup tab and the buttons that display are also available in Print Preview. For example, the tab contains buttons for changing the page size and page layout of the report and displaying the Page Setup dialog box.

Applying Conditional Formatting to a Report

Apply conditional formatting to a report in the same manner as applying conditional formatting to a form (covered in Chapter 5). Click the Conditional Formatting button in the Control Formatting group on the Report Layout Tools Format tab and the Conditional Formatting Rules Manager dialog box displays. Click the New Rule button and then use options in the New Formatting Rule dialog box to specify the conditional formatting.

 Conditional
Formatting

1. With **6-Dearborn.accdb** open, open the 2017Sales report.
2. Display the report in Layout view.
3. Click the Themes button in the Themes group on the Report Layout Tools Design tab and then click *Ion* at the drop-down gallery.
4. Click the Title button in the Header/Footer group (which selects the current title), type 2017 Sales, and then press the Enter key.
5. Insert a row of empty cells in the report by completing the following steps:
   a. Click in the *Representative* cell.
   b. Click the Report Layout Tools Arrange tab.
   c. Click the Insert Above button in the Rows & Columns group.

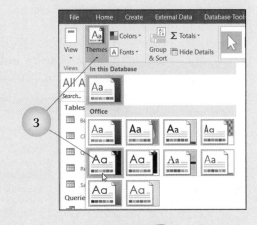

6. Merge the cells in the new row by completing the following steps:
   a. Click in the empty cell immediately above the *Representative* cell.
   b. Press and hold down the Shift key, click immediately above the *Sales 2017* cell, and then release the Shift key. (This selects three cells.)
   c. Click the Merge button in the Merge/Split group.
   d. Type Dearborn 2017 Sales in the new cell.

7. Split a cell by completing the following steps:
   a. Click in the *2017 Sales* title in the *Header* section.
   b. Split the cell containing the title by clicking the Split Horizontally button in the Merge/Split group.
   c. Click in the empty cell immediately right of the cell containing the title *Sales 2017* and then press the Delete key. (Deleting the empty cell causes the date and time to move to the left in the *Header* section.)
8. Change the report table margins and padding by completing the following steps:
   a. Click in any cell in the *Detail* section and then click the table move handle in the upper left corner of the *Dearborn 2017 Sales* cell. (This selects all of the control objects in the report table in the *Detail* section.)
   b. Click the Control Margins button in the Position group and then click *Narrow* at the drop-down list.

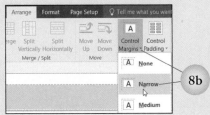

   c. Click the Control Padding button in the Position group and then click *Medium* at the drop-down list.

9. Click in the *Dearborn 2017 Sales* cell and then drag down the bottom border so all of the text in the cell is visible.
10. Change the font for all of the data in the report by completing the following steps:
   a. Press Ctrl + A to select all control objects in the report. (An orange border displays around selected objects.)
   b. Click the Report Layout Tools Format tab.
   c. Click the *Font* option box arrow in the Font group and then click *Cambria* at the drop-down list. (You may need to scroll down the list to display *Cambria*.)

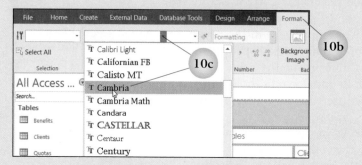

11. Apply bold formatting and change the alignment of the column headings by completing the following steps:
   a. Click *Dearborn 2017 Sales* to select the control object.
   b. Press and hold down the Shift key, click *Sales 2017*, and then release the Shift key. (This selects four cells.)
   c. Click the Bold button in the Font group.
   d. Click the Center button in the Font group.

12. Format and apply conditional formatting to the amounts by completing the following steps:
   a. Click the first field value below the *Sales 2017* column heading. (This selects all of the amounts in the column.)
   b. Click the Decrease Decimals button in the Number group two times.

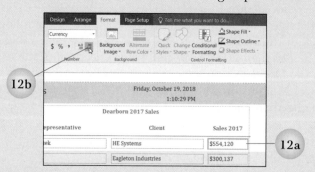

   c. Click the Conditional Formatting button in the Control Formatting group.
   d. At the Conditional Formatting Rules Manager dialog box, click the New Rule button.

e. At the New Formatting Rule dialog box, click the option box arrow for the second option box in the *Edit the rule description* section and then click *greater than* at the drop-down list.

f. Click in the text box immediately right of the option box containing *greater than* and then type 199999.

g. Click the Background color button arrow and then click the *Green 2* color option (seventh column, third row).

h. Click OK.

i. At the Conditional Formatting Rules Manager dialog box, click the New Rule button.

j. At the New Formatting Rule dialog box, click the option box arrow for the second option box in the *Edit the rule description* section and then click *less than* at the drop-down list.

k. Click in the text box immediately right of the option box containing *less than* and then type 200000.

l. Click the Background color button arrow and then click the *Maroon 2* color option (sixth column, third row).

m. Click OK to close the New Formatting Rule dialog box.

n. Click OK to close the Conditional Formatting Rules Manager dialog box.

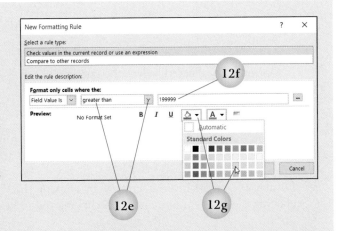

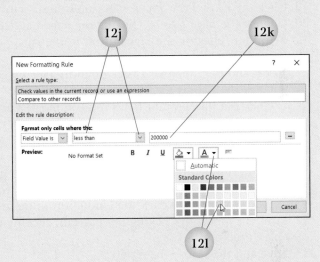

13. Sum the totals in the *Sales 2017* column by completing the following steps:

a. Click in the *Sales 2017* column heading.

b. Click the Report Layout Tools Design tab.

c. Click the Totals button in the Grouping & Totals group and then click *Sum* at the drop-down list.

14. Click in the *Sales 2017* sum amount (at the bottom of the *Sales 2017* column) and then drag down the bottom border so the entire amount is visible in the cell.

15. Change the top margin by completing the following steps:

a. Click in the *Representative* column heading and then click the Report Layout Tools Page Setup tab.

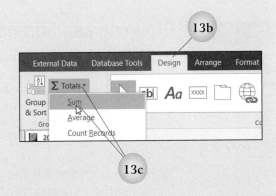

b. Click the Page Setup button in the Page Layout group.

c. At the Page Setup dialog box with the Print Options tab selected, select the current measurement in the *Top* measurement box and then type 0.5.

d. Click OK to close the Page Setup dialog box.

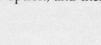

16. Change the page size by clicking the Size button in the Page Size group and and then clicking *Legal* at the drop-down list.

17. Display the report in Print Preview by clicking the File tab, clicking the *Print* option, and then clicking the *Print Preview* option.

18. Click the One Page button in the Zoom group and notice that the entire report will print on one legal-sized page.

19. Click the Close Print Preview button to return to the report.

20. Change the page size by clicking the Page Layout Tools Page Setup tab, clicking the Size button in the Page Size group, and then clicking *Letter* at the drop-down list.

21. Insert and then remove a background image by completing the following steps:

a. Click the Report Layout Tools Format tab.

b. Click the Background Image button in the Background group and then click *Browse* at the drop-down list.

c. At the Insert Picture dialog box, navigate to the AL1C6 folder on your storage medium and then double-click *Mountain.jpg*.

d. Scroll through the report and notice how the image displays in the report.

e. Click the Undo button on the Quick Access Toolbar to remove the background image. (You may need to click the Undo button more than once.)

22. Print the report by clicking the File tab, clicking the *Print* option, and then clicking the *Quick Print* option.

23. Save and then close the report.

Check Your Work

Grouping and Sorting Records in a Report

Tutorial

Grouping and Sorting Records in a Report

 Group & Sort

 Add a group

Quick Steps

Group and Sort Records
1. Open report in Layout view.
2. Click Group & Sort button.
3. Click Add a group button.
4. Click group field.

A report presents database information in a printed form and generally displays data that answers a specific question. To make the data in a report easy to understand, divide the data into groups. For example, data can be divided in a report by regions, sales, dates, or any other division that helps clarify the data for the reader. Access contains a group and sort feature for dividing data into groups and sorting the data.

Click the Group & Sort button in the Grouping & Totals group on the Report Layout Tools Design tab and the Group, Sort, and Total pane displays at the bottom of the work area, as shown in Figure 6.2. Click the Add a group button in the Group, Sort, and Total pane and Access adds a new grouping level row to the pane, along with a list of available fields. Click the field by which data is to be grouped in the report and Access adds the grouping level in the report. With options in the grouping level row, change the group, specify the sort order, and expand the row to display additional options.

Figure 6.2 Group, Sort, and Total Pane

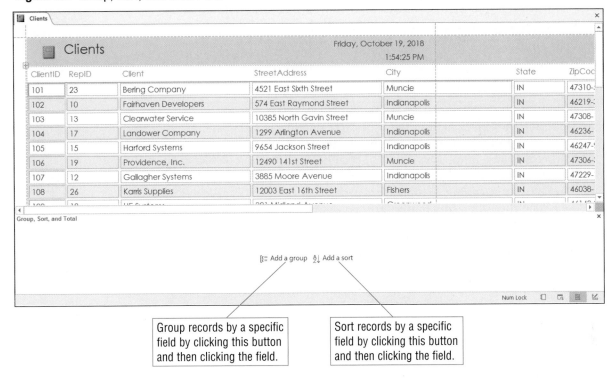

Group records by a specific field by clicking this button and then clicking the field.

Sort records by a specific field by clicking this button and then clicking the field.

When a grouping level is specified, Access automatically sorts that level in ascending order (from A to Z or lowest to highest). Additional data can be sorted within the report by clicking the Add a sort button in the Group, Sort, and Total pane. This inserts a sorting row in the pane below the grouping level row, along with a list of available fields. At this list, click the field by which to sort. For example, in Project 1d, one of the reports will be grouped by city (which will display in ascending order) and then the client names will display in alphabetic order within the city.

Add a sort

Hint Grouping allows you to separate groups of records visually.

To delete a grouping or sorting level in the Group, Sort, and Total pane, click the Delete button at the right side of the level row. After specifying the grouping and sorting levels, close the Group, Sort, and Total pane by clicking the Close button in the upper right corner of the pane or by clicking the Group & Sort button in the Grouping & Totals group.

Project 1d Grouping and Sorting Records in a Report

Part 4 of 5

1. With **6-Dearborn.accdb** open, create a report with the Clients table using the Report button on the Create tab.
2. Click in each column heading individually and then decrease the size of each column so the right border is just right of the longest entry.
3. Change to landscape orientation by completing the following steps:
   a. Click the Report Layout Tools Page Setup tab.
   b. Click the Landscape button in the Page Layout group.
4. Group the report by representative ID and then sort by clients by completing the following steps:
   a. Click the Report Layout Tools Design tab.
   b. Click the Group & Sort button in the Grouping & Totals group.

c. Click the Add a group button in the Group, Sort, and Total pane.

4c

d. Click the *RepID* field in the list box.
e. Scroll through the report and notice that the records are grouped by the *RepID* field. Also, notice that the client names within each *RepID* field group are not in alphabetic order.
f. Click the Add a sort button in the Group, Sort, and Total pane.
g. Click the *Client* field in the list box.
h. Scroll through the report and notice that client names are now alphabetized within *RepID* field groups.
i. Close the Group, Sort, and Total pane by clicking the Group & Sort button in the Grouping & Totals group.

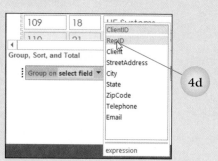

4d

5. Save the report with the name *RepIDGroupedRpt*.
6. Change column width and print the first page of the report by completing the following steps:
   a. Click the File tab, click the *Print* option, and then click the *Print Preview* option.

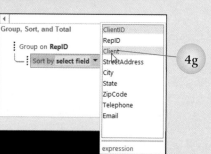

4g

   b. Click the Columns button on the Print Preview tab, select the current measurement in the *Width* measurement box, type 10, and then click OK.
   c. Click the Print button on the Print Preview tab.
   d. At the Print dialog box, click the *Pages* option in the *Print Range* section.
   e. Type 1 in the *From* text box, press the Tab key, and then type 1 in the *To* text box.
   f. Click OK.
7. Close the RepIDGroupedRpt report.
8. Create a report with the InOrMunSalesOver$99999Query query using the Report button on the Create tab. Make sure the report displays in Layout view.
9. Group the report by city and then sort by clients by completing the following steps:
   a. Click the Group & Sort button in the Grouping & Totals group on the Report Layout Tools Design tab.
   b. Click the Add a group button in the Group, Sort, and Total pane.
   c. Click the *City* field in the list box.
   d. Click the Add a sort button in the Group, Sort, and Total pane.
   e. Click the *Client* field in the list box.
   f. Close the Group, Sort, and Total pane by clicking the Group & Sort button in the Grouping & Totals group.
10. Print the first page of the report. (Refer to Step 6.)
11. Save the report, name it *InMunSalesOver$99999*, and then close the report.
12. Close **6-Dearborn.accdb**.
13. Open **6-WarrenLegal.accdb** from the AL1C6 folder on your storage medium and enable the content.

14. Design a query that extracts records from three tables with the following specifications:
    a. Add the Billing, Clients, and Rates tables to the query window.
    b. Insert the *LastName* field from the Clients table field list box in the first field in the *Field* row.
    c. Insert the *Date* field from the Billing table field list box in the second field in the *Field* row.
    d. Insert the *Hours* field from the Billing table field list box in the third field in the *Field* row.
    e. Insert the *Rate* field from the Rates table field list box in the fourth field in the *Field* row.
    f. Click in the fifth field in the *Field* row, type Total: [Hours]*[Rate], and then press the Enter key.

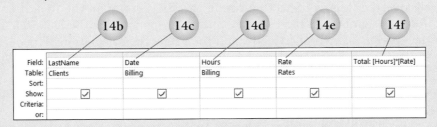

g. Run the query.
h. Save the query with the name *ClientBilling*.
i. Close the query.
15. Create a report with the ClientBilling query using the Report button on the Create tab.
16. Click in each column heading individually and then decrease the size of each column so the right border is near the longest entry.
17. Apply currency formatting to the numbers in the *Total* column by completing the following steps:
    a. Click the Report Layout Tools Format tab.
    b. Click in the first field below the *Total* column (the field containing the number *350*).
    c. Click the Apply Currency Format button in the Number group.
    d. If necessary, increase the size of the *Total* column so the entire amounts (including the dollar symbols ($)) are visible.

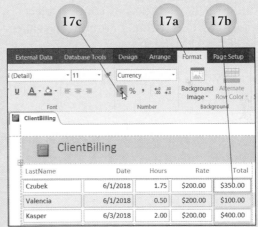

18. Group the report by last name and then sort by date by completing the following steps:
    a. Click the Report Layout Tools Design tab.
    b. Click the Group & Sort button in the Grouping & Totals group.
    c. Click the Add a group button in the Group, Sort, and Total pane.
    d. Click the *LastName* field in the list box.
    e. Click the Add a sort button in the Group, Sort, and Total pane.
    f. Click the *Date* field in the list box.
    g. Close the Group, Sort, and Total pane by clicking the Close button in the upper right corner of the pane.
19. Scroll to the bottom of the report and delete the total amount in the *Rate* column and the line above the total. (Click the line and then press the Delete key.)
20. Save the report with the name *ClientBillingRpt*.
21. Close the report.

Check Your Work

Inserting a Calculation in a Report

Like a form, a calculation can be inserted in a report in a text box control object. To insert a text box control object as well as a label control object, click the Text Box button in the gallery in the Controls group on the Report Layout Tools Design tab, and then click in a location in the report where the two objects are to display. Click in the label control box and then type a label for the calculated field.

Quick Steps

Insert Calculation in Report
1. Click Text Box button on Report Layout Tools Design tab.
2. Click in report to insert label and text box control objects.
3. Click in text box control object.
4. Click Property Sheet button in Tools group.
5. Click Data tab.
6. Click in *Control Source* property box.
7. Type calculation.
8. Click Close button.

Insert a calculation by clicking in the text box control object and then clicking the Property Sheet button in the Tools group on the Report Layout Tools Design tab. At the Property Sheet task pane, click the Data tab, click in the *Control Source* property box, and then type the calculation. Type a calculation in the *Control Source* property box using mathematical operators and type field names in the calculation inside square brackets. Begin the calculation with an equals sign (=). A field name must be typed in the calculation as it appears in the source object.

If a calculation result is currency, apply currency formatting to the text box control object. Apply currency formatting by clicking the Report Layout Tools Format tab and then clicking the Apply Currency Format button in the Number group.

Project 1e Inserting a Calculation in a Report

Part 5 of 5

1. With **6-WarrenLegal.accdb** open, open the ClientBillingRpt report in Layout view.
2. Insert label and text box control objects by completing the following steps:
   a. Click the Text Box button in the gallery in the Controls group on the Report Layout Tools Design tab.
   b. Position the crosshairs to the right of the *Total* field name and then click the left mouse button. (This inserts a label control object and text box object in the report.)

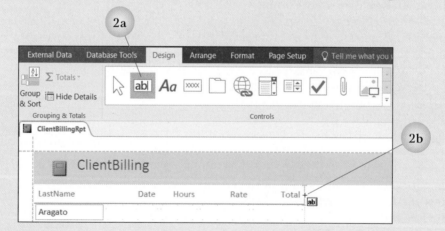

3. Name the new field by clicking in the label control object, double-clicking the text in the label control object, and then typing Total + 9% Tax.

4. Click in the text box control object and then insert a calculation by completing the following steps:

  a. Click the Property Sheet button in the Tools group on the Report Layout Tools Design tab.

  b. At the Property Sheet task pane, click the Data tab.

  c. Click in the *Control Source* property box.

  d. Type =[Total]*1.09 and then press the Enter key.

  e. Close the Property Sheet task pane by clicking the Close button in the upper right corner of the task pane.

5. With the text box control object still selected, apply currency formatting by clicking the Report Layout Tools Format tab and then clicking the Apply Currency Format button in the Number group.

6. Save and then print the report. (The report will print on three pages.).

7. Close the ClientBillingRpt report and then close **6-WarrenLegal.accdb**.

> **Check Your Work**

Project 2 Use Wizards to Create Reports and Labels 3 Parts

You will create reports using the Report Wizard and prepare mailing labels using the Label Wizard.

> **Preview Finished Project**

Creating a Report Using the Report Wizard

Access offers a Report Wizard that provides the steps for creating a report. To create a report using the wizard, click the Create tab and then click the Report Wizard button in the Reports group. At the first Report Wizard dialog box, shown in Figure 6.3, choose a table or query with options from the *Tables/Queries* option box. Specify the fields to be included in the report by inserting them in the *Selected Fields* list box and then clicking the Next button.

At the second Report Wizard dialog box, shown in Figure 6.4, specify the grouping level of data in the report. To group data by a specific field, click the field in the list box at the left side of the dialog box and then click the One Field button. Use the button containing the left-pointing arrow to remove an option as a grouping level. Use the up and down arrows to change the priority of the field.

Figure 6.3 First Report Wizard Dialog Box

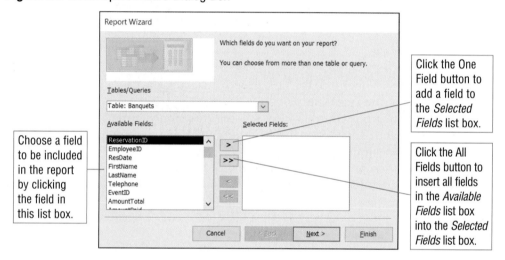

Figure 6.4 Second Report Wizard Dialog Box

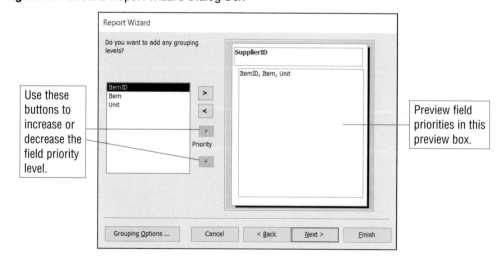

Specify a sort order with options at the third Report Wizard dialog box, shown in Figure 6.5. To specify a sort order, click the option box arrow for the option box preceded by the number *1* and then click the field name. The default sort order is ascending. This can be changed to descending by clicking the button at the right side of the option box. After identifying the sort order, click the Next button.

Use options at the fourth Report Wizard dialog box, shown in Figure 6.6, to specify the layout and orientation of the report. The *Layout* section has the default setting of *Stepped*, which can be changed to *Block* or *Outline*. By default, the report will print in portrait orientation. Change to landscape orientation by clicking the *Landscape* option in the *Orientation* section of the dialog box. Access will adjust field widths in the report so all of the fields fit on one page. To specify that field widths should not be adjusted, remove the check mark from the *Adjust the field width so all fields fit on a page* option.

At the fifth and final Report Wizard dialog box, type a name for the report and then click the Finish button.

Figure 6.5 Third Report Wizard Dialog Box

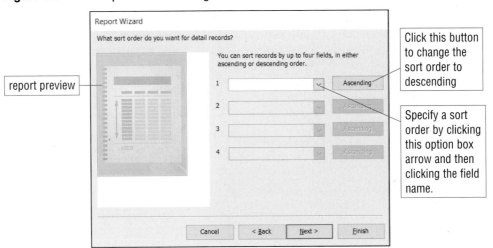

Figure 6.6 Fourth Report Wizard Dialog Box

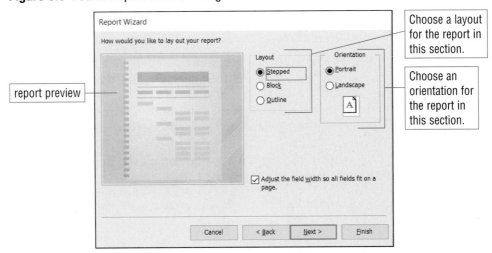

1. Open **6-Skyline.accdb** from the AL1C6 folder on your storage medium and enable the content.
2. Create a report using the Report Wizard by completing the following steps:
   a. Click the Create tab.
   b. Click the Report Wizard button in the Reports group.
   c. At the first Report Wizard dialog box, click the *Tables/Queries* option box arrow and then click *Table: Inventory* at the drop-down list.
   d. Click the All Fields button to insert all of the Inventory table fields in the *Selected Fields* list box.
   e. Click the Next button.
   f. At the second Report Wizard dialog box, make sure *SupplierID* displays in blue at the top of the preview page at the right side of the dialog box and then click the Next button.
   g. At the third Report Wizard dialog box, click the Next button. (You want to use the sorting defaults.)
   h. At the fourth Report Wizard dialog box, click the *Block* option in the *Layout* section and then click the Next button.

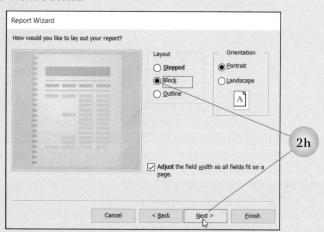

   i. At the fifth Report Wizard dialog box, make sure *Inventory* displays in the *What title do you want for your report?* text box and then click the Finish button. (The report displays in Print Preview.)
3. With the report in Print Preview, click the Print button at the left side of the Print Preview tab and then click OK at the Print dialog box. (The report will print on two pages.)
4. Close Print Preview.
5. Switch to Report view by clicking the View button on the Report Design Tools Design tab.
6. Close the Inventory report.

Check Your Work

If a report is created with fields from only one table, options are specified in five Report Wizard dialog boxes. If a report is created with fields from more than one table, options are specified in six Report Wizard dialog boxes. After choosing the tables and fields at the first dialog box, the second dialog box that displays asks how the data will be viewed. For example, if fields are selected from a Suppliers table and an Orders table, the second Report Wizard dialog box will ask if the data is to be viewed "by Suppliers" or "by Orders."

Project 2b Creating a Report with Fields from Two Tables

Part 2 of 3

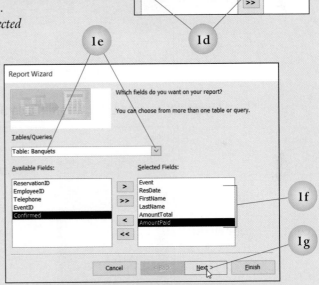

1. With **6-Skyline.accdb** open, create a report with the Report Wizard by completing the following steps:
   a. Click the Create tab.
   b. Click the Report Wizard button in the Reports group.
   c. At the first Report Wizard dialog box, click the *Tables/Queries* option box arrow and then click *Table: Events* at the drop-down list.
   d. Click the *Event* field in the *Available Fields* list box and then click the One Field button.
   e. Click the *Tables/Queries* option box arrow and then click *Table: Banquets* at the drop-down list.
   f. Insert the following fields in the *Selected Fields* list box:
      - *ResDate*
      - *FirstName*
      - *LastName*
      - *AmountTotal*
      - *AmountPaid*
   g. After inserting the fields, click the Next button.
   h. At the second Report Wizard dialog box, make sure *by Events* is selected and then click the Next button.
   i. At the third Report Wizard dialog box, click the Next button. (The report preview shows that the report will be grouped by event.)
   j. At the fourth Report Wizard dialog box, click the Next button. (You want to use the sorting defaults.)
   k. At the fifth Report Wizard dialog box, click the *Block* option in the *Layout* section, click *Landscape* in the *Orientation* section, and then click the Next button.
   l. At the sixth Report Wizard dialog box, select the current name in the *What title do you want for your report?* text box and then type BanquetEvents.
   m. Click the Finish button.
2. Close Print Preview and then change to Layout view.
3. Print and then close the BanquetEvents report.
4. Close **6-Skyline.accdb**.

Check Your Work

Creating Mailing Labels

Access includes a mailing label wizard that provides the steps for creating mailing labels with fields in a table. To create mailing labels, click a table, click the Create tab, and then click the Labels button in the Reports group. At the first Label Wizard dialog box, shown in Figure 6.7, specify the label size, unit of measure, and label type and then click the Next button. At the second Label Wizard dialog box, shown in Figure 6.8, specify the font name, size, weight, and color and then click the Next button.

Labels

Quick Steps

Create Mailing Labels Using the Label Wizard
1. Click table.
2. Click Create tab.
3. Click Labels button.
4. Choose options at each Label Wizard dialog box.

Figure 6.7 First Label Wizard Dialog Box

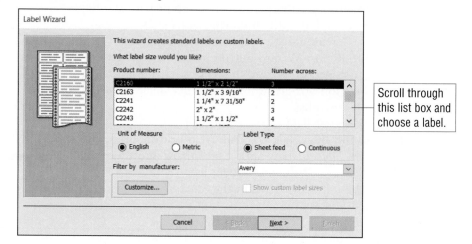

Scroll through this list box and choose a label.

Figure 6.8 Second Label Wizard Dialog Box

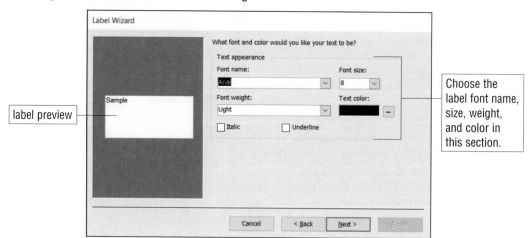

label preview

Choose the label font name, size, weight, and color in this section.

Specify the fields to be included in the mailing labels at the third Label Wizard dialog box, shown in Figure 6.9. To do this, click the field in the *Available fields* list box and then click the One Field button. This moves the field to the *Prototype label* box. Insert the fields in the *Prototype label* box as the text should display on the label. After inserting the fields in the *Prototype label* box, click the Next button.

At the fourth Label Wizard dialog box, shown in Figure 6.10, specify a field from the database by which the labels will be sorted. To sort labels (for example, by last name, postal code, etc.), insert that field in the *Sort by* list box and then click the Next button.

At the last Label Wizard dialog box, type a name for the label report and then click the Finish button. After a few moments, the labels display on the screen in Print Preview. Print the labels and/or close Print Preview.

Figure 6.9 Third Label Wizard Dialog Box

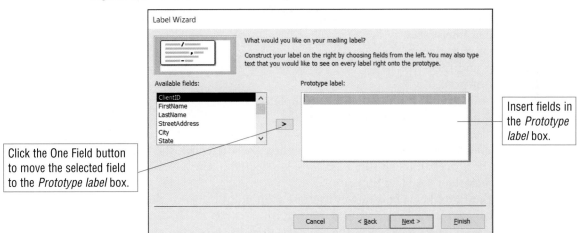

Click the One Field button to move the selected field to the *Prototype label* box.

Insert fields in the *Prototype label* box.

Figure 6.10 Fourth Label Wizard Dialog Box

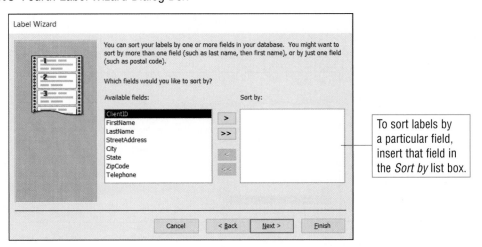

To sort labels by a particular field, insert that field in the *Sort by* list box.

1. Open **6-WarrenLegal.accdb** and enable the content.
2. Click *Clients* in the Tables group in the Navigation pane.
3. Click the Create tab and then click the Labels button in the Reports group.
4. At the first Label Wizard dialog box, make sure *English* is selected in the *Unit of Measure* section, *Avery* is selected in the *Filter by manufacturer* list box, *Sheet feed* is selected in the *Label Type* section, and *C2160* is selected in the *Product number* list box and then click the Next button.
5. At the second Label Wizard dialog box, if necessary, change the font size to 10 points and then click the Next button.
6. At the third Label Wizard dialog box, complete the following steps to insert the fields in the *Prototype label* box:
    a. Click *FirstName* in the *Available fields* list box and then click the One Field button.
    b. Press the spacebar, make sure *LastName* is selected in the *Available fields* list box, and then click the One Field button.
    c. Press the Enter key. (This moves the insertion point down to the next line in the *Prototype label* box.)
    d. With *StreetAddress* selected in the *Available fields* list box, click the One Field button.
    e. Press the Enter key.
    f. With *City* selected in the *Available fields* list box, click the One Field button.
    g. Type a comma (,) and then press the spacebar.
    h. With *State* selected in the *Available fields* list box, click the One Field button.
    i. Press the spacebar.
    j. With *ZipCode* selected in the *Available fields* list box, click the One Field button.

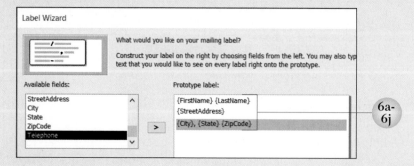

    k. Click the Next button.

7. At the fourth Label Wizard dialog box, sort by zip code. To do this, click *ZipCode* in the *Available fields* list box and then click the One Field button.
8. Click the Next button.
9. At the last Label Wizard dialog box, click the Finish button. (The Label Wizard automatically names the label report *Labels Clients*.)
10. Print the labels by clicking the Print button at the left side of the Print Preview tab and then click OK at the Print dialog box.
11. Close Print Preview.
12. Switch to Report view by clicking the View button on the Report Design Tools Design tab.
13. Close the labels report and then close **6-WarrenLegal.accdb**.

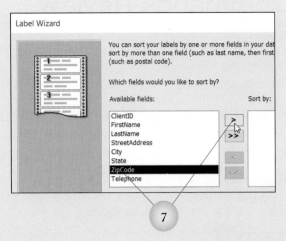

Check Your Work

Chapter Summary

- Create a report with data in a table or query to control how data appears on the page and how the data is formatted when printed.
- Create a report with the Report button in the Reports group on the Create tab.
- Four views are available for viewing a report: Report view, Print Preview, Layout view, and Design view.
- Use options on the Print Preview tab to specify how a report prints.
- In Layout view, a report control object can be selected and then sized or moved.
- One method for changing column width in a report is to click a column heading and then drag the border to the desired width.
- Sort data in a record using the Ascending button or Descending button in the Sort & Filter group on the Home tab.
- Customize a report with options on the Report Layout Tools ribbon with the Design tab, Arrange tab, Format tab, or Page Setup tab selected.
- To make data in a report easier to understand, divide the data into groups using the Group, Sort, and Total pane. Display this pane by clicking the Group & Sort button in the Grouping & Totals group on the Report Layout Tools Design tab.
- Insert a calculation in a report by inserting a text box object, displaying the Property Sheet task pane with the Data tab selected, and then typing the calculation in the *Control Source* property box. If a calculation result is currency, apply currency formatting with the Apply Currency Format button on the Report Layout Tools Format tab.
- Use the Report Wizard to provide the steps for creating a report. Begin the wizard by clicking the Create tab and then clicking the Report Wizard button in the Reports group.
- Create mailing labels with data in a table using the Label Wizard. Begin the wizard by clicking a table, clicking the Create tab, and then clicking the Labels button in the Reports group.

Commands Review

FEATURE	RIBBON TAB, GROUP	BUTTON	KEYBOARD SHORTCUT
Conditional Formatting Rules Manager dialog box	Report Layout Tools Format, Control Formatting		
Find dialog box	Home, Find		Ctrl + F
Group, Sort, and Total pane	Report Layout Tools Design, Grouping & Totals		
Labels Wizard	Create, Reports		
Property Sheet task pane	Report Layout Tools Design, Tools		Alt + Enter
report	Create, Reports		
Report Wizard	Create, Reports		
Sort data in ascending order	Home, Sort & Filter		
Sort data in descending order	Home, Sort & Filter		

Workbook

Chapter study tools and assessment activities are available in the *Workbook* ebook. These resources are designed to help you further develop and demonstrate mastery of the skills learned in this chapter.

Access®

Modifying, Filtering, and Viewing Data

CHAPTER

7

Performance Objectives

Upon successful completion of Chapter 7, you will be able to:

1 Filter records using the Filter button

2 Remove a filter

3 Filter on specific values, by selection, by shortcut menu, and using the *Filter By Form* option

4 View object dependencies

5 Compact and repair a database

6 Encrypt a database with a password

7 View and customize document properties

8 Save a database in an earlier version of Access

9 Save a database object as a PDF or XPS file

10 Backup a database

Precheck

Check your current skills to help focus your study.

Data in a database object can be filtered to view specific records without having to change the design of the object. In this chapter, you will learn how to filter data by selection, by shortcut menu, by form, and how to remove a filter. You will also learn how to view object dependencies, compact and repair a database, encrypt a database with a password, view and customize database properties, save a database in an earlier version of Access, save a database object as a PDF or XPS file, and back up a database.

Data Files

Before beginning chapter work, copy the AL1C7 folder to your storage medium and then make AL1C7 the active folder.

SNAP

If you are a SNAP user, launch the Precheck and Tutorials from your Assignments page.

Tutorial

Filtering Records

Quick Steps

Filter Records

1. Open object.
2. Click in entry in field to filter.
3. Click Filter button.
4. Select sorting option at drop-down list.

 Filter

Filtering Records

A set of restrictions, called a *filter*, can be set on records in a table, query, form, or report to isolate temporarily specific records. A filter, like a query, displays specific records without having to change the design of the table, query, form, or report. Access provides a number of buttons and options for filtering data. Filter data using the Filter button in the Sort & Filter group on the Home tab, right-click specific data in a record and then specify a filter, and use the Selection and Advanced buttons in the Sort & Filter group.

Filtering Using the Filter Button

Use the Filter button in the Sort & Filter group on the Home tab to filter records in an object (a table, query, form, or report). To use this button, open the object, click in any entry in the field column to be filtered, and then click the Filter button. This displays a drop-down list with sorting options and a list of all of the field entries. In a table, display this drop-down list by clicking the filter arrow at the right side of a column heading. Figure 7.1 shows the drop-down list that displays when clicking in an entry in the *City* field and then clicking the Filter

Figure 7.1 *City* Field Drop-down List

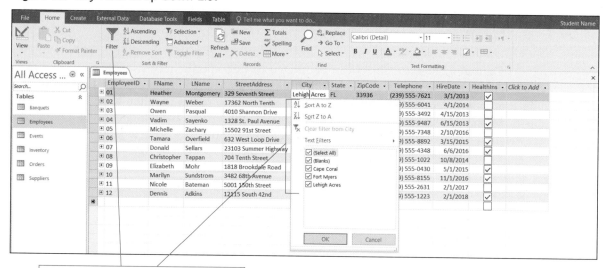

To filter on the *City* field, click in any entry in the field and then click the Filter button. This displays a drop-down list with sorting options and a list of all field entries.

button. To filter on a specific criterion, click the *(Select All)* check box to remove all check marks from the list of field entries. Click the item to filter by in the list box and then click OK.

Open a table, query, or form and the Record Navigation bar contains the dimmed words *No Filter* preceded by a filter icon with a delete symbol (X). If records are filtered, *Filtered* displays in place of *No Filter*, the delete symbol is removed, and the text and filter icon display with an orange background. In a report, apply a filter to records and the word *Filtered* displays at the right side of the Status bar.

Removing a Filter

Toggle Filter

Quick Steps

Remove a Filter
1. Click in an entry in field containing filter.
2. Click Filter button.
3. Click *Clear filter from (name of field)*.
OR
1. Click Advanced button.
2. Click *Clear All Filters* at drop-down list.

When data is filtered, the underlying data in the object is not deleted. Switch back and forth between the data and filtered data by clicking the Toggle Filter button in the Sort & Filter group on the Home tab. Click the Toggle Filter button to turn off the filter and all of the data in the table, query, or form displays and the message *Filtered* in the Record Navigation bar changes to *Unfiltered*.

Clicking the Toggle Filter button may redisplay all of the data in an object, but it does not remove the filter. To remove the filter, click in the field column containing the filter and then click the Filter button in the Sort & Filter group on the Home tab. At the drop-down list that displays, click *Clear filter from xxx* (where *xxx* is the name of the field). Remove all of the filters from an object by clicking the Advanced button in the Sort & Filter group and then clicking the *Clear All Filters* option. When all filters are removed (cleared) from an object, the *Unfiltered* message in the Record Navigation bar changes to *No Filter*.

Project 1a Filtering Records in a Table, Form, and Report   **Part 1 of 4**

1. Open **7-Skyline.accdb** from the AL1C7 folder on your storage medium and enable the content.
2. Filter records in the Employees table by completing the following steps:
   a. Open the Employees table.
   b. Click in any entry in the *City* field.
   c. Click the Filter button in the Sort & Filter group on the Home tab. (This displays a drop-down list of options for sorting and filtering the *City* field.)

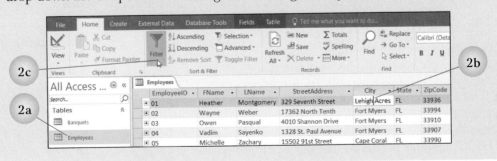

d. Click the *(Select All)* check box in the filter drop-down list box. (This removes all check marks from the list options.)

e. Click the *Fort Myers* check box in the list box. (This inserts a check mark in the check box.)

f. Click OK. (Access displays only those records with a city field entry of *Fort Myers* and also displays *Filtered* and the filter icon with an orange background in the Record Navigation bar.)

g. Print the filtered records by pressing Ctrl + P (the keyboard shortcut to display the print dialog box) and then clicking OK at the Print dialog box.

3. Toggle the display of filtered data by clicking the Toggle Filter button in the Sort & Filter group on the Home tab. (This redisplays all of the data in the table.)

4. Remove the filter by completing the following steps:

a. Click in any entry in the *City* field.

b. Click the Filter button in the Sort & Filter group.

c. Click the *Clear filter from City* option at the drop-down list. (Notice that the message on the Record Navigation bar changes to *No Filter* and dims the words.)

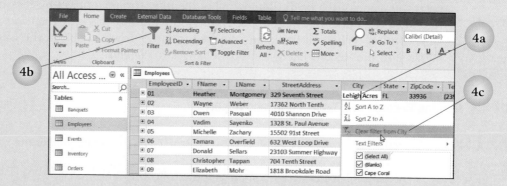

5. Save and then close the Employees table.

6. Create a form by completing the following steps:

a. Click *Orders* in the Tables group in the Navigation pane.

b. Click the Create tab and then click the Form button in the Forms group.

c. Click the Form View button in the view area at the right side of the Status bar.

d. Save the form with the name *Orders*.

7. Filter the records and display only those records with a supplier identification number of 2 by completing the following steps:

a. Click in the *SupplierID* field containing the text *2*.

b. Click the Filter button in the Sort & Filter group.

c. At the filter drop-down list, click *(Select All)* to remove all of the check marks from the list options.

d. Click the *2* option to insert a check mark.

e. Click OK.

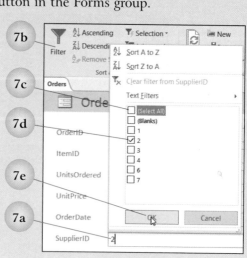

f. Navigate through the records and notice that only the records with a supplier identification number of 2 display.

8. Close the Orders form.

Check Your Work

Filtering on Specific Values

Quick Steps

Filter on Specific Value
1. Click in entry in field.
2. Click Filter button on Home tab.
3. Point to filter option.
4. Click specific value.

When filtering on a specific field, a list of unique values for that field can be displayed. Click the Filter button for a field containing text and the drop-down list for the specific field will contain a *Text Filters* option. Click this option and a values list displays next to the drop-down list. The options in the values list vary depending on the type of data in the field. Click the Filter button for a field containing number values and the option in the drop-down list displays as *Number Filters*. If filtering dates, the Filter button's drop-down list displays as *Date Filters*. Use the options in the values list to refine a filter for a specific field. For example, the values list can be used to display money amounts within a specific range or order dates from a certain time period. The values list can also be used to find fields that are "equal to" or "not equal to" data in the current field.

Project 1b Filtering Records in a Query and Report   Part 2 of 4

1. With **7-Skyline.accdb** open, create a query in Design view with the following specifications:
   a. Add the Banquets and Events tables to the query window.
   b. Insert the *ResDate* field from the Banquets table field list box in the first field in the *Field* row.
   c. Insert the *FirstName* field from the Banquets table field list box in the second field in the *Field* row.
   d. Insert the *LastName* field from the Banquets table field list box in the third field in the *Field* row.
   e. Insert the *Telephone* field from the Banquets table field list box in the fourth field in the *Field* row.
   f. Insert the *Event* field from the Events table field list box in the fifth field in the *Field* row.
   g. Insert the *EmployeeID* field from the Banquets table field list box in the sixth field in the *Field* row.
   h. Run the query.
   i. Save the query with the name *BanquetReservations*.
2. Filter records of reservations on or before June 15, 2018, in the query by completing the following steps:
   a. With the BanquetReservations query open, make sure the first entry is selected in the *ResDate* field.
   b. Click the Filter button in the Sort & Filter group on the Home tab.
   c. Point to the *Date Filters* option in the drop-down list box.
   d. Click *Before* in the values list.

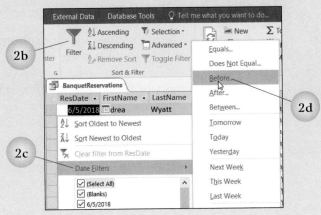

e. At the Custom Filter dialog box, type 6/15/2018 and then click OK.

f. Print the filtered query by pressing Ctrl + P and then clicking OK at the Print dialog box.

3. Remove the filter by clicking the filter icon at the right side of the *ResDate* column heading and then clicking *Clear filter from ResDate* at the drop-down list.

4. Save and then close the BanquetReservations query.

5. Create and format a report by completing the following steps:

   a. Click *BanquetReservations* in the Queries group in the Navigation pane.

   b. Click the Create tab and then click the Report button in the Reports group.

   c. Delete the total amount and line at the bottom of the *ResDate* column.

   d. Delete the page number control object.

   e. With the report in Layout view, decrease the column widths so the right column border displays near the longest entry in each column.

   f. Move the date and time control objects so they align with the last column in the report.

   g. Click the Report Layout Tools Page Setup tab and then click the Columns button in the Page Layout group.

   h. Click the Report View button in the view area at the right side of the Status bar.

   i Save the report with the name *BanquetReport*.

6. Filter the records and display all records of events except *Other* events by completing the following steps:

   a. Click in the first entry in the *Event* field.

   b. Click the Filter button in the Sort & Filter group.

   c. Point to the *Text Filters* option in the drop-down list box and then click *Does Not Equal* at the values list.

   d. At the Custom Filter dialog box, type *Other* and then click OK.

7. Further refine the filter by completing the following steps:

   a. Click in the first entry in the *EmployeeID* field.

   b. Click the Filter button.

   c. At the filter drop-down list, click the *(Select All)* check box to remove all of the check marks from the list options.

   d. Click the *03* check box to insert a check mark.

   e. Click OK.

8. Print the filtered report by pressing Ctrl + P and then clicking OK at the Print dialog box.

9. Save and then close the BanquetReport report.

Check Your Work

Filtering by Selection

Click in a field in an object and then click the Selection button in the Sort & Filter group on the Home tab and a drop-down list displays below the button with options for filtering on the data in the field. For example, click in a field containing the city name *Fort Myers* and then click the Selection button and a drop-down list will display as shown in Figure 7.2. Click one of the options at the drop-down list to filter records.

Specific data can be selected in an object and then filtered by the selected data. For example, in Project 1c, the word *peppers* will be selected in the entry *Green peppers* and then records will be filtered containing the word *peppers*.

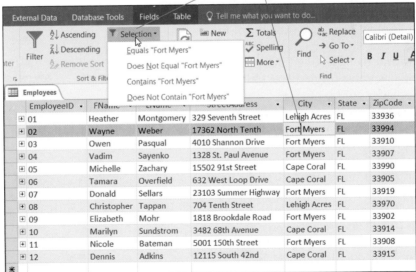

Selection

Quick Steps

Filter by Selection
1. Click in entry in field.
2. Click Selection button.
3. Click filtering option.

Filter by Shortcut Menu
1. Right-click in entry in field.
2. Click filtering option at shortcut menu.

Filtering by Shortcut Menu

Right-click in a field entry, and a shortcut menu displays with options to sort the text, display a values list, or filter on a specific value. For example, right-click in the field entry *Birthday* in the *Event* field and the shortcut menu displays, as shown in Figure 7.3. Click a sort option to sort text in the field in ascending or descending order, point to the *Text Filters* option to display a values list, or click one of the values filters at the bottom of the menu. The shortcut menu can also be displayed by selecting specific text within a field entry and then right-clicking the selection.

Figure 7.2 Selection Button Drop-Down List

Figure 7.3 Filtering Shortcut Menu

> Right-click in a field entry to display a shortcut menu with sorting and filtering options.

BanquetReservations					
ResDate ▾	FirstName ▾	LastName ▾	Telephone ▾	Event ▾	EmployeeID
6/6/2018	Luis	Castillo	(239) 555-4001	Wedding shower	11
6/14/2018	Willow	Earhart	(239) 555-0034	Wedding shower	04
6/9/2018	Joanne	Blair	(239) 555-7783	Birthday	03
6/16/2018	Jason	Haley	(239) 555-6641	Birth	
6/18/2018	Heidi	Thompson	(941) 555-3215	Birth	
6/27/2018	Kirsten	Simpson	(941) 555-4425	Birth	
6/14/2018	Aaron	Williams	(239) 555-3821	Bar	
6/20/2018	Robin	Gehring	(239) 555-0126	Bar	
6/12/2018	Tim	Drysdale	(941) 555-0098	Bat	
6/7/2018	Bridget	Kohn	(239) 551-1299	Othe	
6/12/2018	Gabrielle	Johnson	(239) 555-1882	Othe	
6/13/2018	Tristan	Strauss	(941) 555-7746	Othe	
6/17/2018	Lillian	Krakosky	(239) 555-8890	Othe	
6/20/2018	David	Fitzgerald	(941) 555-3792	Othe	
6/5/2018	Terrance	Schaefer	(239) 555-6239	Wec	
6/12/2018	Cliff	Osborne	(239) 555-7822	Wedding rehearsal dinner	11

Shortcut menu:
- Cut
- Copy
- Paste
- Sort A to Z
- Sort Z to A
- Clear filter from Event
- Text Filters ▸
- Equals "Birthday"
- Does Not Equal "Birthday"
- Contains "Birthday"
- Does Not Contain "Birthday"

Project 1c Filtering Records by Selection

Part 3 of 4

1. With **7-Skyline.accdb** open, open the Inventory table.
2. Filter only those records with a supplier number of 6 by completing the following steps:
   a. Click in the first entry containing *6* in the *SupplierID* field.
   b. Click the Selection button in the Sort & Filter group on the Home tab and then click *Equals "6"* at the drop-down list.
   c. Print the filtered table by pressing Ctrl + P and then clicking OK at the Print dialog box.
   d. Click the Toggle Filter button in the Sort & Filter group.
3. Filter any records in the *Item* field containing the word *peppers* by completing the following steps:
   a. Click in an entry in the *Item* field containing the text *Green peppers*.
   b. Using the mouse, select the word *peppers*.
   c. Click the Selection button and then click *Contains "peppers"* at the drop-down list.
   d. Print the filtered table by pressing Ctrl + P and then clicking OK at the Print dialog box.
4. Close the Inventory table without saving the changes.

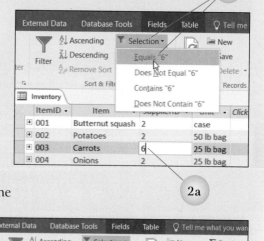

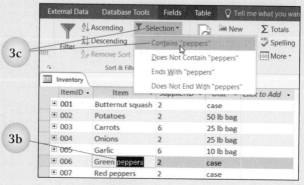

5. Open the BanquetReservations query.
6. Filter the records so that all but those containing *Wedding reception* in the *Event* field display by completing the following steps:
   a. Right-click in the first *Wedding reception* entry in the *Event* field.
   b. Click *Does Not Equal "Wedding reception"* at the shortcut menu.

LastName ⋅	Telephone ⋅		Event ⋅	EmployeeID ⋅
Wyatt	(239) 555-4282	Wec	✂ Cu_t	
Semala	(239) 555-0476	Wec	▤ _Copy	
Satter	(239) 555-8512	Wec	▯ _Paste	
Rivas	(239) 555-9977	Wec	↓ Sort A to Z	
Castillo	(239) 555-4001	Wec	↓ Sort _Z to A	
Earhart	(239) 555-0034	Wec		
Blair	(239) 555-7783	Birtl	Clear filter from Event	
Haley	(239) 555-6641	Birtl	Text _Filters ▶	
Thompson	(941) 555-3215	Birtl	_Equals "Wedding reception"	
Simpson	(941) 555-4425	Birtl	Does _Not Equal "Wedding reception"	
Williams	(239) 555-3821	Bar	Con_tains "Wedding reception"	
Gehring	(239) 555-0126	Bar	_Does Not Contain "Wedding reception"	
Drysdale	(941) 555-0098	Bat		

6a   6b

   c. Print the filtered query.
   d. Click the Toggle Filter button in the Sort & Filter group.
7. Filter the records so that only those containing the word *mitzvah* in the *Event* field display by completing the following steps:
   a. Click in an entry in the *Event* field containing the entry *Bar mitzvah*.
   b. Using the mouse, select the word *mitzvah*.
   c. Right-click in the selected word and then click *Contains "mitzvah"* at the shortcut menu.
   d. Print the filtered query.
8. Close the BanquetReservations query without saving the changes.

Check Your Work

Using the *Filter By Form* Option

Quick Steps

Use the *Filter By Form* Option
1. Click Advanced button.
2. Click *Filter By Form*.
3. Click in empty field below column to filter.
4. Click down arrow.
5. Click item to filter.

One of the options from the Advanced button drop-down list is *Filter By Form*. Click this option and a blank record displays in a Filter by Form window in the work area. In the Filter by Form window, the Look for tab and the Or tab display at the bottom of the form. The Look for tab is active by default and tells Access to look for whatever data is inserted in a field. Click in the empty field below the column and a down arrow displays at the right side of the field. Click the down arrow and then click the item by which to filter. Click the Toggle Filter button to display the desired records. Add an additional value to a filter by clicking the Or tab at the bottom of the form.

1. With **7-Skyline.accdb** open, open the Banquets table.
2. Filter records by a specific employee ID number by completing the following steps:
   a. Click the Advanced button in the Sort & Filter group on the Home tab and then click *Filter By Form* at the drop-down list.

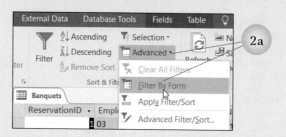

2a

   b. At the Filter by Form window, click in the empty field below the *EmployeeID* column heading.
   c. Click the down arrow at the right side of the field and then click *03* at the drop-down list.
   d. Click the Toggle Filter button in the Sort & Filter group.
3. Print the filtered table by completing the following steps:
   a. Click the File tab, click the *Print* option, and then click the *Print Preview* option.
   b. Change the orientation to landscape and the left and right margins to 0.5 inch.
   c. Click the Print button and then click OK at the Print dialog box.
   d. Click the Close Print Preview button.
4. Close the Banquets table without saving the changes.
5. Open the Inventory table.
6. Filter records by the supplier number 2 or 7 by completing the following steps:
   a. Click the Advanced button in the Sort & Filter group on the Home tab and then click *Filter By Form* at the drop-down list.
   b. At the Filter by Form window, click in the empty field below the *SupplierID* column heading.
   c. Click the down arrow at the right side of the field and then click *2* at the drop-down list.
   d. Click the Or tab at the bottom of the form.
   e. If necessary, click in the empty field below the *SupplierID* column heading.
   f. Click the down arrow at the right side of the field and then click *7* at the drop-down list.
   g. Click the Toggle Filter button in the Sort & Filter group.
   h. Print the filtered table.
   i. Click the Toggle Filter button to redisplay all records in the table.
   j. Click the Advanced button and then click *Clear All Filters* at the drop-down list.
7. Close the Inventory table without saving the changes.

Check Your Work

You will display object dependencies in the Skyline database, compact and repair the database, encrypt it with a password, view and customize database properties, save an object in the database in PDF file format, and save the database in a previous version of Access.

Preview Finished Project

Tutorial

Viewing Object
Dependencies

Viewing Object Dependencies

Quick Steps

**View Object
Dependencies**
1. Open database.
2. Click object in
   Navigation pane.
3. Click Database Tools
   tab.
4. Click Object
   Dependencies
   button.

Object
Dependencies

The structure of a database is comprised of table, query, form, and report objects. Tables are related to other tables by the relationships that have been created. Queries, forms, and reports draw the source data from the records in the tables to which they have been associated, and forms and reports can include subforms and subreports, which further expand the associations between objects. A database with a large number of interdependent objects is more complex to work with than a simpler database. Viewing a list of the objects within a database and viewing the dependencies between objects can be beneficial to ensure an object is not deleted or otherwise modified, causing an unforeseen effect on another object.

Display the structure of a database—including tables, queries, forms, and reports—as well as relationships—at the Object Dependencies task pane. Display this task pane by opening the database, clicking an object in the Navigation pane, clicking the Database Tools tab, and then clicking the Object Dependencies button in the Relationships group. The Object Dependencies task pane, shown in Figure 7.4, displays the objects in the Skyline database that depend on the Banquets table.

Figure 7.4 Object Dependencies Task Pane

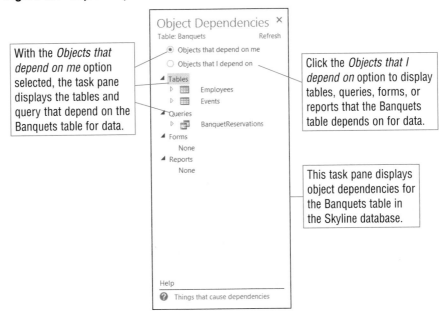

By default, *Objects that depend on me* is selected in the Object Dependencies task pane and the list box displays the names of the objects for which the selected object is the source. Next to each object in the task pane list box is an expand button (a right-pointing, white triangle). Clicking the expand button next to an object shows the other objects that depend on it. For example, if a query is based on the Banquets and Events tables and the query is used to generate a report, clicking the expand button next to the query name will show the report name. Clicking an object name in the Object Dependencies task pane opens the object in Design view.

Project 2a Viewing Object Dependencies

Part 1 of 4

1. With **7-Skyline.accdb** open, display the structure of the database by completing the following steps:
   a. Click *Banquets* in the Tables group in the Navigation pane.
   b. Click the Database Tools tab and then click the Object Dependencies button in the Relationships group. (This displays the Object Dependencies task pane. By default, *Objects that depend on me* is selected and the task pane lists the names of the objects for which the Banquets table is the source.)

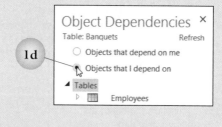

   c. Click the expand button (the right-pointing, white triangle that turns pink when you hover your mouse pointer over it) to the left of *Employees* in the *Tables* section. (This displays all of the objects that depend on the Employees table.)
   d. Click the *Objects that I depend on* option near the top of the Object Dependencies task pane.

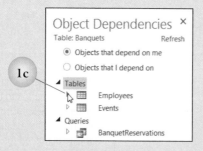

   e. Click *Events* in the Tables group in the Navigation pane. (Make sure to click *Events* in the Navigation pane and not the Object Dependencies task pane.)
   f. Click the Refresh hyperlink in the upper right corner of the Object Dependencies task pane.
   g. Click the *Objects that depend on me* option near the top of the Object Dependencies task pane.
2. Close the Object Dependencies task pane.

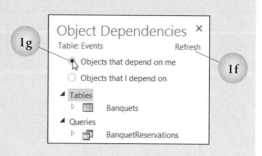

Using Options at the Info Backstage Area

The Info backstage area contains options for compacting and repairing a database, encrypting a database with a password, and displaying and customizing database properties. Display the Info backstage area, shown in Figure 7.5, by opening a database and then clicking the File tab.

Compacting and Repairing a Database

To optimize the performance of a database, compact and repair it on a regular basis. When working in a database on an ongoing basis, data in it can become fragmented, causing the amount of space the database takes on the storage medium or in the folder to be larger than necessary. To compact and repair a database, open the database, click the File tab and then click the Compact & Repair Database button or click the Compact and Repair Database button in the Tools group on the Database Tools tab.

A database can be compacted and repaired each time it is closed. To do this, click the File tab and then click *Options*. At the Access Options dialog box, click the *Current Database* option in the left panel. Click the *Compact on Close* option to insert a check mark and then click OK to close the dialog box. Before compacting and repairing a database in a multi-user environment, make sure that no other user has the database open.

Figure 7.5 Info Backstage Area

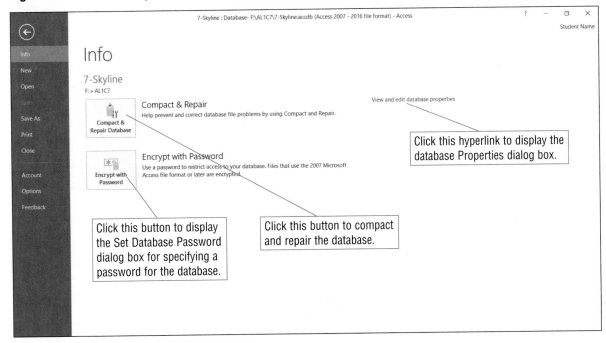

Encrypting a Database with a Password

Tutorial

Encrypting a
Database with a
Password

To prevent unauthorized access to a database, encrypt the database with a password to ensure that it can be opened only by someone who knows the password. Be careful when encrypting a database with a password because if the password is lost, the database will not open.

To encrypt a database with a password, the database must be opened in Exclusive mode. To do this, display the Open dialog box, navigate to the folder containing the database, and then click the database to select it. Click the Open button arrow (in the lower right corner of the dialog box) and then click *Open Exclusive* at the drop-down list. When the database opens, click the File tab and then click the Encrypt with Password button in the Info backstage area. This displays the Set Database Password dialog box, as shown in Figure 7.6. At this dialog box, type a password in the *Password* text box, press the Tab key, and then type the password again. The typed text will display as asterisks. Click OK to close the Set Database Password dialog box.

To remove a password from a database, open the database in Exclusive mode, click the File tab, and then click the Decrypt Database button. At the Unset Database Password dialog box, type the password and then click OK.

 Encrypt with Password

 Decrypt Database

Quick Steps

Open a Database in Exclusive Mode
1. Display Open dialog box.
2. Click database.
3. Click Open button arrow.
4. Click *Open Exclusive.*

Encrypt a Database with a Password
1. Open database in Exclusive mode.
2. Click File tab.
3. Click Encrypt with Password button.
4. Type password, press Tab, and type password again.
5. Click OK.

Hint When encrypting a database with a password, use a password that combines uppercase and lowercase letters, numbers, and symbols.

Figure 7.6 Set Database Password Dialog Box

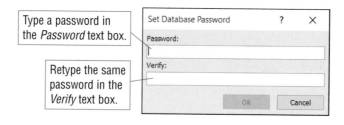

Type a password in the *Password* text box.

Retype the same password in the *Verify* text box.

Project 2b Compacting and Repairing a Database and Encrypting with a Password   Part 2 of 4

1. With **7-Skyline.accdb** open, compact and repair the database by completing the following steps:
   a. Click the File tab. (This displays the Info backstage area.)
   b. Click the Compact & Repair Database button.
2. Close **7-Skyline.accdb**.
3. Open the database in Exclusive mode by completing the following steps:
   a. Display the Open dialog box and make AL1C7 the active folder.
   b. Click **7-Skyline.accdb** in the Content pane to select it.

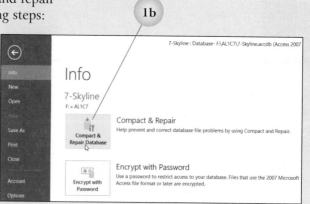

c. Click the Open button arrow (in the lower right corner of the dialog box) and then click *Open Exclusive* at the drop-down list.

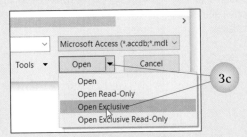

4. Encrypt the database with a password by completing the following steps:
   a. Click the File tab.
   b. At the Info backstage area, click the Encrypt with Password button.
   c. At the Set Database Password dialog box, type your first and last names in all lowercase letters with no space, press the Tab key, and then type your first and last names again in lowercase letters.
   d. Click OK to close the dialog box.
   e. If a message displays with information about encrypting with a block cipher, click OK.
5. Close **7-Skyline.accdb**.
6. Display the Open dialog box with AL1C7 as the active folder and then open **7-Skyline.accdb** in Exclusive mode.
7. At the Password Required dialog box, type your password and then click OK.
8. Remove the password by completing the following steps:
   a. Click the File tab.
   b. Click the Decrypt Database button.
   c. At the Unset Database Password dialog box, type your first and last names in lowercase letters and then press the Enter key.

Tutorial

Viewing and
Customizing
Database Properties

Viewing and Customizing Database Properties

Each database has associated properties, such as the type of file; its location; and when it was created, accessed, and modified. These properties can be viewed and modified at the Properties dialog box. To view properties for the currently open database, click the File tab to display the Info backstage area and then click the <u>View and edit database properties</u> hyperlink at the right side of the backstage area. This displays the Properties dialog box, similar to what is shown in Figure 7.7.

The Properties dialog box for an open database contains tabs with information about the database. With the General tab selected, the dialog box displays information about the database type, size, and location. Click the Summary tab to display fields such as *Title*, *Subject*, *Author*, *Category*, *Keywords*, and *Comments*. Some fields contain data and others are blank. Text can be inserted, edited, or deleted in the fields. Move the insertion point to a field by clicking in the field or by pressing the Tab key until the insertion point is positioned in the field.

Quick Steps

View Database Properties
1. Click File tab.
2. Click <u>View and edit database properties</u>.

Figure 7.7 Properties Dialog Box

Click each tab to display additional information about the database.

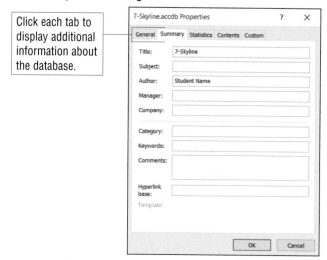

Click the Statistics tab to display information such as the dates the database was created, modified, accessed, and printed. Click the Contents tab and the *Document contents* section displays the objects in the database, including tables, queries, forms, reports, macros, and modules.

Use options at the Properties dialog box with the Custom tab selected to add custom properties to the database. For example, a property can be added that displays the date the database was completed, information on the department in which the database was created, and much more. The list box below the *Name* option box displays the predesigned properties provided by Access. Choose a predesigned property from this list box or create a custom property.

To choose a predesigned property, click a predesigned property in the list box, specify what type of property it is (such as value, date, number, yes/no), and then type a value. For example, to specify the department in which the database was created, click *Department* in the list box, make sure the *Type* displays as *Text*, click in the *Value* text box, and then type the name of the department.

Project 2c Viewing and Customizing Database Properties   Part 3 of 4

1. With **7-Skyline.accdb** open, click the File tab and then click the <u>View and edit database properties</u> hyperlink at the right side of the backstage area.

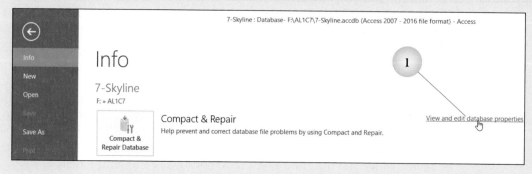

2. At the 7-Skyline.accdb Properties dialog box, click the General tab and then read the information that displays in the dialog box.
3. Click the Summary tab and then type the following text in the specified text boxes:

Title	7-Skyline database
Subject	Restaurant and banquet facilities
Author	(*Type your first and last names.*)
Category	restaurant
Keywords	restaurant, banquet, event, Fort Myers
Comments	This database contains information on Skyline Restaurant employees, banquets, inventory, and orders.

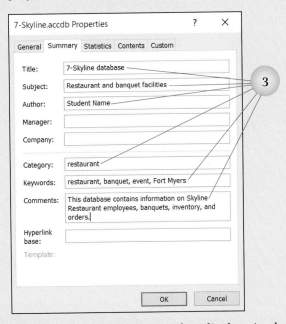

4. Click the Statistics tab and read the information that displays in the dialog box.
5. Click the Contents tab and notice that the *Document contents* section of the dialog box displays the objects in the database.
6. Click the Custom tab and then create custom properties by completing the following steps:
   a. Click the *Date completed* option in the *Name* list box.
   b. Click the *Type* option box arrow and then click *Date* at the drop-down list.
   c. Click in the *Value* text box and then type the current date in this format: *dd/mm/yyyy*.
   d. Click the Add button.
   e. With the insertion point positioned in the *Name* text box, type Course.

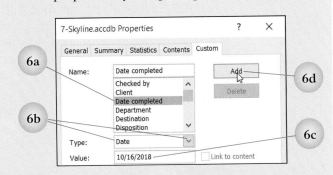

   f. Click the *Type* option box arrow and then click *Text* at the drop-down list.
   g. Click in the *Value* text box, type your current course number, and then press the Enter key.
   h. Click OK to close the dialog box.
7. Click the Back button to return to the database.

Check Your Work

x

x

Tutorial

Saving a
Database and
Database Object
in Different
Formats

Saving a Database and Database Object in Different Formats

An Access 2016, Access 2013, Access 2010, or Access 2007 database is saved with the file extension *.accdb*. Earlier versions of Access (such as 2003, 2002, and 2000) use the file extension *.mdb*. To open an Access 2016, 2013, 2010, or 2007 database in an earlier version of Access, the database must be saved in the .mdb file format.

To save an Access database in the Access 2002 and 2003 file format, open the database, click the File tab, and then click the *Save As* option. This displays the Save As backstage area, as shown in Figure 7.9. Click the *Access 2002-2003 Database (*.mdb)* option in the *Save Database As* section and then click the Save As button at the bottom of the *Save Database As* section. This displays the Save As dialog box with the *Save as type* option set to *Microsoft Access Database (2002-2003) (*.mdb)* and the current database file name with the file extension *.mdb* inserted in the *File name* text box. At this dialog box, click the Save button.

With an object open in a database, clicking the *Save Object As* option in the *File Types* section of the Save As backstage area displays options for saving the object. Click the *Save Object As* option to save the selected object in the database or click the *PDF or XPS* option to save the object in PDF or XPS file format. The letters *PDF* stand for *portable document format*, a file format developed by Adobe Systems that captures all of the elements of a file as an electronic image. An XPS file is a Microsoft file format for publishing content in an easily viewable format. The letters *XPS* stand for *XML paper specification* and the letters *XML* stand for *extensible markup language*, which is a set of rules for encoding files electronically.

Saving an Object in PDF or XPS File Format

To save an object in PDF or XPS file format, open the object, click the File tab, and then click the *Save As* option. At the Save As backstage area, click the *Save Object As* option in the *File Types* section, click the *PDF or XPS* option in the *Save the current database object* section, and then click the Save As button. This displays the Publish as PDF or XPS dialog box with the name of the object inserted in the

Quick Steps

Save a Database in an Earlier Version
1. Open database.
2. Click File tab.
3. Click *Save As* option.
4. Click version in *Save Database As* section.
5. Click Save As button.
6. Click Save button.

Hint An Access 2007, 2010, 2013, or 2016 database cannot be opened with an earlier version of Access.

Quick Steps

Save an Object in PDF or XPS File Format
1. Open object.
2. Click File tab.
3. Click *Save As* option.
4. Click *Save Object As* option.
5. Click *PDF or XPS* option.
6. Click Save As button.

Figure 7.9 Save As Backstage Area with *Save Database As* Option Selected

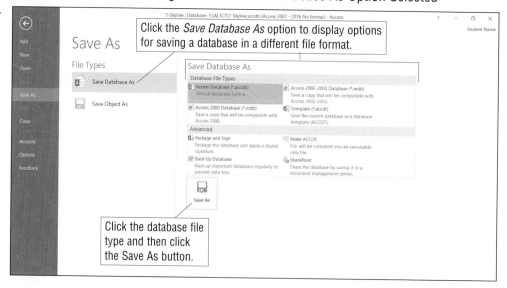

File name text box followed by the file extension *.pdf*, and the *Save as type* option set at *PDF (*.pdf)*. Click the Publish button and the object is saved in PDF file format. To specify that the object should open in Adobe Acrobat Reader, click the *Open file after publishing* check box to insert a check box. With this check box active, the object will open in Adobe Acrobat Reader when the Publish button is clicked.

A PDF file can be opened in Adobe Acrobat Reader, Microsoft Edge, or Word 2016. An XPS file can be opened in Adobe Acrobat Reader, Internet Explorer, or XPS Viewer. One method for opening a PDF or XPS file is to open File Explorer, navigate to the folder containing the file, right-click on the file, and then point to *Open with*. This displays a side menu with the programs that will open the file.

Backing Up a Database

Tutorial

Backing Up a Database

Databases often contain important company information, and loss of this information can cause major problems. Backing up a database is important to minimize the chances of losing critical company data and is especially important when several people update and manage a database.

Quick Steps

Backup Database
1. Click File tab.
2. Click *Save As* option.
3. Click *Back Up Database* option.
4. Click Save As button.
5. Click Save button.

To back up a database, open the database, click the File tab, and then click the *Save As* option. At the Save As backstage area, click the *Back Up Database* option in the *Advanced* section and then click the Save As button. This displays the Save As dialog box with a default database file name, which is the original database name followed by the current date, in the *File name* text box. Click the Save button to save the backup database while keeping the original database open.

Project 2d Saving a Database in a Previous Version, Saving an Object as a PDF File, and Backing Up a Database

Part 4 of 4

1. With **7-Skyline.accdb** open, save the Orders table as a PDF file by completing the following steps:
   a. Open the Orders table.
   b. Click the File tab and then click the *Save As* option.
   c. At the Save As backstage area, click the *Save Object As* option in the *File Types* section.
   d. Click the *PDF or XPS* option in the *Save the current database object* section.
   e. Click the Save As button.

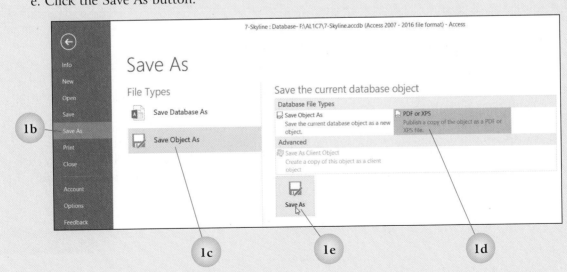

f. At the Publish as PDF or XPS dialog box, make sure the AL1C7 folder on your storage medium is the active folder and then click the *Open file after publishing* check box to insert a check mark. (Skip this step if the check box already contains a check mark.)

g. Click the Publish button.

h. When the Orders table opens in Adobe Acrobat Reader, scroll through the file and then close the file by clicking the Close button in the upper right corner of the screen.

2. Close the Orders table.

3. Save the database in a previous version of Access by completing the following steps:

a. Click the File tab and then click the *Save As* option.

b. At the Save As backstage area, click the *Access 2002-2003 Database (*.mdb)* option in the *Save Database As* section.

c. Click the Save As button.

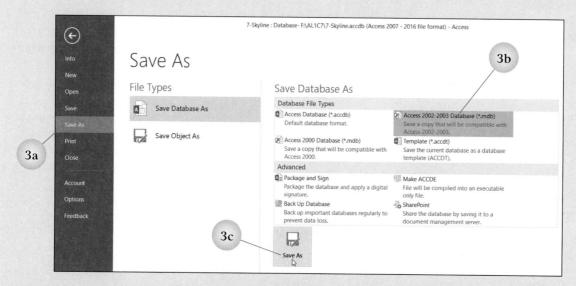

d. At the Save As dialog box, make sure the AL1C7 folder on your storage medium is the active folder and then click the Save button. This saves the database with the same name (**7-Skyline**) but with the file extension *.mdb*.

e. Notice that the Title bar displays the database file name *7-Skyline : Database (Access 2002 - 2003 file format)*.

4. Close the database.

5. Open **7-Skyline.accdb**. (Make sure you open the 7-Skyline database with the .accdb file extension.)

6. Create a backup of the database by completing the following steps:

a. Click the File tab and then click the *Save As* option.

b. At the Save As backstage area, click the *Back Up Database* option in the *Advanced* section and then click the Save As button.

c. At the Save As dialog box, notice that the database name in the *File name* text box displays the original file name followed by the current date (year, month, day).

d. Make sure the AL1C7 folder on your storage medium is the active folder and then click the Save button. (This saves the backup copy of the database to your folder and the original database remains open.)

7. Close **7-Skyline.accdb**.

Check Your Work

Chapter Summary

- A set of restrictions called a filter can be set on records in a table or form. A filter is used to select specific field values.

- Filter records with the Filter button in the Sort & Filter group on the Home tab.

- Click the Toggle Filter button in the Sort & Filter group to switch back and forth between data and filtered data.

- Remove a filter by clicking the Filter button in the Sort & Filter group and then clicking the *Clear filter from xxx* (where *xxx* is the name of the field).

- Another method for removing a filter is to click the Advanced button in the Sort & Filter group and then click *Clear All Filters*.

- Display a list of filter values by clicking the Filter button and then pointing to *Text Filters* (if the data is text), *Number Filters* (if the data is numbers), or *Date Filters* (if the data is dates).

- Filter by selection by clicking the Selection button in the Sort & Filter group.

- Right-click in a field entry to display a shortcut menu with filtering options.

- Filter by form by clicking the Advanced button in the Sort & Filter group and then clicking *Filter By Form* at the drop-down list. This displays a blank record with two tabs: Look for and Or.

- Display the structure of a database and relationships between objects at the Object Dependencies task pane. Display this task pane by clicking the Database Tools tab and then clicking the Object Dependencies button in the Relationships group.

- Click the Compact & Repair Database button in the Info backstage area to optimize database performance.

- To prevent unauthorized access to a database, encrypt the database with a password. To encrypt a database, the database must be opened in Exclusive mode using the Open button drop-down list in the Open dialog box. While in Exclusive mode, encrypt a database with a password using the Encrypt with Password button in the Info backstage area.

- To view properties for the current database, click the <u>View and edit database properties</u> hyperlink in the Info backstage area. The Properties dialog box contains a number of tabs containing information about the database.

- Save a database in a previous version of Access using options in the *Save Database As* section of the Save As backstage area.

- To save a database object in PDF or XPS file format, display the Save As backstage area, click the *Save Object As* option, click the *PDF or XPS* option, and then click the Save As button.

- Backup a database to maintain critical data. Backup a database with the *Back Up Database* option at the Save As backstage area.

Commands Review

FEATURE	RIBBON TAB, GROUP/OPTION	BUTTON, OPTION
filter	Home, Sort & Filter	
filter by form	Home, Sort & Filter	, *Filter By Form*
filter by selection	Home, Sort & Filter	
Info backstage area	File, *Info*	
Object Dependencies task pane	Database Tools, Relationships	
remove filter	Home, Sort & Filter	, *Clear filter from xxx* OR , *Clear All Filters*
toggle filter	Home, Sort & Filter	

Workbook

Chapter study tools and assessment activities are available in the *Workbook* ebook. These resources are designed to help you further develop and demonstrate mastery of the skills learned in this chapter.

Microsoft®

Access®

Exporting and Importing Data

Performance Objectives

Upon successful completion of Chapter 8, you will be able to:

1 Export Access data to Excel

2 Export Access data to Word

3 Merge Access data with a Word document

4 Export an Access object to a PDF or XPS file

5 Import data to a new table

6 Link data to a new table

7 Use the Office Clipboard

Precheck

Check your current skills to help focus your study.

Microsoft Office 2016 is a suite of programs that allows for easy data exchange between programs. In this chapter, you will learn how to export data from Access to Excel and Word, merge Access data with a Word document, export an Access object to a PDF or XPS file, import and link Excel data to a new table, and copy and paste data between applications and programs.

SNAP

If you are a SNAP user, launch the Precheck and Tutorials from your Assignments page.

Data Files

Before beginning chapter work, copy the AL1C8 folder to your storage medium and then make AL1C8 the active folder.

Project 1 **Export Data to Excel and Export and Merge Data to Word** **5 Parts**

You will export a table and query to Excel and export a table and report to Word. You will also merge data in an Access table and query with a Word document.

Preview Finished Project

Exporting Data

One of the advantages of using the Microsoft Office suite is the ability to exchange data between programs. Access, like other programs in the suite, offers a feature to export data from Access into Excel and/or Word. The Export group on the External Data tab contains buttons for exporting a table, query, form, or report to other programs, such as Excel and Word.

Tutorial

Exporting Access Data to Excel

 Excel

Quick Steps

Export Access Data to Excel
1. Click table, query, or form.
2. Click External Data tab.
3. Click Excel button in Export group.
4. Make changes at Export - Excel Spreadsheet dialog box.
5. Click OK.

Insert a check mark in this check box to export all object formatting and layout.

Insert a check mark in this check box to open the file in the destination program.

Exporting Access Data to Excel

Use the Excel button in the Export group on the External Data tab to export data in a table, query, or form to an Excel worksheet. Click the object containing the data to be exported to Excel, click the External Data tab, and then click the Excel button in the Export group. The Export - Excel Spreadsheet dialog box displays, as shown in Figure 8.1.

Figure 8.1 Export - Excel Spreadsheet Dialog Box

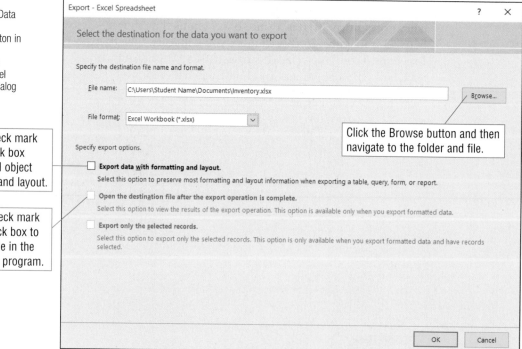

Hint Data exported from Access to Excel is saved as an Excel workbook with the .xlsx file extension.

At the dialog box, Access uses the name of the object as the Excel workbook name. This can be changed by selecting the current name and then typing a new name. The file format also can be changed with the *File format* option. Click the *Export data with formatting and layout* check box to insert a check mark. This exports all data formatting to the Excel workbook. To open Excel with the exported data, click the *Open the destination file after the export operation is complete* option to insert a check mark.

Hint You can export only one database object at a time.

When all changes have been made, click OK. This opens Excel with the data in a workbook. Make changes to the workbook and then save, print, and close the workbook. When Excel is closed, Access displays with a dialog box, asking if the export step should be saved. At this dialog box, insert a check mark in the *Save export steps* check box to save the export steps or leave the check box blank and then click the Close button.

Project 1a Exporting a Table and Query to Excel

Part 1 of 5

1. Open **8-Hilltop.accdb** from the AL1C8 folder on your storage medium and enable the content.
2. Save the Inventory table as an Excel workbook by completing the following steps:
   a. Click *Inventory* in the Tables group in the Navigation pane.
   b. Click the External Data tab and then click the Excel button in the Export group.
   c. At the Export - Excel Spreadsheet dialog box, click the Browse button.
   d. At the File Save dialog box, navigate to the AL1C8 folder on your storage medium and then click the Save button.

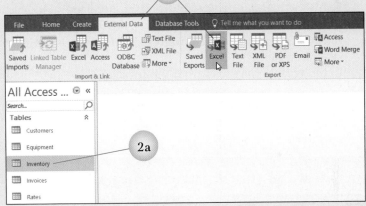

   e. Click the *Export data with formatting and layout* option to insert a check mark in the check box.
   f. Click the *Open the destination file after the export operation is complete* option to insert a check mark in the check box.

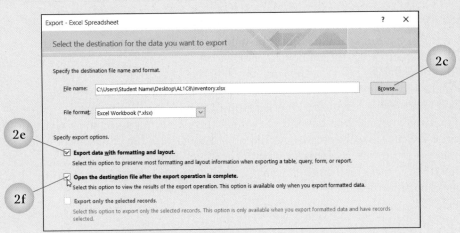

g. Click OK.

h. When the data displays on the screen in Excel as a worksheet, select the range A2:A11 and then click the Center button in the Alignment group on the Home tab.

i. Select the range D2:F11 and then click the Center button.

j. Click the Save button on the Quick Access Toolbar.

k. Print the worksheet by pressing Ctrl + P and then clicking the Print button at the Print backstage area.

l. Close the worksheet and then close Excel.

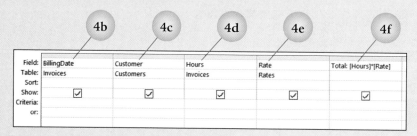

	A	B	C	D	E	F
1	EquipmentID	PurchaseDate	PurchasePrice	AvailableHours	ServiceHours	RepairHours
2	10	01-Sep-13	$65,540.00	120	15	10
3	11	01-Feb-14	$105,500.00	125	20	15
4	12	01-Jun-14	$55,345.00	140	10	10
5	13	05-May-15	$86,750.00	120	20	20
6	14	15-Jul-16	$4,500.00	160	5	5
7	15	01-Oct-16	$95,900.00	125	25	20
8	16	01-Dec-16	$3,450.00	150	10	5
9	17	10-Apr-17	$5,600.00	160	5	10
10	18	15-Jun-17	$8,000.00	150	5	5
11	19	30-Sep-18	$42,675.00	120	20	25
12						

3. In Access, click the Close button to close the dialog box.

4. Design a query that extracts records from three tables with the following specifications:

a. Add the Invoices, Customers, and Rates tables to the query window.

b. Insert the *BillingDate* field from the Invoices table field list box in the first field in the *Field* row.

c. Insert the *Customer* field from the Customers table field list box in the second field in the *Field* row.

d. Insert the *Hours* field from the Invoices table field list box in the third field in the *Field* row.

e. Insert the *Rate* field from the Rates table field list box in the fourth field in the *Field* row.

f. Click in the fifth field in the *Field* row, type Total: [Hours]*[Rate], and then press the Enter key.

	4b	4c	4d	4e	4f

Field:	BillingDate	Customer	Hours	Rate	Total: [Hours]*[Rate]
Table:	Invoices	Customers	Invoices	Rates	
Sort:					
Show:	☑	☑	☑	☑	☑
Criteria:					
or:					

g. Run the query.

h. If necessary, automatically adjust the column width of the *Customer* field.

i. Save the query with the name *CustomerInvoices*.

j. Close the query.

5. Export the CustomerInvoices query to Excel by completing the following steps:

a. Click *CustomerInvoices* in the Queries group in the Navigation pane.

b. Click the External Data tab and then click the Excel button in the Export group.

c. At the Export - Excel Spreadsheet dialog box, click the *Export data with formatting and layout* option to insert a check mark in the check box.

d. Click the *Open the destination file after the export operation is complete* option to insert a check mark in the check box.

e. Click OK.

f. When the data displays on the screen in Excel as a worksheet, select the range C2:C31 and then click the Center button in the Alignment group on the Home tab.

g. Click the Save button on the Quick Access Toolbar.

h. Print the worksheet by pressing Ctrl + P and then clicking the Print button at the Print backstage area.

i. Close the worksheet and then close Excel.

6. In Access, click the Close button to close the dialog box.

Check Your Work

Exporting Access Data to Word

Tutorial

Exporting Access Data to Word

 More

Export data from Access to Word in a similar manner as exporting to Excel. To export data to Word, click the object in the Navigation pane, click the External Data tab, click the More button in the Export group, and then click *Word* at the drop-down list. At the Export - RTF File dialog box, make changes and then click OK. Word automatically opens and the data displays in a Word document that is saved automatically with the same name as the database object. The difference is that the file extension *.rtf* is added to the name. An RTF file is saved in rich-text format, which preserves formatting such as fonts and styles. A document saved with the .rtf extension can be exported in Word and other Windows word processing or desktop publishing programs.

Quick Steps

Export Data to Word
1. Click table, query, form, or report.
2. Click External Data tab.
3. Click More button in Export group.
4. Click *Word*.
5. Make changes at Export - RTF File dialog box.
6. Click OK.

Project 1b Exporting a Table and Report to Word

Part 2 of 5

1. With **8-Hilltop.accdb** open, click *Invoices* in the Tables group in the Navigation pane.

2. Click the External Data tab, click the More button in the Export group, and then click *Word* at the drop-down list.

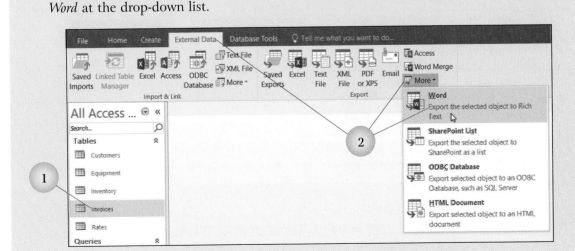

3. At the Export - RTF File dialog box, click the Browse button.
4. At the File Save dialog box, make sure the AL1C8 folder on your storage medium is active and then click the Save button.
5. At the Export - RTF File dialog box, click the *Open the destination file after the export operation is complete* check box to insert a check mark.

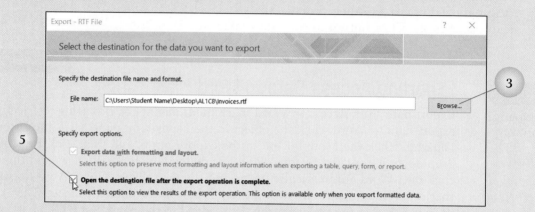

6. Click OK.
7. With **Invoices.rtf** open in Word, print the file by pressing Ctrl + P and then clicking the Print button at the Print backstage area.
8. Close **Invoices.rtf** and then close Word.
9. In Access, click the Close button to close the dialog box.
10. Create a report with the Report Wizard by completing the following steps:
    a. Click the Create tab and then click the Report Wizard button in the Reports group.
    b. At the first Report Wizard dialog box, insert the following fields in the *Selected Fields* list box:

    From the Customers table:
    Customer
    From the Equipment table:
    Equipment
    From the Invoices table:
    BillingDate
    Hours

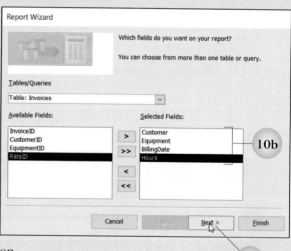

    c. After inserting the fields, click the Next button.
    d. At the second Report Wizard dialog box, make sure *by Customers* is selected in the list box in the upper left corner and then click the Next button.
    e. At the third Report Wizard dialog box, click the Next button.
    f. At the fourth Report Wizard dialog box, click the Next button.
    g. At the fifth Report Wizard dialog box, click *Block* in the *Layout* section and then click the Next button.
    h. At the sixth and final Report Wizard dialog box, select the current name in the *What title do you want for your report?* text box, type CustomerReport, and then click the Finish button.
    i. When the report displays in Print Preview, click the Print button at the left side of the Print Preview tab and then click OK at the Print dialog box.
    j. Save and then close the CustomerReport report.

11. Export the CustomerReport report to Word by completing the following steps:
    a. Click *CustomerReport* in the Reports group in the Navigation pane.
    b. Click the External Data tab, click the More button in the Export group, and then click *Word* at the drop-down list.
    c. At the Export - RTF File dialog box, click the *Open the destination file after export operation is complete* option to insert a check mark in the check box and then click OK.
    d. When the data displays on the screen in Word, print the document by pressing Ctrl + P and then clicking the Print button at the Print backstage area.
    e. Save and then close the CustomerReport document.
    f. Close Word.
12. In Access, click the Close button to close the dialog box.

> **Check Your Work**

  Tutorial

Merging Access Data with a Word Document

Merging Access Data with a Word Document

Data from an Access table or query can be merged with a Word document. When merging data, the data in the Access table is considered the data source and the Word document is considered the main document. When the merge is completed, the merged documents display in Word.

Word Merge

To merge data in a table, click the table in the Navigation pane, click the External Data tab, and then click the Word Merge button. When merging Access data, either type the text in the main document or merge Access data with an existing Word document.

Project 1c Merging Access Table Data with a Word Document   Part 3 of 5

1. With **8-Hilltop.accdb** open, click *Customers* in the Tables group in the Navigation pane.
2. Click the External Data tab.
3. Click the Word Merge button in the Export group.

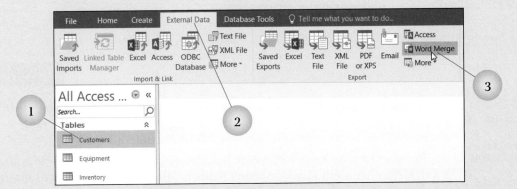

4. At the Microsoft Word Mail Merge Wizard dialog box, make sure *Link your data to an existing Microsoft Word document* is selected and then click OK.
5. At the Select Microsoft Word Document dialog box, make sure the AL1C8 folder on your storage medium is the active folder and then double-click the document named **8-HilltopLetter.docx**.
6. Click the Word button on the taskbar.

7. Click the Maximize button that displays in the *8-HilltopLetter.docx* Title bar and then close the Mail Merge task pane.
8. Press the Down Arrow key six times (not the Enter key) and then type the current date.
9. Press the Down Arrow key four times and then insert fields for merging from the Customers table by completing the following steps:

   a. Click the Insert Merge Field button arrow in the Write & Insert Fields group and then click *Customer* in the drop-down list. (This inserts the «Customer» field in the document.)

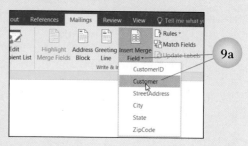

9a

   b. Press the Enter key, click the Insert Merge Field button arrow, and then click *StreetAddress* in the drop-down list.

   c. Press the Enter key, click the Insert Merge Field button arrow, and then click *City* in the drop-down list.

   d. Type a comma (,) and then press the spacebar.

   e. Click the Insert Merge Field button arrow and then click *State* in the drop-down list.

   f. Press the spacebar, click the Insert Merge Field button arrow, and then click *ZipCode* in the drop-down list.

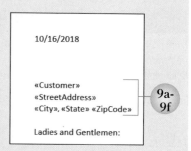

10/16/2018

«Customer»
«StreetAddress»
«City», «State» «ZipCode»

Ladies and Gentlemen:

9a-
9f

   g. Replace the letters *XX* at the bottom of the letter with your initials.

   h. Click the Finish & Merge button in the Finish group and then click *Edit Individual Documents* in the drop-down list.

   i. At the Merge to New Document dialog box, make sure *All* is selected and then click OK.

   j. When the merge is completed, save the new document and name it **8-HilltopLtrs** in the AL1C8 folder on your storage medium.

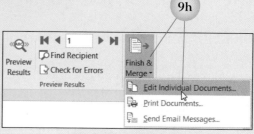

9h

10. Print just the first two pages (two letters) of **8-HilltopLtrs.docx**.
11. Close **8-HilltopLtrs.docx** and then close **8-HilltopLetter.docx** without saving the changes.
12. Close Word.
13. Close **8-Hilltop.accdb**.

Check Your Work

Quick Steps

Merge Data with Word
1. Click table or query.
2. Click External Data tab.
3. Click Word Merge button.
4. Make choices at each dialog box.

 Address Block

A query in a database can be used to merge with a Word document. In Project 1c, a table was merged with an existing Word document. A table or query also can be merged and then the Word document typed.

In Project 1c, a number of merge fields were inserted for the inside address of a letter. Another method for inserting fields for the inside address is to insert the «AddressBlock» field, which inserts all of the fields required for the inside address. Insert the «AddressBlock» composite field by clicking the Address Block button in the Write & Insert Fields group on the Mailings tab. Clicking the button displays the Insert Address Block dialog box with a preview of how the fields will be inserted in the document to create the inside address. The dialog box also contains buttons and options for customizing the fields. Click OK and the «AddressBlock» field is inserted in the document. The «AddressBlock» field is an example of a composite field, which groups a number of fields together.

In Project 1c, the «AddressBlock» composite field could not be used because the *Customer* field was not recognized by Word as a field for the inside address. In Project 1d, a query will be created that contains the *FirstName* and *LastName* fields, which Word recognizes and uses for the «AddressBlock» composite field.

Project 1d Performing a Query and then Merging with a Word Document

Part 4 of 5

1. Open **8-CopperState.accdb** from the AL1C8 folder on your storage medium and enable the content.
2. Perform a query with the Query Wizard and modify the query by completing the following steps:
   a. Click the Create tab and then click the Query Wizard button in the Queries group.
   b. At the New Query dialog box, make sure Simple Query Wizard is selected and then click OK.
   c. At the first Simple Query Wizard dialog box, click the *Tables/Queries* option box arrow and then click *Table: Clients*.
   d. Click the All Fields button to insert all of the fields in the *Selected Fields* list box.
   e. Click the Next button.
   f. At the second Simple Query Wizard dialog box, make the following changes:
      1) Select the current name in the *What title do you want for your query?* text box and then type ClientsPhoenix.
      2) Click the *Modify the query design* option.
      3) Click the Finish button.
   g. At the query window, click in the *City* field in the *Criteria* row, type Phoenix, and then press the Enter key.
   h. Click the Run button in the Results group. (Only clients living in Phoenix will display.)
   i. Save and then close the query.
3. Click *ClientsPhoenix* in the Queries group in the Navigation pane.
4. Click the External Data tab and then click the Word Merge button in the Export group.
5. At the Microsoft Word Mail Merge Wizard dialog box, click the *Create a new document and then link the data to it* option and then click OK.
6. Click the Word button on the taskbar.

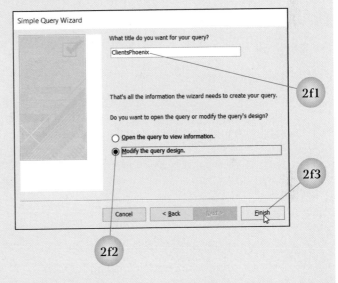

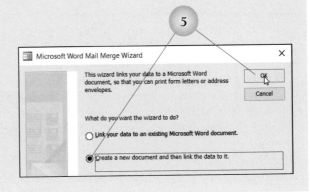

7. Click the Maximize button that displays in the Document1 Title bar and then close the Mail Merge task pane.

8. Complete the following steps to type text and insert the «AddressBlock» composite field in the blank Word document:

   a. Click the Home tab and then click the *No Spacing* style in the Styles group.

   b. Press the Enter key six times.

   c. Type the current date.

   d. Press the Enter key four times.

   e. Click the Mailings tab.

   f. Insert the «AddressBlock» composite field by clicking the Address Block button in the Write & Insert Fields group on the Mailings tab and then clicking OK at the Insert Address Block dialog box. (This inserts the «AddressBlock» composite field in the document.)

   g. Press the Enter key two times and then type the salutation Ladies and Gentlemen:.

   h. Press the Enter key two times and then type the following paragraphs of text (press the Enter key two times after typing the first paragraph):

   At the Grant Street West office of Copper State Insurance, we have hired two additional insurance representatives as well as one support staff member to ensure that we meet all your insurance needs. To accommodate the new staff, we have moved to a larger office just a few blocks away. Our new address is 3450 Grant Street West, Suite 110, Phoenix AZ 85003. Our telephone number, (602) 555-6300, has remained the same.

   If you have any questions or concerns about your insurance policies or want to discuss adding or changing current coverage, please stop by or give us a call. We are committed to providing our clients with the most comprehensive automobile insurance coverage in the county.

   i. Press the Enter key two times and then type the following complimentary close at the left margin (press the Enter key four times after typing *Sincerely,*):

   Sincerely,

   Lou Galloway
   Manager

   XX (Type your initials instead of XX.)
   8-CSLtrs.docx

   j. Click the Finish & Merge button in the Finish group on the Mailings tab and then click *Edit Individual Documents* in the drop-down menu.

   k. At the Merge to New Document dialog box, make sure *All* is selected, and then click OK.

   l. When the merge is complete, save the new document in the AL1C8 folder on your storage medium and name it **8-CSLtrs**.

9. Print the first two pages (two letters) of **8-CSLtrs.docx**.

10. Close **8-CSLtrs.docx**.

11. Save the main document as **8-CSMainDoc** in the AL1C8 folder on your storage medium and then close the document.

12. Close Word.

Check Your Work

Quick Steps

Export an Access Object to a PDF or XPS File

1. Click object in the Navigation pane.
2. Click External Data tab.
3. Click PDF or XPS button.
4. Navigate to folder.
5. Click Publish button.

PDF or XPS

Exporting an Access Object to a PDF or XPS File

With the PDF or XPS button in the Export group on the External Data tab, an Access object can be exported to a PDF or XPS file. As explained in Chapter 7, the letters *PDF* stand for *portable document format*, which is a file format that captures all of the elements of a file as an electronic image. The letters *XPS* stand for *XML paper specification* and the letters *XML* stand for *extensible markup language*, which is a set of rules for encoding files electronically.

To export an Access object to the PDF or XPS file format, click the object, click the External Data tab, and then click the PDF or XPS button in the Export group. This displays the Publish as PDF or XPS dialog box with the *PDF (*.pdf)* option selected in the *Save as type* option box. To save the Access object in XPS file format, click the *Save as type* option box and then click *XPS Document (*.xps)* at the drop-down list. At the Save As dialog box, type a name in the *File name* text box and then click the Publish button.

To open a PDF or XPS file in a web browser, open the browser and then press Ctrl + O to display the Open dialog box. At the Open dialog box, change the *Files of type* to *All Files (*.*)*, navigate to the folder containing the file, and then double-click the file.

Project 1e Exporting an Access Object to a PDF File

Part 5 of 5

1. With **8-CopperState.accdb** open, export the Coverage table to a PDF file by completing the following steps:
   a. Click *Coverage* in the Tables group in the Navigation pane.
   b. Click the External Data tab.
   c. Click the PDF or XPS button in the Export group.
   d. At the Publish as PDF or XPS dialog box, navigate to the AL1C8 folder on your storage medium, click the *Open file after publishing* check box to insert a check mark, and then click the Publish button.

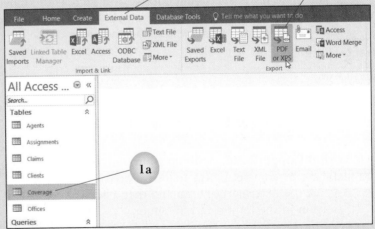

   e. When the Coverage table data displays in Adobe Acrobat Reader, scroll through the file to see how it looks.
   f. Print the PDF file by clicking the Print button on the menu bar and then clicking the Print button at the Print dialog box.
   g. Close Adobe Acrobat Reader by clicking the Close button in the upper right corner of the window.
2. In Access, click the Close button to close the dialog box.

Check Your Work

You will import an Excel worksheet into an Access table. You will also link an
Excel worksheet to an Access table and then add a new record to the Access
table.

Preview Finished Project

Importing and Linking Data to a New Table

♀ Hint Store data in
Access and analyze it
using Excel.

In addition to exporting Access data to Excel or Word, data from other programs
can be imported into an Access table. For example, data from an Excel worksheet
can be imported to create a new table in a database. Data in the original program
is not connected to the data imported into an Access table. If changes are made to
data in the original program, those changes are not reflected in the Access table.
To connect the imported data with the data in the original program, link the data.

Tutorial

Importing Data to
a New Table

Importing Data to a New Table

To import data, click the External Data tab and then determine where to retrieve
data with options in the Import & Link group. At the Import dialog box that
displays, click the Browse button and then double-click the file name. This activates
the Import Wizard and displays the first wizard dialog box. The appearance of the
dialog box varies depending on the file selected. Complete the steps of the Import
Wizard, specifying information such as the range of data, whether the first row
contains column headings, whether to store the data in a new table or existing
table, the primary key, and the name of the table.

Q̄uick Steps

Import Data into a
New Table
1. Click External Data tab.
2. Click application in
   Import & Link group.
3. Click Browse button.
4. Double-click file name.
5. Make choices at each
   wizard dialog box.

Project 2a Importing an Excel Worksheet to an Access Table   Part 1 of 2

1. With **8-CopperState.accdb** open, import an Excel worksheet into a new table in the
   database by completing the following steps:
   a. Click the External Data tab and then click the Excel
      button in the Import & Link group.
   b. At the Get External Data - Excel
      Spreadsheet dialog box, click the Browse
      button and then make the AL1C8 folder
      on your storage medium the active folder.
   c. Double-click *8-Policies.xlsx* in the list box.
   d. Click OK at the Get External Data - Excel
      Spreadsheet dialog box.
   e. At the first Import Spreadsheet Wizard dialog box, make sure the *First Row Contains
      Column Headings* check box contains a check mark and then click the Next button.

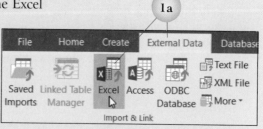

f. At the second Import Spreadsheet Wizard dialog box, click the Next button.
g. At the third Import Spreadsheet Wizard dialog box, click the *Choose my own primary key* option (which inserts *PolicyID* in the option box to the right of the option) and then click the Next button.

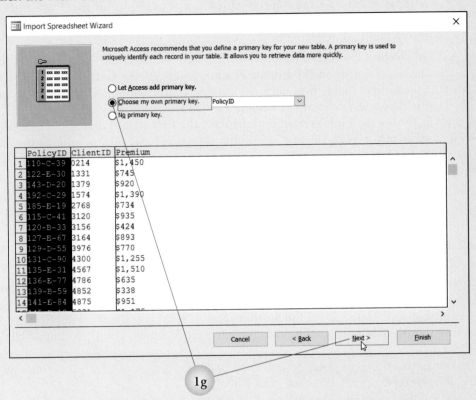

1g

h. At the fourth Import Spreadsheet Wizard dialog box, type Policies in the *Import to Table* text box and then click the Finish button.

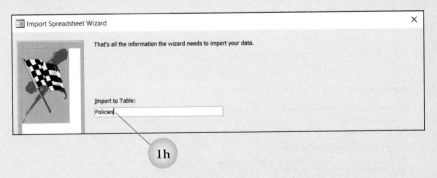

1h

i. At the Get External Data - Excel Spreadsheet dialog box, click the Close button.
2. Open the new Policies table in Datasheet view.
3. Print and then close the Policies table.

Check Your Work

Linking Data to an Excel Worksheet

Imported data is not connected to the source program. If the data will only be used in Access, import it. However, to update the data in a program other than Access, link the data. Changes made to linked data in the source program file are reflected in the destination program file. For example, an Excel worksheet can be linked with an Access table and, when changes are made to the Excel worksheet, the changes are reflected in the Access table.

To link Excel data to a new table, click the External Data tab and then click the Excel button in the Import & Link group. At the Get External Data - Excel Spreadsheet dialog box, click the Browse button, double-click the file name, click the *Link to a data source by creating a linked table* option, and then click OK. This activates the Link Wizard and displays the first wizard dialog box. Complete the steps of the Link Wizard, specifying the same basic information as the Import Wizard.

 Excel

Project 2b Linking an Excel Worksheet to an Access Table

Part 2 of 2

1. With **8-CopperState.accdb** open, click the External Data tab and then click the Excel button in the Import & Link group.
2. At the Get External Data - Excel Spreadsheet dialog box, click the Browse button, make sure the AL1C8 folder on your storage medium is active, and then double-click **8-Policies.xlsx**.
3. At the Get External Data - Excel Spreadsheet dialog box, click the *Link to the data source by creating a linked table* option and then click OK.

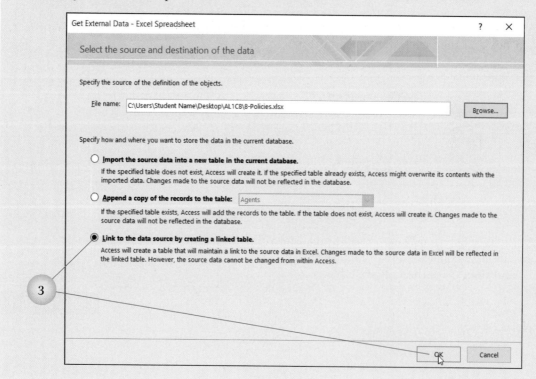

4. At the first Link Spreadsheet Wizard dialog box, make sure the *First Row Contains Column Headings* option contains a check mark and then click the Next button.
5. At the second Link Spreadsheet Wizard dialog box, type LinkedPolicies in the *Linked Table Name* text box and then click the Finish button.
6. At the message stating the linking is finished, click OK.
7. Open the new LinkedPolicies table in Datasheet view.
8. Close the LinkedPolicies table.
9. Open Excel, open the **8-Policies.xlsx** workbook, and then make the following changes:
   a. Change the amount *$745* in cell C3 to *$850*.
   b. Add the following information in the specified cells:

22	170-C-20	7335	$ 875
23	173-D-77	7521	$ 556
24	180-E-05	8223	$ 721
25	188-D-63	8854	$ 1,384
26	190-C-28	3120	$ 685.00
27			

   A26: 190-C-28
   B26: 3120
   C26: 685

   9b

10. Save, print, and then close **8-Policies.xlsx**.
11. Close Excel.
12. With Access as the active program and **8-CopperState.accdb** open, open the LinkedPolicies table. Notice the changes you just made in Excel are reflected in the table.
13. Close the LinkedPolicies table.
14. Close **8-CopperState.accdb**.

Check Your Work

Project 3 **Collect Data in Word and Paste It into an Access Table** **1 Part**

You will open a Word document containing Hilltop customer names and addresses and then copy the data and paste it into an Access table.

Preview Finished Project

Using the Office Clipboard

Use the Office Clipboard to collect and paste multiple items. Up to 24 different items can be collected and pasted in Access or other programs in the Office suite. To copy and paste multiple items, display the Clipboard task pane, shown in Figure 8.2, by clicking the Clipboard group task pane launcher on the Home tab.

Select the data or object to be copied and then click the Copy button in the Clipboard group on the Home tab. Continue selecting text or items and clicking the Copy button. To insert an item from the Clipboard task pane to a field in an Access table, make the destination field active and then click the button in the task pane representing the item. If the copied item is text, the first 50 characters display in the Clipboard task pane. After items have been inserted, click the Clear All button to remove any remaining items from the Clipboard task pane.

Data can be copied from one object to another in an Access database or from a file in another program to an Access database. In Project 3, data from a Word document will be copied and then pasted into an Access table. Data also can be collected from other programs, such as PowerPoint and Excel.

Figure 8.2 Office Clipboard Task Pane

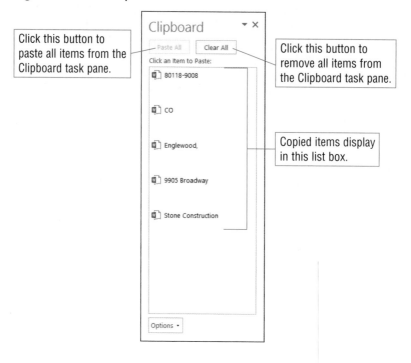

Click this button to paste all items from the Clipboard task pane.

Click this button to remove all items from the Clipboard task pane.

Copied items display in this list box.

Project 3 Collecting Data in Word and Pasting It into an Access Table

Part 1 of 1

1. Open **8-Hilltop.accdb** and then open the Customers table.
2. Copy data from Word and paste it into the Customers table by completing the following steps:
   a. Open Word, make AL1C8 the active folder, and then open **8-HilltopCustomers.docx**.
   b. Make sure the Home tab is active.
   c. Click the Clipboard group task pane launcher to display the Clipboard task pane.
   d. Select the first company name, *Stone Construction*, and then click the Copy button in the Clipboard group.

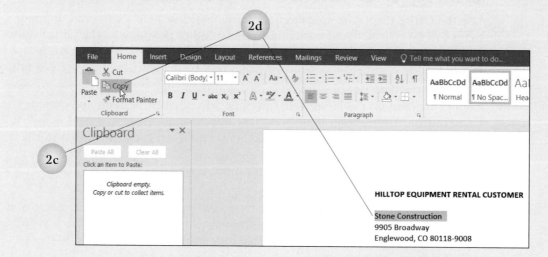

e. Select the street address, *9905 Broadway*, and then click the Copy button.

f. Select the city, *Englewood* (selecting only the city and not the comma after the city), and then click the Copy button.

g. Select the state, *CO* (selecting only the two letters and not the space after the letters), and then click the Copy button.

h. Select the zip code, *80118-9008*, and then click the Copy button.

i. Click the button on the taskbar representing Access. (Make sure the Customers table is open and displays in Datasheet view.)

j. Click in the first empty field in the *CustomerID* field column and then type 178.

k. Display the Clipboard task pane by clicking the Home tab and then clicking the Clipboard group task pane launcher.

l. Close the Navigation pane by clicking the Shutter Bar Open/Close Button.

m. Click in the first empty field in the *Customer* field column and then click *Stone Construction* in the Clipboard task pane.

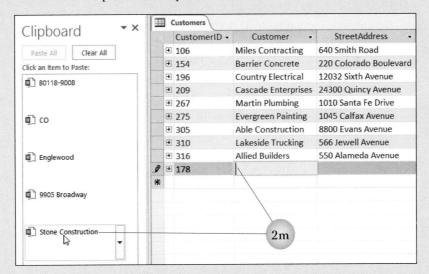

n. Click in the *StreetAddress* field and then click *9905 Broadway* in the Clipboard task pane.

o. Click in the *City* field and then click *Englewood* in the Clipboard task pane.

p. Click in the *State* field and then click *CO* in the Clipboard task pane.

q. Click in the *ZipCode* field, make sure the insertion point is positioned at the left side of the field, and then click *80118-9008* in the Clipboard task pane.

r. Click the Clear All button in the Clipboard task pane. (This removes all entries from the Clipboard.)

3. Complete steps similar to those in 2d through 2q to copy the information for Laughlin Products and paste it into the Customers table. (The customer ID number is 225.)

4. Click the Clear All button in the Clipboard task pane.

5. Close the Clipboard task pane by clicking the Close button (which contains an *X*) in the upper right corner of the task pane.

6. Save, print, and then close the Customers table.

7. Open the Navigation pane by clicking the Shutter Bar Open/Close Button.

8. Make Word the active program, close **8-HilltopCustomers.docx** without saving changes, and then close Word.

9. Close **8-Hilltop.accdb**.

Check Your Work

Chapter Summary

- Use the Excel button in the Export group on the External Data tab to export data in a table, query, or form to an Excel worksheet.

- Export data in a table, query, form, or report to a Word document by clicking the More button and then clicking *Word* at the drop-down list. Access exports the data to an RTF (rich-text format) file.

- Access data can be merged with a Word document. The Access data is the data source and the Word document is the main document. To merge data, click the table or query, click the External Data tab, and then click the Word Merge button in the Export group.

- Export an Access object to a PDF or XPS file with the PDF or XPS button in the Export group on the External Data tab.

- Use the Excel button in the Import group on the External Data tab to import Excel data to an Access table.

- Imported data can be linked so that changes made to the data in the source program file are reflected in the destination source file.

- To link imported data, click the *Link to the data source by creating a linked table* option at the Get External Data dialog box.

- Use the Clipboard task pane to collect up to 24 different items in Access or other programs and paste them in various locations.

- Display the Clipboard task pane by clicking the Clipboard group task pane launcher on the Home tab.

Commands Review

FEATURE	RIBBON TAB, GROUP	BUTTON, OPTION
Clipboard task pane	Home, Clipboard	
export object to Excel	External Data, Export	
export object to PDF or XPS	External Data, Export	
export object to Word	External Data, Export	, *Word*
import Excel data	External Data, Import & Link	
merge Access data with Word	External Data, Export	

Workbook

Chapter study tools and assessment activities are available in the *Workbook* ebook. These resources are designed to help you further develop and demonstrate mastery of the skills learned in this chapter.

Unit assessment activities are also available in the *Workbook*. These activities are designed to help you demonstrate mastery of the skills learned in this unit.

Index

sorting in records, 117
database
    backing up, 219–220
    closing, 7–9
    compacting and repairing,
        213–215
    creating new database, 4
    defined, 4
    design principles for, 21–22
    encrypting with password,
        214–215
    naming, 4
    opening, 4–6, 8–9
    pinning/unpinning to *Recent*
        option list, 6
    relational, 21
    saving, 4, 218–220
    viewing and customizing
        database properties, 215–
        217
    viewing object dependencies,
        211–212
Database Password dialog box,
    214–215
Database Tools tab, 211
Datasheet view, 10
    creating split forms and,
        162–163
    creating tables in, 22–31
        assigning default value,
            27–28
        assigning field size, 28
        changing AutoNumber
            field, 28
        data types, 22–24
        defining the table structure,
            22
        inserting field name,
            caption, description,
            26–27
        inserting Quick Start fields,
            28–29
        renaming field heading, 26
    formatting table data in,
        118–121
data types, 22–24, 103
Date and Time button, 143
Date Filters, 205
Date/Time data type, 103
Date & Time data type, 23
Decrypt Database button, 214

default value, assigning, 27–28,
    106
Default Value button, 27–28
defining the table structure, 22
Delete button, 10, 139, 177
Delete Columns button, 71
Delete Rows button, 113
deleting
    control object, 143
    fields, 12–14
        in Design View, 112–117
    forms, 137–138
    query, 75
    records, 10–12
        in forms, 139–140
        in related tables, 50–51
    relationships, 46
    report, 177
    table, 16
Descending button, 117, 139,
    177
Description text box, 26
Design view, 136
    creating tables in, 102–105
        assigning default value, 106
        inserting, moving and
            deleting fields, 112–117
        inserting Total row, 113
        overview, 102–105
        using Input Mask, 106–107
        using Lookup Wizard,
            111–112
        validating field entries, 111
    determining primary key, 37
    displaying table in, 37
    Properties table in, 102–103
Detail section, 137, 143, 176
dialog box, getting help in,
    128–129

E

editing, relationships, 46–49
Edit Relationships button, 46
Edit Relationships dialog box,
    40–41
Enable Content button, 5
encrypting database with
    password, 214–215
Encrypt with Password button,
    214

Enforce Referential Integrity,
    41, 50
Enter Fields Properties dialog
    box, 26
entity integrity, 37
Excel button, 224, 236
Excel worksheet
    exporting data to, 224–227
        Word document, 227–229
    linking data to, 236–237
expand indicator, 55
exporting
    Access object to PDF or XPS
        file, 233
    data to Excel document,
        224–227
    data to Word document,
        227–229
Expression Builder dialog box,
    86–87
External Data tab, 224, 227

F

Field List task pane, 157–158
field names, 9
    inserting, 26–27
    renaming, 26
fields
    assigning default value, 27–28
    assigning size, 28
    calculated field, 86–88
    creating, in Design view,
        102–103
    data types, 22–24
    defined, 22
    deleting, 12–14
        in Design View, 112–117
    filtering on specific field,
        205–206
    inserting, 12–14
        in Design View, 112–117
        in forms, 157–160
        name, caption and
            description, 26–27
        in query design grid, 63–64
        Quick Start fields, 28–29
    moving, 12–14
        in Design View, 112–117
    primary key field, 36–39
    in query

Report button, creating report with, 174–176
Report Layout Tools Arrange tab, 182
Report Layout Tools Design tab, 174, 182
Report Layout Tools Format tab, 182
Report Layout Tools Page Setup tab, 182
reports, 173–199
  creating
    with fields from multiple tables, 195
    with Report button, 174–176
    with Report Wizard, 192–195
  customizing, 182–191
  as database object, 7
  description of, 7
  filtering records in, 203–205, 205–206
  formatting, 182–191
    conditional formatting, 182–186
    grouping and sorting records, 186–189
    inserting calculator, 190–191
  modifying, 176–181
    control objects, 176–177
    deleting, 177
    displaying and customizing, in print preview, 177–178
    finding data in, 177–181
    sorting records, 177
  modifying record source, 175
  purpose of, 174
Report Wizard, creating report with, 192–195
Report Wizard dialog box, 192–193
ribbon, 5, 6
Run button, 63

S

Save As option, 218, 219
saving
  database, 4, 218–220

object in PDF or XPS file format, 218–220
security message warning bar, 5
Select All button, 151
Select button, 144
Select Column button, 147
selection, filtering by, 207–209
Selection button, 207
Select Row button, 147
shortcut menu, filtering by, 207–208
Short Text button, 28
Short Text data type, 23, 103
showing, fields in query, 71
Show Table button, 46
Show Table dialog box, 46, 62
Shutter Bar Open/Close button, 7
Simple Query Wizard, performing queries with, 80–86
Simple Query Wizard dialog box, 80–81
Size button, 17
sorting
  data in records, 117
  fields in query, 71–74
  records and fields in tables, 119–121
  records in forms, 139
  records in reports, 177, 186–189
Spelling button, 122
spelling check feature, 122–123
Spelling dialog box, 122
split form, creating, 162–165
Split Horizontally button, 147
Split Vertically button, 147
Status bar, 5, 6
subdatasheet
  defined, 54
  displaying related records in, 54–57
synchronous, 162

T

Table button, 22, 102
table move handle, 137, 147, 176, 182
tables

collecting data in Word and pasting in, 238–239
columns
  hiding, unhiding, freezing and unfreezing, 14–16
  width changes, 14–16
creating in Datasheet view, 22–31
  assigning default value, 27–28
  assigning field size, 28
  changing AutoNumber field, 28
  data types, 22–24
  defining the table structure, 22
  inserting field name, caption, description, 26–27
  inserting Quick Start fields, 28–29
  renaming field heading, 26
creating in Design View, 102–117
  assigning default value, 106
  inserting, moving and deleting fields, 112–117
  inserting Total row, 113
  overview, 102–105
  using Input Mask, 106–107
  using Lookup Wizard, 111–112
  validating field entries, 111
database design principles, 21–22
as database object, 7
defined, 22
deleting, 16
description of, 7
exporting, to Excel, 224–227
fields
  deleting, 12–14
  inserting, 12–14
  moving, 12–14
filtering records in, 203–205
finding and replacing data in, 123–126
formatting data in, 118–121
importing data into new, 234–235

linking Excel worksheet to, 236–237
performing queries on, 65–67
primary table, 40
printing, 16–20
   changing page layout, 18–20
   changing page size and margins, 17
   previewing, 17
records
   adding, 10–12
   deleting, 10–12
   inserting, 10–12
related tables
   creating, 36–54
   creating form with, 140–142
   defined, 40
   renaming, 16
   showing, 46
   spell checking, 122–123
Table Tools Design tab, 112
Table Tools Fields tab, 26, 28
tabs, 5, 6
Tell Me feature, 5, 6
   using, 129
Text Box button, 144

text box control object, 143, 144
Text Filter option, 205
Text Formatting buttons, 118
Theme button, 150
themes, applying to forms, 150
Title bar, 5, 6
Title button, 143
Toggle Filter button, 203
Total row, inserting, 113
Totals button, 89, 113, 182

U

Underline button, 118
unfreezing, columns, 14–16
unhiding, columns, 14–16
unpinning, database file, 6

V

Validation Rule property box, 111
View button, 102, 136, 177
viewing, database properties, 215–217

W

wildcard character, 64
Word document
   collecting data in, and pasting in Access table, 238–239
   exporting data to, 227–229
   merging Access data with, 229–230
   merging query data with, 230–232
Word Merge button, 229
Work area, 5, 6

X

XPS file format
   exporting Access object to, 233
   saving object as, 218–219

Y

Yes/No data type, 23, 103

Z

Zoom box, 68